The Invisible Minority

The Invisible Minority
Urban Appalachians

WILLIAM W. PHILLIBER
& CLYDE B. McCOY, Editors
with HARRY C. DILLINGHAM

THE UNIVERSITY PRESS OF KENTUCKY

ISBN: 0-8131-1395-4
Library of Congress Catalog Card Number: 79-4008

Copyright © 1981 by The University Press of Kentucky

Scholarly publisher for the Commonwealth,
serving Berea College, Centre College of Kentucky,
Eastern Kentucky University, The Filson Club,
Georgetown College, Kentucky Historical Society,
Kentucky State University, Morehead State University,
Murray State University, Northern Kentucky University,
Transylvania University, University of Kentucky,
University of Louisville, and Western Kentucky University.

Editorial and Sales Offices: Lexington, Kentucky 40506

Chapter 5 was written under the auspices
of the Appalachian Regional Commission
and is in the public domain.

Contents

Tables

Maps

Acknowledgments

Those whose names appear on the title page of a book or as authors of papers always owe a debt to many others who contributed to the final product. This book is perhaps even more heavily indebted than most because it is the result of a conference which involved the efforts of many. In particular we would like to acknowledge the contributions of Harry C. Dillingham, who chaired the Conference Planning Committee for the conference on Appalachians in Urban Areas and who first began to organize those papers in a form suitable for publication; Ralph R. Widner, director of the Academy for Contemporary Problems, who provided facilities and served as host to the conference; Virginia McCoy Watkins and Kathleen Sowders, of Cincinnati's Appalachian Committee (now the Urban Appalachian Council), who served as organizers of the conference; the Research Department of the Urban Appalachian Council, who assisted the editors in conference follow up; and Naomi Silverman, who typed the final manuscript.

Introduction   WILLIAM W. PHILLIBER

Urban Appalachians: Unknown and Unnoticed

Since 1950 over three million people have migrated from the Appalachian region to the cities of the southern, eastern, and midwestern United States. In size, this migration compares to the total Irish immigration of 4.7 million or the Italian immigration of 5.0 million between 1820 and 1970 and is far larger than the Puerto Rican postwar migration of 1.0 million. Perhaps because it occurred entirely within the boundaries of the continental United States or because it involved people who already spoke the language and shared many of the national customs, it has remained a largely ignored aspect of changing America. What happened to the people who moved and to the areas where they located has not attracted the attention given other migrations.

The area that Ford (1967) called Appalachia and Campbell (1921) called the Southern Highlands was settled in the late eighteenth century principally by people of British and northern European heritage. The Blue Ridge Mountains separated them from the Eastern Seaboard while the Allegheny-Cumberland Plateau cut off areas to the west. These two ranges joined in the foothills of Alabama, forming a triangle which served to isolate the Appalachian people from the influences of the industrialized urban areas which developed around them. For many years they functioned in relatively closed systems, having little contact with outsiders (Ergood, 1976).

The ability of the area to support a large population declined over the years. The once large farms were subdivided by generations of inheritance into small tracts of worn-out land. The forests were harvested of their trees and left as rocky hillsides. Coal mines, which for a time involved large numbers of workers, increased automation and decreased total production, resulting in a substantial reduction in the number of employees. Appalachians turned to urban areas outside the region in an effort to provide for themselves. In the twenty-year span from 1950 through 1969, 3.3 million Appalachians migrated to other areas.

Much of the knowledge we have about Appalachian migrants in urban areas is based on the impressions of social workers and journalists. Their writings develop the thesis that Appalachians have migrated to ghettos where they are unable to adjust to urban life. Montgomery's (1968) description of Chicago, Henderson's (1966) story of Detroit, and Adams's (1971) portrayal of Cincinnati are examples of the type of work which has been done. In the absence of hard quantitative data, the writers have been forced to rely upon their own impressions or those of their informants.

Some noteworthy exceptions exist to the type of studies cited above. In Cincinnati, Schwarzweller, Brown, and Mangalam (1971) studied migrants from a community in Appalachia. They concluded that Appalachians do not experience serious problems of assimilation but take roles in urban areas which are of similar status to those they or their parents occupied before migrating. The ability to generalize these findings is limited both by the small number of people studied and by the reliance upon migrants from a single community. Maloney (1974) also included Appalachians in his analysis of the social areas of Cincinnati. He found that areas believed to be populated by Appalachians were the lowest in socioeconomic status and had the highest school dropout rates in the city. It is impossible, however, to disaggregate the data to determine if indeed it is the Appalachians in those areas who disproportionately experience poverty and withdraw from school. In fact, it is unclear how the reader can be sure the areas so identified are populated by Appalachians.

In Cleveland, Photiadis (1970) compared migrants from West Virginia to nonmigrants who remained behind and to migrants who returned home. He described the assimilation of migrants as a two-stage process in which West Virginians first moved to the ghettos of Cleveland, where they remained until they were able to move to better areas of the city. The result was an average level of economic attainment among migrants above that of people who remained in or returned to West Virginia. No comparisons were made between migrants and natives to the Cleveland area.

What emerges is a confused picture. On the one hand there is the impression that Appalachians have migrated to urban ghettos where they experience low achievement and high unemployment and grow wary of institutionalized attempts to assist them (e.g., Henderson, 1966; Montgomery, 1968; Maloney, 1974). Contrasted with this is the position that Appalachians migrate out of the ghettos and move to suburban areas characteristic of stereotypic middle-class America (Photiadis, 1970). Still others have the view that many Appalachians never experience life in urban ghettos; instead they are believed to distribute themselves initially throughout the cities, taking positions comparable to those they left (Schwarzweller et al., 1971). What remains is the realization that so little actual research has been done that no one really knows what happened to the 3.3 million people who left the Appalachian region nor what problems and contributions were created in the cities which were receiving centers.

The absence of much actual scholarship in the study of Appalachian migrants has not kept people from speculating about the consequences, particularly the negative ones. For example, a sociologist employed by the U. S. Bureau of the Census speculated recently in the major journal in that field that the reason higher proportions of white southern migrants to urban areas receive public assistance is because Appalachians have moved where public assistance benefits are better (Long, 1974). This speculation was made despite the fact that no data were available to identify people of Appalachian heritage. Clearly, as has happened so many times in the past, when real facts and information are absent, stereotypes are formed and used as the basis of judgments about people.

Recognizing the absence of scholarly attention to Appalachian migrants, the Academy for Contemporary Problems and the Urban Appalachian Council organized a conference of scholars and practitioners designed to encourage further work on the topic. Held at the Academy for Contemporary Problems in Columbus, Ohio, March 27–29, 1974, the conference attracted many of the recognized scholars who had written on the topic. An invited group of seventy-five people were presented with both the scholarly knowledge in the field and the need for further research as perceived by social practitioners. Most of the chapters which make up this book were originally presented at that conference. Two have been written since that time.

The two papers of Part I present arguments and evidence for considering Appalachian migrants as an urban ethnic group. It became clear at the time of the conference that the distinctiveness of Appalachians must be considered before undertaking specialized studies of the experiences they have encountered through migration. It was felt important to understand whether the issue was one of simple rural-to-urban migration or if there were factors peculiar to Appalachians which made their experience of migration different. Obermiller considers the definition of an ethnic group and the importance of the issue to Appalachians. His perspective is to consider the way Appalachians view themselves and the emergence of ethnicity through the process of group formation. The paper on stereotypes by McCoy and Watkins approaches the issue of ethnic group formation from the perspective of other persons. They use jokes told about Appalachians to show that others in the areas of destination treat Appalachians as a distinctive group who have traits undesirable in the urban environment. These papers thus may be seen as studying ethnic group formation from opposite sides of the issue.

The papers of Part II are concerned with the process of migration and its consequences for the urban areas where Appalachians have settled and for the Appalachian communities left behind. McCoy and Brown take up the question of where Appalachians go when they leave Appalachia. They uncover the migratory streams from particular regions within Appalachia to particular cities outside the area, notably within the Midwest. The persistence of these patterns is demonstrated to exist over a thirty-year span. It becomes possible through their data to obtain an understanding of the extensiveness of the migration which took place during that period and the consequences of the creation of large Appalachian subpopulations within the cities surrounding Appalachia. Fowler turns to the settlement patterns of Appalachians within a city. Looking at Cincinnati, Ohio, he discovers that Appalachians are residentially segregated from others in the community. He explains the characteristics of those neighborhoods and explanations for the settlement of Appalachians there. Pickard's paper focuses attention upon the consequences of migration for the communities within Appalachia. The selectivity in both the people who migrated and the counties from which they moved have produced definite demographic changes within the region. Further changes continue to be produced by recent in-migration to areas experiencing economic growth through increased coal production, industrialization, and recreational development. McCoy, Brown, and Watkins consider the implications of the impact of the Appalachian migration for both the cities where migrants have gone and the communities they have left behind.

Most of those who migrated chose to do so in the belief that economic opportunities in the urban areas outside the region were better than those where they lived. The papers of Part III turn to the experiences of the people from Appalachia in their search for a better life. Morgan analyzes the experiences of a group of migrants from Eastern Kentucky who moved either to Cincinnati, Ohio, or to Lexington, Kentucky. He shows that for those people the migration experience has been a positive one resulting in higher incomes which make possible better standards of living. Schwarzweller discusses the process of socio-economic attainment from the time of the migrants' initial entrance into the urban labor force. He points to the assets and liabilities of the migrants and shows that over a period of time the migrant develops skills applicable to the urban labor market. The migrants are seen to adapt while still retaining strong Appalachian characteristics. Photiadis compares the attainments of Appalachians who migrated to those who either remained in Appalachia or returned there. His data show that in Cleveland, Appalachians first migrate to low-income ghettos before moving into better suburban neighborhoods. The experiences of the migrants have generally been favorable, resulting in a favorable outlook on life and an improved standard of living as compared to those who remained in West Virginia. Philliber compares Appalachian migrants to non-Appalachians living in the inner city of Cincinnati. He finds that Appalachians are less successful than other groups in those neighborhoods in obtaining better jobs. He points to the rural backgrounds and limited education of Appalachian migrants as serious liabilities in competing with others for jobs within the city.

In this last selection of papers our strongest conflicts emerge. From the perspective of people living in Appalachia, those who migrate seem to have made financial gains. Compared to others in the city of destination, however, Appalachian migrants are not doing as well. Whether migrants are seen as "successful" depends upon the reference group to which they are compared. Even these conclusions are tentative at best. Morgan is restricted to a sample of Eastern Kentucky migrants who moved to one of two cities; Philliber is limited to people living in three inner-city neighborhoods; and Photiadis's data were collected from people on an availability basis. No one has data drawn from a representative sample of the population in an area of destination. In short, we know where the migrants came from; we know where they went; but we are only beginning to learn how well they are doing there.

The final section of the book turns to the need to know more about Appalachians in urban areas. It is written by Michael Maloney, director of the Urban Appalachian Council, which is probably the leading advocacy group for Appalachians in urban areas. Maloney reviews what we know as a result of both the papers here and those which have come before, and then points toward what is still needed.

Since the time of the conference the Appalachian region has experienced economic growth brought about by the increased demand for coal to meet the needs of the nation's energy crisis. Several papers— notably those by Pickard, Schwarzweller, and Photiadis—have been expanded to take into account those changes. Although they are speculative in some sense, they provide the best estimates by people who study the area of what the consequences have been for the Appalachians who have migrated to urban areas outside their native region.

Part I

Appalachians as an Urban Ethnic Group

1   PHILLIP J. OBERMILLER

The Question of Appalachian Ethnicity

Considerable confusion exists as to whether Appalachians can legiti-
mately be included among the ethnic groups of this nation. This essay
attempts to deal with the more salient questions which flow through
the discussion of Appalachians as an ethnic group. Regional, cultural,
and class issues will be examined, a working definition of ethnicity presented, and both the positive and negative aspects of Appalachian ethnicity investigated. Finally, I will offer a few suggestions for research
based on the perspective of Appalachians as an ethnic group. Perhaps a
brief survey of what is being said and written on this topic will help to
outline the question.

A number of professional academics and practitioners believe that
Appalachians are an ethnic group on a par with other recognized minorities. After examining the evidence for and against "homogeneity"
presented by Arthur Estabrook and John Day, Cratis Williams
(1976:47) concludes: "As a result of isolation, economic depravity [sic],
struggles, hardships and common interests, the sons of mountain pi-
oneers of from five to eight generations back are now blended into a
somewhat homogeneous people. But it must be remembered that although a homogeneity of the *ethical and ethnic character of the mountain people may more or less exist, there is no homogeneity of social and
economic status*." (Emphasis added) James Branscome (1976:73) describes Appalachians as "a culturally distinct group who do not share
the life goals and cultural aspirations of the dominant middle class in
America or, for that matter, those of other minorities." The sociologist
Robert Paul Sessions (1977:94) believes that Appalachians have a
"common bond" with other Americans yet notes the "many unique

qualities of mountain life and numerous characteristics which set the mountaineers off from other Americans."

Others who assert that Appalachians are ethnics include Ann Orlov (1976), managing editor of the *Harvard Encyclopedia of American Ethnic Groups*, who has "never doubted that we should regard the Appalachians as an ethnic group [although] my view is not universally shared." Andrew Greeley (1976), a leader in ethnic research and director of the Center for the Study of American Pluralism, apparently shares her opinion. Stanley Arnowitz of the New School for Social Research in New York refers in his book *False Promises* (1973:27–28) to the "young white workers . . . from the coal mining communities of Virginia, West Virginia and Southeastern Kentucky . . . [whom] the natives of the Ohio Valley called . . . 'hillbillies' " as "this new 'ethnic minority.' " Michael Maloney (1976) of Cincinnati's Urban Appalachian Council considers Appalachian migrants to be an "urban ethnic minority" because they clearly fit the commonly understood definitions of each of those three words. The council itself was described by the *Cincinnati Post* (1976) as "an advocate organization for Appalachians, contending that the immigrants from the southern mountains are as much of an ethnic group as are blacks and Indians."

The position of most people who have given the question any thought at all is that Appalachians are indeed distinct but are not an ethnic group. Jim Wayne Miller's (1976:24) familiarity with Appalachian studies and his personal investigation of the concept of ethnicity led him to conclude that:

while Appalachians are in no legitimate sense an ethnic group, they are classified by other Americans as something quite similar to an ethnic group; and have many of the same problems—economic, social, and psychological—as members of various ethnic groups. But there is an important difference. Appalachians have none of the obvious distinguishing features of most ethnic groups—no distinguishing racial or physical features, no different language or religion. Because of this, Appalachians bear a special stigma. To have none of the marks of an "ethnic"—which serves as an explanation of different attitudes and value emphases—and yet to be so different.

Miller believes that Appalachian values are at heart quite similar to general American values, and that there is no basis for speaking of a distinctive Appalachian ethnicity. John Stephenson (1976b) also is not convinced that Appalachians are an ethnic group and does not see how ethnicity can be a "useful metaphor" in the Appalachian cause. Nonetheless, he, like Jim Wayne Miller, is quite clear on the fact that Appalachians are a distinctive group in and of themselves, however hard that distinctiveness may be to define.

Soundings, an interdisciplinary journal based in Nashville, Tennessee, published a special issue in 1973 entitled "The Rediscovery of Ethnicity: Its Implications for Culture and Politics in America." In that issue David Whisnant (1973: 124) writes: "Appalachian people are among the growing number of ethnic and cultural groups which are rejecting the melting pot—together with its associated ideology—and consciously returning to their historical and cultural roots as a source of pride, strength, and political identity." Whisnant clearly considers Appalachians to be an ethnic group but, without actually defining it, goes on to reject ethnicity as an adequate basis for Appalachian identity: "anyone who wishes to understand the current movement toward regional identity must look beyond simple ethnicity, however strictly or loosely defined" (p. 124).

The geographer Charles Lieble (1976: 99) regards it as presumptuous for anyone to think Appalachians possess any strong degree of cultural unity. He goes on to conclude: "Adherence to the idea that the Appalachian Region is a tightly knit cultural entity, displaying a high degree of cultural cohesion, is nothing more than a nostalgic fancy that allows . . . retreat into the glorious unadulterated past while ignoring present-day reality" (Lieble, 1976: 98).

Those who share this approach to Appalachian ethnicity ignore the seven million people who have departed the Appalachian region since 1940, many of whom are living in major metropolitan areas among the other racial and cultural minorities who preceded them (see Pickard, chapter 5, below). Moreover, many experts on ethnicity maintain that culture is not the sole criterion for calling a group "ethnic." Charles Keyes (1976: 210), a member of the Committee for Comparative Studies in Ethnicity and Nationality at the University of Washington, states simply that "an ethnic group cannot be defined in cultural terms alone." In this light, Fred Snuffer (1976: 101) finds that Appalachia is "a bicultural region characterized by relative degrees of traditional and progressive values and beliefs as well as degrees of affluence and poverty."

A third perspective on Appalachian ethnicity rejects the concept entirely and concludes instead that class analysis is more appropriate to the study of the people of Appalachia. David Walls (1976: 42), for example, states, "The national context for Appalachian problems suggests that class is a more relevant analytic concept than culture."

Two points can be made in response to the arguments that a class analysis should replace an ethnic understanding. The first is stated by Pierre van den Berghe (1976: 251–52), also of the Committee for Comparative Studies in Ethnicity and Nationality: "The appeal and salience of ethnicity as a basis for political action seems to be roughly inverse to those of class. Indeed, it may well be generally the case that class organization being based on the rather abstract notion of interest, is intrinsically more difficult to achieve than ethnic organization, based as it is on recognition of readily identifiable cultural symbols."

Moreover, a class analysis which does not take into account ethnic reality soon encounters serious problems, as the leaders of the Chinese People's Republic, a relatively classless society with fifty-four minority ethnic groups, have belatedly discovered (Dreyer, 1977).

As a further argument against ethnicity, Walls (1977: 71) points out that " 'Appalachian' after all, has never become a symbol of self-identification for the vast majority of the region's people, for whom the community, county, state, and nation remain more important units of political identity." This argument, however, focuses on political identity. There are anthropological studies in Thailand, for instance, which show that ethnic groups of distinct culture, language, and nationality frequently adopt categories similar to those Walls mentions for reasons of functional convenience rather than linking themselves to their tacitly recognized ethnic identity (Keys, 1976: 206–07).

Only one study to date has considered the ethnicity of Appalachians in urban areas. Tommie Miller's (1976: 24) master's thesis at the University of Cincinnati, entitled "Urban Appalachians: Cultural Pluralism and Ethnic Identity in the City," gives an urban perspective on Appalachian ethnicity: "An examination of past and present data on urban Appalachians reveals that many of the conditions which have been cited for the formation of ethnic group identification are applicable to the urban Appalachian situation." Miller's survey consisted of telephone interviews with 170 randomly chosen residents in Norwood, Ohio, an independent municipality surrounded by the city of Cincinnati, which is commonly thought to have large numbers of Appalachian residents. She asked the question, "Are Appalachians an ethnic group in the city?" and discovered that there existed "considerable ambiguity over and rejection of the concept of 'ethnicity.' " She goes on to say:

A culturally pluralistic approach to community was not found among the respondents, but rather ethnicity was denied, maligned, or feared. At the same time, however, over forty percent of the respondents identified Appalachians as an ethnic group in the community, and even among those who claimed Appalachians were not an ethnic group were many who were able to cite 'characteristics' of the group. Thus, evidence of other-definition of Appalachians as an ethnic group was established. Self-definition lagged behind other-definition, however, with the majority of Appalachian respondents rejecting both ethnic and Appalachian identities. Whether this rejection reflects a lack of awareness of their cultural history and its sociological significance, or whether it is a conscious rejection of cultural pluralism in favor of assimilation is not clear from this research.

Further investigation of urban Appalachian ethnic identity is needed to answer many questions raised by this research. [Miller, 1976: 26]

Without settling the issue definitively, Miller's study adds substantive information in favor of considering Appalachians in urban areas as part of an ethnic group.

Part of the difficulty in deciding whether to regard Appalachians as an ethnic group arises from confusion over the meaning of "ethnic group." Wasvelod Isajiw (1974: 117) surveyed sixty-five studies of ethnicity and found twenty-seven different definitions of the term. Among those definitions, twelve attributes of ethnicity appeared fairly constantly. They were, in order of frequency of use: common national or geographic origin or common ancestors; same culture or customs; same religion; same race or physical characteristics; same language; consciousness of kind; "we feeling," sense of peoplehood, loyalty; *Gemeinschaft* relations; common values or ethos; separate institutions; minority or subordinate status or majority or dominant status; and immigrant group.

Although there are obviously many possible definitions and attributes of ethnicity to choose from, there is a need to agree upon some working definition so that when we tell each other that Appalachians are or are not or may be an ethnic group, we all know what we are talking about. In order to synthesize the most significant constitutive elements into a single comprehensive definition, Isajiw (1974: 122) defines "ethnic collectivity" as "an involuntary group of people who share the same culture or [the] descendents of such people who identify themselves and/or are identified by others as belonging to the same involuntary group." This definition encompasses both the subjective and the objective (self-definition and other-definition), both "the ethnic boundary that defines the group" and the "cultural stuff that it encloses" (Isajiw, 1974: 115).

Agreement on such a definition would be a helpful beginning, but would not necessarily settle the question of Appalachian ethnicity. The most convincing argument for Appalachian ethnicity is the extensive recognition that a distinct group does exist, whether its members are called Appalachians, southern highlanders, or mountaineers. Although we may not be able to distill satisfactorily the essence of "Appalachianness," we are able to recognize its existence. Charles Keyes (1976: 210) following Shils and Geertz, recognizes a " 'primordial' quality" in each ethnic group. Van den Berghe (1976: 243) writes: "New ethnic definitions are always grounded in pre-existing ethnic realities." These "realities" or "qualities" are implicitly acknowledged throughout the literature on Appalachia—if not, there would be no such literature.

The issues at stake in the whole discussion of Appalachian ethnicity are quite significant. Thomas Sowell (1978: 213) puts it succinctly: "Ethnicity remains a major factor in such objective variables as income, education, fertility, unemployment, and crime, as well as in such subjective variables as general opinions, and political preferences." He could well have extended his list of important "variables" influenced by ethnicity to include religious preference, occupational status, career aspirations, and mental health. In addition, ethnicity is a commonly used category for recognizing groups of people for various political and social purposes. As Harvard sociologist Mark Granovetter (1975: 5) puts it, "It is not an accident that those ethnic groups which have embraced ethnicity most warmly are those which have felt disadvantaged in the American political arena. They are groups which had previously been unable to achieve the kind of solidarity needed to exert genuine political influence."

To a certain extent, Appalachians need to be recognized by the researchers—sociologists, demographers, geographers, anthropologists, economists, political scientists, and others who do the studies and produce the data which influence policy decisions at all levels. What will it mean to the millions of Appalachians living outside of the Appalachian Regional Commission boundaries that the 1980 census will ask ethnic and racial questions which completely ignore them (Novak, 1976: 4-5)? In positive terms, what will it mean to the Appalachian advocacy effort that the Center for the Study of American Pluralism at the National Opinion Research Center now recognizes Appalachians as an ethnic group, and will begin including them in major surveys (Greeley, 1976)? Obviously, to be recognized as an ethnic collectivity by serious academicians, both inside and outside of the region, can add a substantial amount of information, and therefore potency, to the Appalachian movement.

Major social programs sponsored by governmental and private agencies are usually designated for target groups which are defined not only by socioeconomic status but also by racial and ethnic identity. Nathan Glazer (1976: 121) holds that "public action [is] determined directly by [these programs]: quotas in higher education, quotas in government employment and programs, and funds specifically earmarked for one group or another." Laws are being enacted to ensure that equal rights are granted to members of minority groups. Frequently these groups are specified by race, sex, or ethnicity. All too often Appalachians find themselves excluded from such legislation.

It was not until the militant black pride of the 1960s showed the power of ethnic cohesiveness that racial and ethnic groups openly began to reject the ideal of assimilation. Because of this, the direct social benefits of ethnicity are now more numerous than ever before, particularly through the antipoverty and antidiscriminatory legislation of the last fifteen years. "Originally affirmative action was meant to apply to blacks, American Indians, the Spanish-surnamed, and Asian Americans. . . . Polish Americans, Indians (from India), and other groups are either on the way to being included in some affirmative action plans, or are arguing that they should be" (Glazer, 1976: 126). In this perspective, ethnicity becomes a "set of symbols used to appeal to constituencies in order to organize them politically for the capture of resources within an existing state and social system" (van den Berghe, 1976: 250). This highly utilitarian view of Appalachian ethnicity is valid and necessary, but limited. It carries with it the dangers of mere tokenism and the prolongation of internal colonialism by dominant groups.

Appalachian self-identity is still rare because acknowledging oneself as a "hillbilly" means subjecting oneself to ridicule, derision, and, in some cases, outright discrimination in many areas of American society. There is a fear of being "different." People who fear difference either attack it or try to suppress it; social norms are to be observed, standards of correctness must be maintained. As Nathan Glazer (1976: 121) puts it, "Difference itself is the enemy." He goes on to say that, even academically, it is "retrograde to speak of culture . . . that groups may differ in tastes, values, practices, stemming from history and custom is considered almost as dangerous a suggestion as the idea that groups may differ because of genetic selection."

But there are deeper, more significant dangers involved in ethnicity. Ethnocentrism is an exaggeration of ethnicity, an "illusion of the center" that leads one to exercise value judgments about all others solely according to the restricted norms of a single group, one's own. Racism is a natural corollary to ethnocentrism. Ethnicity is feared because it has led in some cases to polarization, exclusion, discrimination, hatred, and violence (Jackson, 1973). But to condemn the encouragement of group pride and cultural consciousness on the grounds that undesirable consequences may result is to fear history rather than to learn from it.

The dangers of ethnicity act to reinforce the conviction that it is indeed a powerful reality, whether employed for good or for evil. In probing the consequences of enlightened ethnic consciousness among predominantly white groups, the American Jewish Committee's Task Force on Group Life in America (1972: 28) reported that "the failure of the racial backlash to emerge as a major phenomenon of white society has been documented in detail in a series of national surveys taken by the National Opinion Research Center since World War II." The power of ethnic consciousness can be respected and channeled creatively for the benefit of Appalachians if they so choose.

Some Appalachians fear ethnicity because they associate it with a distortion of the Appalachian experience that is usually referred to as "museum-piece romanticism." This approach idealizes Appalachian history and tends to focus myopically on the arts and crafts of Appalachia to the exclusion of all other concerns. David Walls (1976: 42) recognizes that "a social movement must draw selectively from a living working-class subculture, not romanticize everything folksy and traditional." Gunnar Myrdal (1974: 28) has written "The Case against Romantic Ethnicity" to condemn "the writers on historical identity [who] rather systematically avoid the problem of poverty and all that is related to it."

In most instances, however, ethnic consciousness can be a fulcrum for social change. Based in Washington, D.C., the National Center for

Urban Ethnic Affairs specializes in encouraging and advising community organization in ethnic neighborhoods in 110 cities across the country. The National Center has shown that respect for a group's ethnic heritage does not necessarily have to result in a dysfunctional kind of romanticism. Rather, as recent history has shown, the quantum release of human energy that is associated with the coming to ethnic self-consciousness can be and frequently is harnessed for the achievement of social justice.

Appalachians, prompted especially by their experiences as relatively recent urban migrants, are in the process of ethnogenesis and are still coming to know themselves as an ethnic minority. In the words of Emma Bell Miles (1976: 200): "From the mountains will yet arise a quickening of American ideals and American life. But before such renaissance the Mountaineers must awaken to consciousness of themselves as people. For . . . we are yet a people asleep, a race without knowledge of its own existence." If, as David Walls (1976), John Stephenson (1976 a), James Branscome (1976), and others have indicated, Appalachia's problems are national problems, to be faced and resolved at the national level, then the nation too must come to know the Appalachian people.

For those of us working in the cities, Appalachian ethnicity is not a "fotched-on" scholarly concept—it is a basic social reality. The research needs of Appalachians in the city are based on that reality.

Multigenerational research among Appalachians is needed. Comparing Appalachians with mainstream norms seems to be of minimal utility, and in some cases can be harmful. It is more practical for the purpose of setting policy and program design to know as precisely as possible the situation among Appalachians themselves. This kind of research has been carried out effectively among other ethnic groups (by Paul Campisi, Lydio Tomasi, Richard Gambino, and others) and is particularly helpful in detecting "natural" adaptations of the culture to urban environments as well as finding the specific problems which affect different generations. Tommie Miller's study of Appalachians in Norwood, despite difficulties in obtaining third-generation data, is a good beginning in multigenerational research among urban Appalachians and needs to be followed up.

Research should include both personal (value expressive) and psychological indicators as well as the standard socioeconomic and political indicators among Appalachians. Standard social indicators give only a one-sided view of lives which are often rich and complex. Personal satisfaction should be taken into account in determining the quality of life of urban Appalachians, especially before any planning is done which will affect them.

We must begin to look at Appalachian success patterns and social competence, and not just the social disorganization that is present within some segments of the Appalachian community. Our research efforts should document the severe problems which affect great numbers of urban Appalachians, but to spend all of our energy in pursuit of pathology can be a disservice to Appalachian people. There are two sides to victim blaming: one is to discover social dysfunction and to blame it on the individual or individuals involved; the other is to note success and attribute it solely to the individual or individuals achieving it. The successful Appalachian has manipulated the "system" for his or her own benefit, implying that to a certain extent the system does work. We should begin therefore to examine those instances in which the system has been successfully exploited by Appalachians, and look for patterns which can be reinforced by policy and planning decisions. We need to add the Appalachian middle class to our studies so that the opportunity structures they have either built or discovered can be made available to all.

Research, especially in the cities, should take into consideration the concept of neighborhood. It is necessary in developing social policy and programs, and for setting priorities, to have some idea of the relative vitality and continuing viability of the neighborhoods in which our people live. Michael Maloney's *The Social Areas of Cincinnati* (1974) is a good example of how the importance of neighborhoods can be recognized in research methodology. Data as they pertain to individual Appalachian neighborhoods can be factored out of gross statistics or developed independently for analysis before being correlated to other neighorhoods or the city as a whole.

Information is urgently needed on the present situation of the Appalachian family. That the family is a central institution in Appalachian life and has been the key survival mechanism for migrants has been adequately documented by Schwarzweller, Brown, and Mangalam (1971). However, it is encountering severe stress in the urban setting, and signs of family breakdown are becoming all too frequent. Current data on the condition and needs of the urban Appalachian family should be a high research priority.

NOTE

An earlier version of this paper was published under the title "Appalachians as an Urban Ethnic Group: Romanticism, Renaissance, or Revolution?" in *Appalachian Journal* 5:1 (Autumn 1977). It appears here with permission of the publisher.

2 CLYDE B. McCOY & VIRGINIA McCOY WATKINS

Stereotypes of
Appalachian Migrants

Jokes about Appalachian migrants illustrate the many negative stereotypes about them held by much of the native population in the midwestern cities to which they have migrated. The social implications of
such ethnic jokes are an important issue.

Since sensitivity is required in discussing these jokes (as with black,
Polish, or any other ethnic jokes), the reader should realize that no
offense is intended; the jokes are used here simply to demonstrate how
the image of a population can be established and reinforced. It should
also be known that the authors, being children of a coal miner from
Gobblers Knob up Convict Hollow in Buchanan County, Virginia, and
having descended from the "Real McCoys" of Pike County, Kentucky,
and Mingo County, West Virginia, are bona fide hillbillies who are
sensitive to how hillbilly jokes are used and perceived within the culture.

Much of the material discussed in this paper comes from the twelve
years' experience of the authors in Cincinnati, Ohio, and their initial
years of adjustment to urban life in Norfolk, Virginia. Both of these
cities are among the most popular destinations of Appalachian
migrants, as can be seen from the data. In preparation for discussing
the ethnic humor about Appalachians, we asked several native Ohioans
who possessed a storehouse of "hillbilly" jokes to share with us as many
of these as possible. The jokes were provided in both oral and written
form and served to confirm the type of humor heard by the authors
over the years.

It is not unusual in Cincinnati and other midwestern cities to hear a
joke like the following: "Know what is the best thing to come out of
Kentucky?" asks the native Ohioan. "No," responds another Ohioan.

"An empty greyhound bus" is furnished as the punchline for the joke. More often than not, it is followed by: "Know the best thing to ever leave Ohio?" "What?" "A full bus." This is only one of many jokes that illustrate the imagery about thousands of Appalachians, called by various appellations, such as "hillbillies," "ridgerunners," and "briar-hoppers." The implication of this and other similar repartee, of course, is that there are too many of these Kentuckians and West Virginians in places like Cincinnati and Columbus and that the cities would be better off if most of these "hillbillies" went back home to the mountains.

This type of humor is common among urbanites and reveals some images they hold about Appalachians. The stereotype that the Appalachian would much rather be in the mountains than in Ohio is one of these images. Some of the most common jokes heard in Ohio concern the frequency of "visiting down home."

When St. Peter was showing some visitors through heaven, he was showing off the lavishly furnished rooms and the excellent attention given to all the people. Of course, the visitors were very impressed by the heavenly living arrangements of all the people until they came upon the Ohio room where they were astonished to find that about half the people were tied up and not permitted to move. St. Peter assured the visitors that this was not normal, but this was the weekend, and if these Kentucky hillbillies were not tied up, they would leave heaven and go back to Kentucky.

A more localized humor in Cincinnati is expressed by the many jokes concerning the hillbillies' creating traffic jams on the Brent Spence, a two-tiered bridge spanning the Ohio River, connecting Kentucky and Ohio. One such version states, "Know the reason for building the Brent Spence bridge with two levels? . . . . So that all of the hillbillies leaving Ohio can take off their shoes and pass them below to their cousins leaving Kentucky for Ohio." A somewhat more crude, and possibly more popular, version asks, "Did you know that Kentuckians could walk on water to cross the Ohio River? . . . . Yes, they walk across all the scum left by the other hillbillies." In addition to addressing the "nostalgia for down home" stereotype, these jokes indicate a general awareness of the fact that there are large numbers of Appalachians (particularly from Kentucky) living in Cincinnati, Dayton, and Hamilton, Ohio, and a dislike for their concentration in these cities.

Some of the prevalent stereotypes concerning Kentuckians which are subtly communicated by native urban Ohioans through their ethnic jokes present the negatively caricatured image that the migrants are threatening, not only because of their numbers, but because of their lack of urban sophistication, their lack of cleanliness, and their general lack of high morals. Some jokes in the southwestern Ohio area most assuredly express these negative images of hillbillies, especially persons from Kentucky. Caricatures of questionable morality and cleanliness seem to be communicated in the following type of humor: "Do you know what a virgin in Kentucky is? . . . . The ugliest girl in the fifth grade." The joke that "A virgin in Kentucky is the sister who can out-run her brothers" expresses the often-held incest stereotype. A similarly demeaning caricature is revealed in the inquiry, "Why was Jesus Christ not born in Kentucky? God replies that he had searched diligently in Kentucky but could not find three wise men nor a virgin."

The stereotypic lack of cleanliness is portrayed in the bet between a Kentuckian, a West Virginian, and an Ohioan: "There was a pig pen and a barn which had not been cleaned for years, so the bet was on who could stay in the barn the longest. The Ohioan had barely entered, when he had to escape the stench; the West Virginian emerged choking and gasping about five minutes later; after about thirty seconds of silence all thunder broke loose, all the pigs squealing out of the barn—of course, to escape the Kentuckian." One prominent joke in the Cincinnati and Hamilton area communicates a similar stereotype by involving a well-known local personality who is both a highly publicized fundamentalist preacher and a very successful businessman (and also an Appalachian migrant): "Did you know that the old country preacher was arrested?" "No." "Yes, he was arrested for polluting the Ohio River." "How did that happen?" "He was baptizing hillbillies in the river."

The caricature of ignorance appears in this retreaded Polish joke: "An Ohioan had hired a Kentuckian and West Virginian to build a house. The Kentuckian would drive a few nails and throw away practically an entire handfull of nails. When the West Virginian inquired as to why he was doing that, the Kentuckian answered that the heads were on the wrong end. The West Virginian indignantly replied, 'You must have been born stupid. We always save those and use them on the other side of the house.' "

A general recognition of (and, for some, a certain distaste for) hillbilly migrants is revealed in the joke which starts by asking, "Did you realize that there are only forty-eight states now?" "No, how did that happen?" "All of Kentucky moved to Ohio, and Ohio went to hell." It is interesting that Lewis Killian (1970: 98) reports a much earlier version of this joke circulating in Detroit at a time when there were only forty-eight states; it differed only in that forty-five states remained because all of Kentucky and Tennessee had moved to Michigan and Michigan went to hell. As interesting as the fact that this joke about Appalachians has survived so long is that the referent varies in different cities and for different periods of time. Information from our research on migration streams shows that most of the Appalachian migrants to the southwestern Ohio cities of Cincinnati, Dayton, and Hamilton are from Kentucky, while those in the north-central Ohio cities of Columbus and Cleveland are largely from West Virginia. Detroit has always drawn a considerable number of Appalachian migrants from Kentucky and Tennessee but now attracts many West Virginians. Apparently the general population has some awareness of the origin of the migrants. Most of the hillbilly jokes in southwestern Ohio refer to Kentuckians while in Columbus and Cleveland they usually concern West Virginians. Earlier jokes in Detroit were about Kentuckians and Tennesseans, but today they also include West Virginians.

An important consideration in discussing this type of ethnic humor is whether it is truly indicative of the general stereotype held by the urban population concerning the Appalachian migrant. Does it not indicate that the urbanites responded to the Appalachian in the same way as to other migrant groups—the Irish, German, Jewish, Polish, Puerto Rican, and black migrants? In fact, many of the so-called "hillbilly" jokes are simply retreaded applications from a former migrant group to a newer one. Hillbillies seem to be favorite targets of retreaded Polish jokes. For example, "How do you tell the groom at a hillbilly wedding? . . . . The one in the clean bowling shirt." "Do you know what to do if a hillbilly throws a stick of dynamite at you? . . . . You light it and throw it back at him." In Indianapolis one of the favorites today is: "Did you hear about the hillbilly driver in the Indianapolis 500 who made fifty pit stops? . . . . Three were for gas and forty-seven for directions."

Each of these jokes demonstrates one of the common stereotypes—ignorance, laziness, uncleanliness, immorality, etc.—generally held by a sizable proportion of the urban population. They are similar to the images of earlier migrant populations. The most socially dangerous aspect of these ethnic jokes and the sterotypes they represent is that they portray a singularly negative image about the referent group. Few jokes present positive characteristics of migrant groups. Most of the attitudes toward Appalachians and other migrant groups which are perpetuated by ethnic humor do not lead to positive acceptance. These jokes become expressions of fear, dislike, and a desire to get rid of the unacceptable differences believed to be present in the new migrants. The extent of the low-status image of hillbillies in urban areas is indicated in one research study reported by Killian (1970). Respondents in Detroit were asked to identify the most undesirable people or those people who were not good to have in the city. Only one group was considered more undesirable than the hillbilly; and that was criminals or gangsters. Whereas 26 percent indicated that gangsters were the most undesirable, 21 percent responded that hillbillies were the most undesirable, and 13 percent that Negroes were the most undesirable. Although this survey was done in the 1950s, the stereotyped image of the Appalachian hillbilly persists in many cities where large numbers of Appalachian migrants reside.

Though black migrants are discriminated against in part because of their color, the Appalachian migrant suffers discrimination because of cultural differences—or at least what are perceived to be differences. The mannerisms, customs, and, in particular, speech patterns of Appalachians are perceived as foreign and cause the urban native to react according to established stereotypes. Some behavioral expressions, such as a particular way of talking, generate a host of traits which have been reinforced by comic strips like "Snuffy Smith" and "L'il Abner," television shows like the "Beverly Hillbillies," and movies like "Deliverance," which usually concentrate on the naive, ignorant, nonsophisticated image of the Appalachian. That they are violence-prone and great knife-wielders are also characteristics applied to the hillbilly. Even commercials like the 1974 Dodge take-off on "Deliverance," in which two mountain men are pictured driving a Ram-charger truck through mountainous country while engaged in a dialogue which reveals their cunning yet threatening manner, reinforces the caricature of hillbillies as being rough, crude, and potentially dangerous, enough so that one must protect oneself when dealing with them.[1]

Perceived ignorance in hillbillies was used by Woody Hayes, former football coach at Ohio State University, to illustrate how his football team overcame their mistakes. "It was like the census-taker who went to this shack up in the Tennessee hills," Hayes said. "The woman came to the door and said, 'There's me and pappy and thirteen kids and there won't be any more.' The census-taker asked how come she was so sure, and she said, 'Because we found out what was causing them' " (Pille, 1978).

Such a caricature can be transferred to hillbillies in an urban area, as was revealed in an unpublished report in Cincinnati by Police Captain Robert Roncker (Maloney and Huelsman, 1972). The report is replete with negative stereotypes of Appalachians, emphasizing particularly their supposed proneness to violence as it related to the ubiquity and agility of knife-wielding. The image of Kentuckians as troublemakers led the captain to suggest that most crimes in Cincinnati were committed by Kentuckians. The final tribute to the hillbilly in the report would lead people to believe that the hillbilly was so tough and immune to pain as not to be seriously affected by a police club.

This type of stereotypic belief has not been limited to police reports. Maloney and Huelsman's (1972: 25) critique of an article in *Harper's* which appeared a year earlier than the police report in Cincinnati, is an example.

We find no particular correlation between the poor quality of the stereotyped literature on migrants and the source of publication. One of the most inaccurate, insulting, and infuriatingly juvenile pieces of all time was written in 1958 by Albert Votaw in *Harper's* (CCXVI, Feb. 1958) and was called "Hillbillies Invade Chicago." We get the impression from reading this pathetically biased piece of reporting that Chicago might well have become a kind of Utopia, if it just had not been for those unwelcome, impossible-to-assimilate hillbillies! Whether he realized it or not, Votaw was subscribing to a theory of culture-conflict between the mountain subculture and that of the urban society of Chicago, but he seemed to feel that in most cases, the hard-drinking, hard-fighting hillbilly was to blame for the conditions he tried to describe for the Uptown area to his literary readers in a high-prestige magazine.

Police officials in particular seem to subscribe to these stereotypes of Appalachians in scapegoating many urban problems onto the uneducated, nonskilled, welfare-seeking, unsanitary migrants. It seems that many public officials believe that many of the unsanitary conditions of the cities are caused by the migrant who has to be enculturated and taught to use the urban "john" and garbage cans instead of using the streets for a toilet and for tossing the garbage. The stereotype that Appalachians are unsanitary and unkempt, both in dress and in housekeeping, continues to be one of the most prevalent myths about the migrants. It seems difficult to convince some people, even today, that hillbillies do have commodes and do not keep chickens in their homes nor pigs under the house.

Ethnic jokes are merely one way of expressing these stereotypic attitudes in a somewhat exaggerated form. The specific content of the joke is not as important as the general image and attitude communicated. The jokes generally contain some small grain of truth about at least some small part of the population, as do most stereotypes. Neither the listener nor the joke-teller is interested in the reality-testing of jokes, since good jokes depend in large part upon the extreme exaggeration of some trait or characteristic that can be identified, even mythically, with the group to which the jokes apply. The most important aspect of the content of the joke is that it can be somehow associated in the minds of the listener with the referents of the joke. Of course, the fact that the truth of the content of the joke is not expected to be tested permits its most dangerous consequence: that it only expresses general, negative, mythical images concerning the group being joked about.

There are no positive reinforcers to counteract negative information or images that are being communicated through humor. Mythical stereotypes exist because little contradictory information is permitted to discredit the believed stereotype. When a little positive information is revealed, even though it represents the fact rather than the more commonly communicated mythical trait, it can be treated as an exception to the generality of the believed stereotype. This has been one of the major difficulties in improving the image of both Appalachians and blacks. Much of the information which is communicated about them is based on that which portrays a negative image. For example, both Appalachian and black migrants are frequently identified as welfare recipients, bearers of large families, unemployed, and poorly educated, factors believed to create problems for the urban areas which have to be paid for by the native urban population. Most of the carriers of these stereotypes neither talk about nor joke about the successful Appalachians or blacks, as both groups are typically outside the limits the stereotypes permit.

The most harmful social implication of ethnic humor is that it reinforces the singularly negative stereotype of the referents. Ethnic humor permits few, if any, redeeming qualities of the referents to be portrayed. All the media forms which portray ethnic images seem to be less singularly negative than the jokes. Television shows like "The Waltons" serve to balance the negative stereotypes of mountaineers by revealing them as sensitive, warm, dedicated, and hard-working, whereas most jokes portray a sharp, definitive caricature that stands alone without any positive attributes. Even the simple, naive, unkempt, unsophisticated, moonshine-making, pig-keeping, ill-accented "Beverly Hillbillies" are shown to be overly honest and possessed with a rural "country" wisdom that outwits the urbanites. Even these redeeming qualities are not expressed in most of the jokes.

Merely reinforcing existing attitudes is not the only social implication of ethnic humor. Another serious potential is that jokes present a way of establishing stereotypes about a group where none existed, or giving rise to more entrenched attitudes than were held before being involved in an ethnic humor session.

For the joke-tellers and listeners of ethnic humor, a certain aspect of small group solidarity is established and maintained through depreciating another group. If the joked-about group is seen as a threat because of its cultural differences, the joking group seems to reinforce the superiority of its own way of life by demeaning the "foreigners" through exaggerated negativism. Such demeaning expressions create great embarrassment and potential interpersonal conflict when one of the foreign referents is present or happens unknowingly on the scene of such a joke session. The opposite effect is noted in the amount of peer pressure that can be exerted to participate in this form of verbal and attitudinal competition, which usually demands that more crude and negative caricatures be expressed with each successive joke. Anyone unwilling to participate is, to borrow an ethnophalism, a "nigger lover." Of course, the social pressure to engage in such ethnic humor is indicative of the social implications arising from the activity itself. Although the joke-tellers gain peer acceptance and ego strengthening, there are few social rewards for the objects of ethnic humor, since positive information or attitudes are seldom communicated through this medium.

There does seem to be some very positive outgrowth of ethnic humor when the referents themselves use the humor. It is common for ethnic minorities to use the ethnic jokes among themselves. Recognizing the existence of the jokes and being willing to express them among themselves are possibly ways of denying their truth, providing release of frustration and tension, and promoting group solidarity.

Ethnic humor also seems to have a positive role at certain stages in interethnic relations. Particularly important, and probably occurring first, is the ability to display and share humor with people outside the ethnic group. The confidence to laugh at oneself or one's group can go far toward reducing tension and creating acceptance. A later stage in interethnic acceptance occurs when the nonminority person or outsider can tactfully use ethnic humor without rejection. This use can be a way of testing the social bond and of saying, "We know the existence of such stereotypes, but we reject them and accept you." It is a way of putting out into the open the underlying tensions present in interethnic relations. However, this use of ethnic humor can be risky and dangerous; it seems to be appreciated only when bonds of acceptance have been previously established. The lack of acceptance of such humor, particularly in public situations, has been demonstrated by the widely publicized Earl Butz affair and by the national attention given to Johnny Bench's attempt at ethnic humor during remarks made at a symphony performance. Bench, a superstar with the Cincinnati Reds baseball team, made an appearance with the Cincinnati Symphony Orchestra where he attempted humorous remarks of an ethnic nature. The audience present at the time, and later press coverage of the event, decried such poor taste by the well-known local and national celebrity (Gianutsos, 1978). Media coverage and public displeasure at this kind of behavior indicate the existence of social tension in interethnic relations. Of course, media representatives decry the inability of our society to appreciate ethnic humor and to be able to laugh at one's self. The acceptance of ethnic humor in public can only occur in particular social situations at a particular time of interethnic acceptance.

The preceding discussion has been intended to show that the existence and functions of ethnic humor are indicative of a false stereotypic image, particularly as it concerns Appalachian migrants. The Appalachian migrant too often is viewed only through the image of the poverty-stricken, unskilled, uneducated migrant who comes to the inner city without a job and has great difficulty coping with the urban institutions. There has been a failure to recognize the many different types of Appalachians, both the heterogeneity of cultures and peoples in the mountains and the variety among the migrants in the cities. Although most Appalachians do not fit the stereotypes, false precepts prevail because undue emphasis has been placed upon the poor migrants who are perceived as failures. There has been particular focus upon the inner-city areas, where the adjustment of Appalachians to urban institutions, particularly to slum living and poor schools, has been portrayed as presenting serious problems for the migrants, for the cities, and for the native citizenry. Native inhabitants see themselves as victims of problems created by the migrants.

The Appalachian is similar to the black in the need for a more positive role identity, and if Appalachian identity is to be changed, we must provide more positive role models than at present prevail in the media. The research presented in this volume will do much to project a more correct image of the Appalachian migrant. In addition to the writings and research presented, many of the participants are themselves Appalachians who represent a contrasting image to the typical stereotype of the uneducated, unskilled hillbilly migrant. The Appalachian scholars do not differ greatly from many other Appalachians in their lifestyle in the mountains, or in their experience of the migration process and the consequent adjustment to urban life.

During the last few years a considerable amount of excellent research has been done by such persons as James S. Brown, Harry Schwarzweller, J. J. Mangalam, Robert Coles, John Photiadis, Gary Fowler, Mike Maloney, Larry Morgan, William Philliber, Brady Deaton, Laura Sharp, and Dorothy Kunkin; examples of this type of research are presented in this volume, and are extremely important in correcting the myths contained in the stereotypes of Appalachians and in replacing those myths with facts, or at least in posing appropriate questions that will lead us to truer facts about Appalachians in urban areas.

The type of research that will destroy many myths contained in the Appalachian stereotypes is exemplified by a statewide study sponsored by the Columbus, Ohio, Chamber of Commerce which found that:

One of three factory workers in Ohio are Appalachians. The author-economist, Kenneth Danter, states that the Ohio economy depends heavily on Appalachia as a source of labor. Statistically, Appalachian workers surveyed had held their jobs longer than non-Appalachians, had bought more houses per capita, and had provided "a stable labor force for Ohio manufacturing." Employers' attitudes about Appalachian employees were generally favorable. They were impressed by the migrants' willingness to work. [Kunkin and Byrne, 1973: 8]

Based on the evidence reported in the Cleveland studies, the authors conclude: "It is inaccurate to characterize Appalachian migrants to Cleveland as shiftless, 'poor whites.' Studies by the Institute of Urban Studies, the Labor Department, and Professor Photiadis provide factual information which discounts many commonly held myths about Appalachian migrants" (Kunkin and Byrne, 1973: 30).

The research of the past few years shows that most Appalachian migrants have been much more successful (even by their own definition of success) than most people—writers, antagonists, and activists—have represented them to be. Even some of the strongest Appalachian advocates leave the impression in oral and written comments that the migrant has been forced to remain in cities which are too foreign and hostile for Appalachians to possibly adjust to. In exaggerating the evils of the cities and in presenting a picture of urban life destroying the beauties and strengths of the Appalachian culture, advocates too often only project the image of maladjustment and malcontent which leads to the same distorted stereotypes portraying the Appalachian as unsuccessful.

It is understandable that many, in advocating the Appalachian cause, emphasize the evils of the urban areas and the many ills confronted by the migrants. And in the process of convincing others of the evils meted to the migrants, they also leave the false impression that most Appalachians are doing miserably in the cities and wish to return to the mountains at all costs. No doubt such statements are based upon a desire to compensate and correct the real ills faced by the mountaineers, and are grounded in the sincere wish that there had been revolutionary developments in Appalachia, particularly concerning those who control the energy complex and thereby control so many Appalachian lives, and the wish that Appalachians could have more power to control their own lives and more alternatives, including the choice not to migrate. But the fact remains that for many Appalachians the only alternative to a life of unemployment, poor education, poverty, poor health, and poor housing in the mountains has been to migrate to the urban areas in search of a means to survive and possibly provide better lives for their families. In doing so, many have been able to accomplish unfulfilled dreams and hopes which could never have been realized in Appalachia.

It is time to recognize that many Appalachians will never return to the mountains, even if it becomes possible, because they enjoy a high level of living and prefer the lifestyle of the urban environment. For too long the injustices of the system have overshadowed the deserved recognition of the fortitude and strength of many of the migrants who have made a successful adjustment to difficult situations. Their adjustment is more remarkable when one considers the lack of support from outside sources, either in the mountains or in the cities (unless the controversial support of the Appalachian Regional Commission is considered, and their expenditure of millions of dollars, at a late date, mostly for highways and other projects unrelated to support for individuals). In their tragedies the Appalachian families have relied upon their own cultural heritage for strength and support. Rather than seek outside aid, the Appalachians, like preceding migrant groups, have been able to depend upon strong kinship ties and the many ramifications of kinship support. Additional cultural supports have been available in a religious tradition which has provided standards of behavior and direction of daily activities that have shielded many from the potential anomic conditions of the adjustment process.

In suggesting that we improve our perceptions of Appalachians in urban areas by ridding ourselves of an unbalanced and distorted image of them, we do not suggest a cessation of efforts to improve the many poor conditions still abundant for many urban Americans. There are those who both need and deserve support and appropriate services through equal opportunities in both public and private sectors. But it is equally important to correct the myths that distort the image of the Appalachian, and to replace those mythical images with facts and role models that permit the development of a positive Appalachian identity.

NOTE

1. A representative of the advertising agency which developed the "mountain folk" commercial revealed that the commercial ran for only a very short time, since the client asked that it be pulled. Even an uninitiated executive found the material to be public degradation of mountain people.

Part II

Migration of Appalachians to Urban Areas

3 CLYDE B. McCOY & JAMES S. BROWN

Appalachian Migration
to Midwestern Cities

During the three decades from 1940 to 1970, the processes of migration within, to, and from Southern Appalachia were among the most important consequences as well as causes of regional social change. Appalachia, like any area, is significantly altered, for example, when a large proportion of its population, particularly the young, productive persons, find it necessary and desirable to leave. The enormous migration from Southern Appalachia is, then, a reflection—indeed an index—of the tremendous social changes in the region.

Brown and Hillery (1962) have documented Appalachia's great loss through migration from 1940 to 1960, but the extent and effect of this vast movement have yet to be fully appreciated. The net loss through migration from the Southern Appalachians was more than three million persons during the three decades between 1940 and 1970 (Table 3.1). Half of that loss occurred during the 1950s, when the region had a net loss of over one and a half million persons due to migration. The Appalachian portion of Kentucky had a startling loss in that decade, equal to almost one-third of its population of 1950. Appalachian West Virginia and Virginia had losses equivalent to one-fifth of their 1950 populations.

Appalachian Kentucky and West Virginia were severely depleted during the 1960s, too, when about 15 percent of their populations were lost due to the excess of out-migration over in-migration. The serious social and economic consequences for West Virginia and Kentucky become obvious when one realizes the enormity of the loss through migration during those three decades: The Appalachian parts of these two states had net losses through migration of about 1,645,000 persons

Table 3.1: Net Migration from Southern Appalachian Counties, 1940-70, by Decade

State	No. of counties†	Net Migration* 1940-50 Number	Rate**	1950-60 Number	Rate**	1960-70 Number	Rate**
Alabama	35	−137,010	−8.0	−205,821	−10.4	−73,463	−3.7
Georgia	34	−60,854	−10.5	−53,656	−31.8	+52,446	+7.8
Kentucky	49	−246,227	−22.1	−340,876	−31.8	−146,597	−15.9
Maryland	3	−10,543	−5.9	−14,751	−7.8	−2,057	−1.1
Mississippi	20	−94,878	−20.7	−90,324	−21.2	−34,861	−8.6
N.Carolina	29	−77,124	−9.4	−84,691	−9.6	−4,485	−0.5
S.Carolina	6	−23,578	−5.1	−40,593	−7.8	−3,807	−0.6
Tennessee	50	−62,162	−4.6	−173,871	−11.4	−45,514	−2.8
Virginia	21 (+5††)	−69,234	−13.7	−117,798	−22.2	−74,133	−14.8
W.Virginia	55	−204,763	−10.7	−446,711	−22.3	−259,528	−13.9
Total	303 (+5††)	−986,373	−10.9	−1,569,092	−16.3	−591,999	−6.1

* See note 4.
† Delineation I; see note 1.
** Net migration expressed as a percentage of the population at the beginning of the specified decade.
†† Independent cities, with separate units of government.

Sources: Data for 1940-50: University of Michigan Political Science Consortium.
Data for 1950-60: U.S. Bureau of the Census, *Current Population Reports,* Series P-23, No. 7, *Components of Population Change, 1950 to 1960, for Counties, Standard Metropolitan Statistical Areas, State Economic Areas, and Economic Subregions, November, 1962.*
Data for 1960-70: Estimates by the Department of Sociology, University of Kentucky, Agricultural Experiment Station. For a discussion of these data, see James S. Brown, "Southern Appalachian Population Change, 1960 to 1970," in David S. Walls and John B. Stephenson, eds., *Appalachia in the Sixties* (Lexington: University Press of Kentucky, 1972, pp. 130-44).

(the equivalent of 55 percent of the 1940 population of these areas), and the average loss for each of the 103 counties of Appalachian West Virginia and Kentucky for this period was 15,968, though their average population in 1940 was only 29,245. Both because more than half of all Southern Appalachia's loss due to out-migration from 1940 to 1950 was from West Virginia and Eastern Kentucky and because these two states are the primary sources of migrants to the Midwest, we will pay particular attention here to the destinations of out-migrants from these states.

Some of the social and economic conditions in the Appalachian state economic areas contributing to this phenomenal exodus are given in Table 3.2. [1] Obviously many areas, even in 1970, showed evidence

Table 3.2: Socioeconomic Characteristics of Appalachian SEAs, 1970, and Rates of Out-migration, 1955-60 and 1965-70

SEA	Rate of out-migration* 1955-60	Rate of out-migration* 1965-70	Males completing high school (%)	Males in labor force (%)	Median family income (in dollars)	Families below poverty level (%)	Families with income above $15,000 (%)
Alabama							
1	11.5	11.4	43.5	75.7	7,576	22.6	10.31
2	14.6	12.5	30.3	71.9	6,114	25.0	5.92
3	15.6	11.6	38.1	73.2	7,090	22.9	8.37
4	16.2	14.8	37.2	69.0	6,778	26.2	8.03
5	16.7	12.6	33.5	68.1	6,003	30.9	6.12
A	12.9	12.9	46.8	75.1	8,562	18.8	15.34
E	13.9	15.8	43.7	61.1	7,435	25.8	12.29
F	11.7	25.8	66.4	83.6	10,439	14.1	28.02
Georgia							
1	13.1	10.5	31.7	78.9	8,004	15.6	10.27
2	15.6	11.9	26.3	69.0	6,150	24.5	5.96
3	12.8	10.4	29.7	78.5	7,589	17.8	8.71
A	17.5	17.5	34.3	77.6	8,111	15.3	8.90
Kentucky							
5	15.8	12.7	20.8	64.2	5,855	40.0	5.22
8	17.3	14.6	23.8	58.3	5,977	40.3	4.78
9	19.6	16.9	21.9	54.0	5,597	40.3	4.78
C	19.7	19.9	48.9	70.9	9,623	14.6	14.53
Maryland							
1	13.3	14.1	44.7	71.8	7,681	17.1	8.97
N.Carolina							
1	14.8	13.2	31.8	68.3	6,103	26.0	5.96
2	11.4	8.6	28.0	77.6	7,673	16.0	7.39
A	15.2	14.8	44.5	74.7	7,742	16.1	11.83
B	11.7	14.1	45.7	77.9	9,286	14.3	17.83

(continued)

Table 3.2 (continued)

SEA	Rate of out-migration* 1955-60	Rate of out-migration* 1965-70	Males completing high school (%)	Males in labor force (%)	Median family income (in dollars)	Families below poverty level (%)	Families with income above $15,000 (%)
S.Carolina							
1	13.5	10.6	30.8	73.7	7,854	16.0	8.69
2	12.4	9.5	33.2	78.4	8,060	16.7	10.22
D	16.5	13.2	43.4	80.8	8,775	14.8	14.37
Tennessee							
6	13.8	13.3	31.1	69.8	5,851	27.0	6.76
7	16.8	14.7	23.2	63.8	5,135	36.2	3.81
8	12.4	9.5	34.9	72.9	6,683	23.6	7.58
C	17.8	17.0	51.1	76.9	8,609	16.6	15.73
D	17.0	13.3	51.4	72.1	8,200	17.7	14.06
Virginia							
1	19.5	16.7	22.1	62.6	5,802	32.1	5.29
2	15.5	11.8	24.9	69.9	6,436	22.9	6.20
3	16.7	15.4	38.0	70.3	7,772	16.4	10.46
4	10.2	11.1	38.4	77.1	8,057	14.3	11.49
A	14.7	14.0	50.4	77.7	9,145	11.2	16.36
W.Virginia							
1	14.2	13.0	47.6	76.1	9,015	12.7	13.62
2	18.3	15.8	32.5	61.7	6,224	30.5	5.41
3	16.0	13.6	45.6	65.3	7,374	19.8	8.70
4	22.3	16.4	29.8	59.0	6,492	28.7	6.54
5	17.6	15.1	35.4	65.8	5,891	28.8	5.75
6	12.4	10.9	38.0	73.3	7,726	17.0	10.27
A	13.6	13.0	44.7	72.2	8,649	13.8	12.94
B	17.6	16.2	46.1	69.1	7,803	19.9	11.93
C	18.2	19.9	53.4	73.8	8,669	16.5	15.34

* Number of out-migrants expressed as a percentage of the total population 5 years old and over in 1960 or 1970.

Sources: U.S. Bureau of the Census, U.S. Census of Population: 1960, Subject Reports, Final Report PC(2)-2E, *Migration between State Economic Areas* (Washington, D.C.: G.P.O., 1967).

Idem, U.S. Census of Population: 1970, Subject Reports, Final Report PC(2)-2E, *Migration between State Economic Areas;* Final Report PC(2)-108, *State Economic Areas* (Washington, D.C.: G.P.O., 1972).

of scarcities of social and economic opportunity. In the adjacent coal mining areas, Va. 1 and Ky. 9, for example, only 22 percent of the males twenty-five years old and over had completed high school; median annual income was less than $6,000; more than a third of the persons lived in poverty; and only about 5 percent of the families had annual incomes of $15,000 or more. These statistics paint a grim picture and strongly suggest why there were, and continue to be, so many leaving Appalachia.

The situation in the 1960s, then, remained very similar to that in the 1950s as summarized by Brown and Hillery (1962: 55): "In actuality, Appalachian people desiring higher levels of living have had few alternatives to migration. The prospects for commercial farming have not been bright, industry has been reluctant to settle in the Region, and coal mining has proved to be an undependable and inadequate source of employment even in the areas richest in coal resources. For many, migration offers the only alternative to a life of material and cultural poverty."

Southern Appalachia has long been surrounded by areas more highly developed economically, with important cities and metropolitan areas offering many jobs suitable for relatively unskilled and inadequately educated persons. Consequently, for decades Appalachia has been *a* major, and, since immigration from abroad has all but stopped, *the* major labor pool for industrial metropolises, especially in the Midwest.

Appalachia's own metropolitan areas lies mostly within the Great Valley—Birmingham and Huntsville, Alabama; Chattanooga and Knoxville, Tennessee; and Roanoke, Virginia—or along the fringes of the Southern Appalachians. For a number of reasons Eastern Kentucky and West Virginia have never developed large cities with industries employing great numbers of unskilled people. Consequently, since metropolitan areas are where the jobs are these days, migrants from Kentucky and West Virginia have had to leave their home states and Appalachia entirely. Modern migratory-stream systems[2] tend to center mainly on metropolitan areas. Since Appalachian Kentucky's and West Virginia's migrants have gone mainly to cities in the East North Central states, especially to Cincinnati, Dayton, Hamilton, Columbus, Cleveland, Akron, Canton, Indianapolis, Chicago, and Detroit, migratory streams involving these midwestern cities will be described and analyzed here in some detail.

Our major objective in this paper is to describe and interpret patterns of Appalachian migration, concentrating on migration to metropolitan areas,[3] especially to Midwestern metropolises. Our prime question is: Where did migrants go when they left Appalachia? To answer this question, we attempt to (1) indicate the main destinations of Southern Appalachian migrants, (2) show that the migratory streams have had a definite pattern, (3) point out the persistence of these patterns over three decades, and (4) place Appalachian migration in the context of the total migratory-stream systems centering around its principal metropolitan destinations.

To learn where the migrants went, we used migration data derived from the census question, in both the 1960 and the 1970 census, that asked persons where they had lived five years earlier, and in the 1950 census, where they had lived one year earlier.[4] One of the major limitations of these migration data is that they do not indicate total volume, nor can one easily estimate total volume for the decade (e.g., by multiplying by two or ten years).[5] We know only in what state economic area (SEA) persons residing in a specific state economic area in 1960 and 1970 lived five years earlier, or one year earlier for the 1950 data. Given this limitation, we look for patterns that persisted over the years and compare the patterns of different areas and different groupings of the population. Percentage comparisons, as well as correlations, are therefore used as important descriptive tools in interpreting the data.

To interpret properly the various tables and data, three characteristics of the data must be described:

(1) The smallest units for which the Bureau of the Census has published migratory stream data are state economic areas, which are groupings of relatively homogeneous counties or metropolitan areas (Bogue, 1951). For our purposes, therefore, Appalachia had to be defined as a collection of SEAs.

(2) The data indicate the number of persons who reported having moved but do not always report their former place of residence. (Approximately 13 percent of those who had moved by 1970 did not report place of residence in 1965.) No allocations were made of these persons, so their distributions are not reflected in the stream data we report here.[6]

(3) Because of data and time limitations we have had to use several different delineations, as indicated in note 1.

The twenty-six-SEA delineation (I) is used only in the first section, in which Appalachian migration to selected midwestern metropolitan areas is discussed. The twenty-six SEAs in this delineation are more significant than the others in the larger region, since they include those whose primary migratory ties are with the Midwest. Out-migration from the twenty-six SEA's constituted a little less than two-thirds of the total migrants from the larger (forty-three-SEA) region (Delineation II) (65 percent, 1960; 51 percent, 1970). Out-migrants from the twenty-six SEAs to midwestern metropolitan areas constituted high proportions of the total out-migrants to these metropolises from the forty-three SEAs in the larger delineation (Dayton: 84 percent in 1960 and 1970; Cincinnati: 88 percent in 1960 and 72 percent in 1970). Actually, migration to the Midwest even from the twenty-six-SEA region was highly concentrated; for instance, the Appalachian portions of Kentucky, Tennessee, West Virginia, and to a lesser degree Virginia, were the only SEAs of major significance to the midwestern metropolises. All twenty-six SEAs are included, however, in order to maintain comparability with other studies using this delineation.

Again, we must emphasize, these figures should not be interpreted as measures of the total number of out-migrants from Southern Appalachia to other areas, as is evident when comparing 1960 or 1970 data with 1950 data, since the data for the latter concern a different time period (one year compared to five years). One can, however, gain much understanding of the magnitude of in- and out-migration by comparisons of percentages: between different population groups (e.g., Appalachian whites and blacks), and between different areas of origin and/or destination.

Though caution is called for, we believe that when percentages are used, valid comparisons can be made between the one-year (1949–50) and the five-year (1955–60 and 1965–70) data because the patterns for all three periods are so constant. The consistency of these patterns is further confirmed by strong Pearsonian correlations between 1949–50 and 1955–60 data (.88) and between 1949–50 and 1965–70 data (.93).

We wish also to note briefly several general patterns evident in the out-migration from the twenty-six SEAs.

First, comparison of the proportions of the total out-migration from each SEA of origin shows great consistency for the three decades (Table 3.3).[7] For example, the migrants from the Eastern Kentucky Hills (Ky. 8) to other SEAs in the United States made up 4.45, 3.90, and 3.91 percent of the total out-migration from Southern Appalachia dur-

Table 3.3: Migration from Specified Southern Appalachian SEAs to All Other SEAs, 1949-50, 1955-60, and 1965-70

| SEA of residence in 1949, 1955, or 1965 | Residence in all other SEAs in the U.S. | | | | | |
| | 1950 | | 1960 | | 1970 | |
	Number	Percent	Number	Percent	Number	Percent
Alabama 2	11,865	4.88	25,728	3.04	24,629	3.34
Georgia 1	11,675	4.80	28,671	3.39	27,318	3.70
2	4,770	1.96	12,002	1.42	10,202	1.38
A	2,715	1.11	7,051	.83	8,105	1.10
Total	19,160	7.88	47,724	5.64	45,625	6.18
Kentucky 8	10,815	4.45	33,001	3.90	28,852	3.91
9	16,945	6.97	69,075	8.17	52,767	7.15
C	2,790	1.15	9,131	1.08	9,600	1.30
Total	30,550	12.56	111,207	13.15	91,219	12.35
N.Carolina 1	13,300	5.47	35,273	4.17	34,413	4.66
2	5,745	2.36	19,398	2.29	17,072	2.31
A	6,055	2.49	17,833	2.11	19,764	2.68
Total	25,100	10.32	72,504	8.58	71,249	9.65
Tennessee 7	5,160	2.11	16,697	1.97	14,888	2.02
8	22,135	9.10	76,694	9.07	65,628	8.89
C	11,240	4.62	37,672	4.46	39,757	5.38
D	16,225	6.67	55,880	6.61	49,226	6.67
Total	54,760	22.52	186,943	22.11	169,499	22.95
Virginia 1	7,395	3.04	30,363	3.59	22,644	3.07
2	8,740	3.59	29,585	3.50	22,691	3.07
3	8,080	3.32	27,777	3.29	28,659	3.88
4	6,480	2.67	20,604	2.44	25,985	3.52
A	5,700	2.34	20,933	2.48	23,333	3.16
Total	36,395	14.97	129,262	15.29	123,312	16.70
W.Virginia 2	10,710	4.40	40,218	4.76	33,776	4.28
3	9,695	3.99	36,848	4.36	31,569	4.28
4	15,120	6.22	87,802	10.38	55,219	7.48
5	4,595	1.89	36,368	4.30	21,845	2.96
6	6,115	2.51	6,771	.80	6,557	.89
B	6,360	2.62	23,306	2.76	21,590	2.92
C	12,720	5.23	40,830	4.83	42,313	5.73
Total	65,315	28.86	272,143	32.19	212,869	28.83
Total	243,145	100.	845,511	100.	738,402	100.

Sources: Data for 1949-50: Special tabulations by the U.S. Bureau of the Census for the Agricultural Experiment Station, University of Kentucky.
Data for 1955-60: U.S. Bureau of the Census, U.S. Census of Population: 1960, Subject Reports, Final Report PC(2)-2E, *Migration between State Economic Areas* (Washington, D.C.: G.P.O., 1967).
Data for 1965-70: U.S. Bureau of the Census, U.S. Census of Population: 1970, Subject Reports, Final Report PC(2)-2E, *Migration between State Economic Areas* (Washington, D.C.: G.P.O., 1972).

ing the 1949–50, 1955–60, and 1965–70 periods, respectively. Correlations show somewhat higher similarity of the 1955–60 and 1965–70 proportions (.95) and of 1949–50 and 1965–70 proportions (.93) than of 1949–50 and 1955–60 proportions (.87), but all are very high.

The overall Appalachian out-migration pattern, then, is consistent for the three decades. But how consistent is it when one views out-migration from Appalachia to specific metropolises?

The data for ten midwestern metropolises show that each metropolitan area received very similar proportions of migrants from the same areas of origin for each of the three decades. A strong association of the patterns of out-migration from Appalachia to the specified midwestern metropolises is evident in all three decades. For example, correlations between Appalachian SEAs contributing most to Cincinnati in 1949–50 and 1955–60 (.98), 1949–50 and 1965–70 (.96), and 1955–60 and 1965–70 (.98) were all high, as they also were for Dayton (.84, .85, and .87, respectively).

Ten midwestern metropolises were major focal areas for Appalachian migration in all three decades. General patterns (see Table 3.4) are evident in the migration from the twenty-six Appalachian SEAs to each of the ten metropolises for all three decades. Eastern Kentucky, Eastern Tennessee, and West Virginia were the areas supplying most of the migrants to the Midwest. Alabama and Georgia contributed very few; and North Carolina, though sending slightly more than the three smallest contributors, sent significantly fewer migrants than the three most important contributors.

Detailed observation of each metropolis reveals, then, that each received most of its migrants over the years from specific areas. Because of the heterogeneity of culture within Southern Appalachia, it is important to note, therefore, that persons and agencies in most metropolises need only concern themselves with *particular* rather than *all* the areas in Appalachia. Those in Cincinnati wanting to understand their Appalachian migrants, for instance, should especially study the culture of Eastern Kentucky, whereas those in Columbus and especially Cleveland should be more concerned with West Virginia's culture.

As an example, Cincinnati (Table 3.5) received for each decade more than 30 percent of its Appalachian migrants from the coal fields of Eastern Kentucky (Ky. 9). Another 17 percent of Cincinnati's Appalachian migrants came from the subsistence-farming area adjacent to the coal fields (Ky. 8), and East Tennessee migrants have con-

Table 3.4: Percentage of Southern Appalachian* Migrants to Ten Metropolitan Areas, 1949-50, 1955-60, and 1965-70

Destination	Alabama	Georgia	Kentucky	North Carolina	Ten- nessee	Virginia	West Virginia
Cincinnati							
1950	†	†	57	2	16	5	20
1960	†	1	63	1	15	6	14
1970	†	1	50	†	16	6	23
Dayton							
1950	†	†	54	2	25	5	13
1960	†	†	47	1	24	9	18
1970	†	†	52	†	17	11	18
Hamilton							
1950			85	†	4	3	8
1960		†	77	1	8	5	9
1970	1	3	42	7	11	8	28
Columbus							
1950		†	28	3	7	5	58
1960	†	†	30	†	5	6	59
1970	†	†	26	1	5	4	64
Cleveland							
1950	1	2	8	3	22	6	58
1960	†	1	7	2	14	7	68
1970	†	†	5	2	14	6	72
Akron							
1950	3	5	7	6	9	7	64
1960	2	†	7	2	12	7	70
1970	†	2	6	1	6	6	79
Canton							
1950	2	8	18	10	†	11	52
1960	0	†	3	7	3	4	82
1970	0	0	7	3	6	5	78
Indianapolis							
1950	1	0	37	2	31	9	19
1960	†	2	35	1	27	10	25
1970	†	3	46	2	24	8	16
Chicago							
1950	5	4	16	6	33	10	27
1960	5	4	17	9	26	7	32
1970	3	2	17	4	25	11	38
Detroit							
1950	3	9	26	7	32	6	17
1960	2	5	29	6	22	10	28
1970	2	3	35	5	18	10	27

* Delineation IV (see note 1).   † Less than 1 percent.

Sources: Data for 1940-50: University of Michigan Political Science Consortium.

Data for 1950-60: U.S. Bureau of the Census, *Current Population Reports,* Series P-23, No. 7, *Components of Population Change, 1950 to 1960, for Counties, Standard Metropolitan Statistical Areas, State Economic Areas, and Economic Subregions, November, 1962.*

Data for 1960-70: Estimates by Department of Sociology, University of Kentucky, Agricultural Experiment Station. For a discussion of these data, see James S. Brown, "Southern Appalachian Populations Change, 1960 to 1970," in David S. Walls and John B. Stephenson, eds., *Appalachia in the Sixties* (Lexington: University Press of Kentucky, 1972), pp. 130-44.

Table 3.5: Appalachian Migrants to Selected Metropolises from Specified Southern Appalachian SEAs, Percentage Comparisons for 1950, 1960, and 1970

Residence in Southern Appalachia*		Residence in Cincinnati			Residence in Dayton			Residence in Hamilton			Residence in Columbus		
		1950	1960	1970	1950	1960	1970	1950	1960	1970	1950	1960	1970
Alabama	2	.30	.06	.48	.30	.15	.18	.00	.00	1.26	.00	.06	.19
Georgia	1	.50	.50	.87	.05	.18	.66	.00	.08	2.21	.00	.51	.24
	2	.00	.10	.00	.00	.06	.00	.00	.00	.00	.00	.03	.08
	A	.00	.36	.61	.00	.06	.00	.00	.00	.44	.00	.00	.07
	Total	.50	.96	1.49	.05	.30	.66	.00	.08	2.65	.00	.54	.39
Kentucky	8	20.80	17.40	17.22	32.30	17.98	20.60	49.40	39.34	24.64	12.90	8.43	8.03
	9	34.10	43.63	30.63	19.70	27.94	30.52	32.30	36.15	16.11	14.20	18.86	12.48
	C	1.80	1.55	2.21	2.40	1.54	1.19	3.20	1.56	1.58	1.30	2.44	4.62
	Total	56.70	62.58	50.06	54.40	47.46	52.31	84.90	77.05	42.33	28.40	29.73	25.13
N.Carolina	1	.80	.47	.61	1.00	.72	.88	.00	.62	5.18	1.70	.31	.33
	2	.50	.00	.00	.30	.04	.00	.00	.07	.00	.40	.11	.29
	A	.80	.97	.22	.30	.29	.00	.60	.45	1.70	.40	.22	.41
	Total	2.10	1.44	.83	1.60	1.05	.88	.60	1.14	6.88	2.50	.64	1.03
Tennessee	7	3.80	2.98	2.17	8.40	5.38	4.38	.60	.27	.00	.00	.22	.06
	8	5.30	6.14	5.53	9.20	12.42	8.40	1.30	4.03	2.84	4.60	1.80	1.88
	C	2.50	1.14	2.99	2.10	.53	.36	.00	.45	4.04	1.70	.42	.73
	D	4.00	5.07	5.42	5.20	5.24	3.61	2.50	2.80	3.85	.80	2.26	1.82
	Total	15.60	15.33	16.11	24.90	23.57	16.75	4.40	7.55	10.73	7.10	4.70	4.49
Virginia	1	2.80	4.05	2.34	2.40	5.43	6.68	.60	2.98	6.44	1.30	2.18	2.02
	2	.00	.60	.30	.80	2.06	1.44	.60	1.65	.00	1.70	1.30	.77
	3	.80	.48	.94	.50	.61	1.55	.60	.53	.44	.80	1.00	.29
	4	1.00	.11	.53	.50	.56	.93	.00	.09	1.20	.00	.21	.56
	A	.80	.67	1.55	.80	.29	.45	.60	.00	.38	1.30	.85	.79
	Total	5.40	5.91	5.66	5.00	8.95	11.05	2.40	5.25	8.46	5.10	5.54	4.43
W.Virginia	2	1.80	.52	1.26	1.00	2.01	2.36	.00	.33	2.97	10.80	8.08	5.52
	3	2.50	1.72	3.30	1.80	2.29	2.34	1.30	.93	1.20	5.00	2.69	3.54
	4	5.80	4.71	6.23	3.90	8.99	7.49	1.30	3.41	3.66	12.90	29.03	28.69
	5	.30	.68	.12	.30	1.28	.47	.60	1.25	.76	.80	2.76	2.51
	6	1.00	.19	.11	1.30	.07	.06	.60	.26	.00	2.90	.00	.21
	B	3.50	2.57	4.41	3.10	1.58	2.27	.00	1.54	5.87	7.10	8.01	13.46
	C	5.00	3.44	9.95	1.80	2.32	3.16	3.80	1.47	13.20	17.90	8.22	10.07
	Total	19.90	13.83	23.38	13.20	18.54	18.15	7.60	9.19	27.66	57.40	58.79	64.00
Total number		1,995	13,077	5,839	1,905	11,226	7,961	790	4,492	1,583	1,200	13,384	9,134

* Residents in specified metropolitan areas in 1950, 1960, and 1970 had their residence in the specified Southern Appalachian SEA in 1949, 1955, and 1965, respectively.

(continued)

Table 3.5 (continued)

Residence in Southern Appalachia*	Residence in Cleveland 1950	1960	1970	Residence in Akron 1950	1960	1970	Residence in Canton 1950	1960	1970	Residence in Indianapolis 1950	1960	1970
Alabama 2	1.30	.77	.72	2.90	1.83	.14	1.60	.00	.00	1.00	.72	.00
Georgia 1	1.70	1.05	.08	2.20	.13	1.26	4.80	.41	.00	.00	.87	3.09
2	.00	.20	.15	2.90	.64	.19	3.20	.27	.00	.00	1.02	.21
A	.00	.20		.00	.00	.19	.00	.00	.00	.00	.00	.19
Total	1.70	1.45	.23	5.10	.77	1.64	8.00	.68	.00	.00	1.89	3.49
Kentucky 8	2.60	1.18	1.22	2.20	1.21	.19	6.50	1.30	2.82	19.20	10.89	17.64
9	3.80	4.84	3.04	3.60	5.32	4.21	6.50	1.64	2.62	18.20	23.64	28.30
C	1.70	.51	.88	1.40	.49	1.54	4.80	.14	1.97	.00	.54	
Total	8.10	6.53	5.14	7.20	7.02	5.94	17.80	3.08	7.41	37.40	35.07	45.94
N.Carolina 1	2.60	.76	1.03	4.30	1.43	1.10	9.70	6.21	1.53	.00	.64	1.03
2	.00	.48	.06	1.40	.00	1.10	.00	.72	1.08	1.00	.23	.54
A	.40	.41	.77	.00	.21	.33	.00	.00	.16	1.00	.16	.81
Total	3.00	1.65	1.86	5.70	1.64	1.43	9.70	6.93	2.77	2.00	1.03	2.38
Tennessee 7	2.10	1.93	1.51	.70	1.00	.49	.00	.17	.28	3.00	4.10	5.58
8	9.80	6.72	4.77	3.60	5.27	1.43	.00	.92	2.58	14.10	11.86	9.70
C	4.70	1.65	2.07	2.20	2.59	2.01	.00	.68	1.08	4.00	2.09	3.71
D	5.60	3.78	5.77	2.20	3.18	2.17	.00	1.43	2.46	10.10	8.65	5.44
Total	22.20	14.08	14.12	8.70	12.04	6.10	.00	3.20	6.40	31.20	26.70	24.43
Virginia 1	1.70	3.83	2.22	3.60	2.66	1.76	1.60	2.66	.48	3.00	6.49	2.90
2	1.30	1.17	.51	2.20	2.05	.99	4.80	.51	.00	1.00	1.17	1.03
3	.00	1.53	.98	.70	.51	.57	4.80	.00	2.29	4.00	1.23	3.09
4	1.30	.50	1.22	.00	.90	.71	.00	.10	.00	1.00	.44	.29
A	1.70	.39	.84	.00	.72	2.09	.00	.99	2.54	.00	.69	.48
Total	6.00	7.42	5.77	6.50	6.84	6.12	11.20	4.26	5.33	9.00	10.02	7.79
W.Virginia 2	9.00	8.13	8.88	32.40	24.77	32.29	14.50	32.64	20.08	1.00	2.09	1.03
3	13.70	9.52	11.03	13.70	17.39	12.09	17.70	19.51	27.58	3.00	2.12	1.22
4	12.40	31.13	26.57	1.40	9.11	9.39	3.20	17.09	11.94	8.10	8.93	4.63
5	1.30	5.59	4.11	2.90	8.52	7.57	1.60	8.08	4.24	.00	.01	.57
6	3.40	.07	.33	4.30	.00	.22	6.50	.14	3.35	.00	.87	.56
B	8.10	3.63	5.26	2.90	2.56	3.30	4.80	1.33	4.76	3.00	4.07	2.35
C	9.80	10.12	16.23	6.50	7.51	12.91	3.20	3.21	9.48	4.00	6.59	5.53
Total	57.70	68.19	72.41	64.10	69.86	78.77	51.50	82.00	78.07	19.10	24.68	15.89
Total number	1,170	18,128	9,873	695	6,095	3,631	310	2,932	2,480	495	3,931	3,689

Sources: Data for 1949–50: Special tabulations by the U.S. Bureau of the Census for the Agricultural Experiment Station, University of Kentucky.

Data for 1955–60: U.S. Bureau of the Census, U.S. Census of Population: 1960, Subject Reports, Final Report PC(2)-2E, *Migration between State Economic Areas* (Washington, D.C.: G.P.O., 1967).

(continued)

Table 3.5 (continued)

Residence in Southern Appalachia*		Residence in Chicago			Residence in Detroit			Residence in Atlanta		
		1950	1960	1970	1950	1960	1970	1950	1960	1970
Alabama	2	5.20	5.26	2.77	3.20	1.58	2.45	4.20	3.30	4.70
Georgia	1	2.80	2.79	1.19	5.50	2.94	2.14	37.80	33.70	23.20
	2	.80	.49	.25	2.90	1.53	.37	14.60	16.70	10.80
	A	.00	.52	.15	.30	.08	.46	2.90	1.80	1.60
Total		3.60	3.80	1.59	8.70	4.55	2.97	55.30	52.20	35.60
Kentucky	8	3.60	1.96	2.53	3.60	3.22	5.10	.30	.20	.40
	9	10.80	15.04	13.97	20.90	25.14	27.78	.90	1.40	1.20
	C	1.40	.48	.89	1.20	.64	1.96	.60	.10	.10
Total		15.70	17.48	17.39	25.70	29.00	34.84	1.80	1.70	1.70
N.Carolina	1	3.60	2.01	1.94	4.60	4.16	2.49	3.50	5.50	6.20
	2	1.10	.95	.78	.50	.62	.71	.20	.90	.80
	A	1.50	5.83	1.52	1.60	1.19	1.45	3.00	2.80	3.30
Total		6.20	8.79	4.24	6.70	5.97	4.65	6.70	9.20	10.30
Tennessee	7	1.70	3.36	2.69	4.60	2.80	2.89	1.10	.70	1.20
	8	11.00	9.81	10.33	13.00	9.02	8.45	5.90	9.20	14.00
	C	9.40	4.51	2.10	7.30	3.68	2.95	9.10	8.10	9.40
	D	10.50	8.69	9.60	7.50	6.20	3.58	10.60	8.50	13.90
Total		32.60	26.37	24.72	32.40	21.70	17.87	26.70	26.50	38.50
Virginia	1	1.70	3.05	4.10	2.20	5.26	6.24	.20	.50	.30
	2	2.20	1.16	1.69	1.60	1.72	1.49	.60	.60	.80
	3	2.80	1.05	1.79	1.40	1.02	1.13	.60	.70	.90
	4	2.20	.72	2.19	.30	.53	.86	.60	.20	.50
	A	1.40	.84	1.16	.70	1.12	.18	.60	.90	1.80
Total		10.30	6.82	10.93	6.20	9.65	9.90	2.60	2.90	4.30
W.Virginia	2	1.40	.91	3.57	1.50	2.03	1.40	.30	.10	.30
	3	5.00	.82	5.65	2.80	2.87	2.06	.30	1.00	.70
	4	7.70	22.57	17.06	5.00	14.85	13.06	.00	.80	1.10
	5	1.40	1.59	1.74	.60	1.72	1.18	.50	.50	.20
	6	.80	.02	.00	1.20	.00	.00	.80	.10	.10
	B	2.80	1.60	4.32	2.50	2.50	3.63	.20	.80	.80
	C	7.50	4.09	5.92	3.40	3.68	6.07	.80	1.00	1.60
Total		26.60	31.58	38.26	17.00	27.63	27.40	2.90	4.30	4.80
Total number		1,810	15,838	9,389	4,670	13,013	15,220	3,295	18,439	21,075

Sources (continued): Data for 1965–70: U.S. Bureau of the Census, U.S. Census of Population: 1970, Subject Reports, Final Report PC(2)-2E, *Migration between State Economic Areas* (Washington, D.C.: G.P.O., 1972).

sistently been about 15 percent of Cincinnati's total Appalachian in-migrants.

The major changes in Cincinnati's pattern over the three decades were that West Virginians came to form a higher proportion of Appalachian migrants while the coal fields of Eastern Kentucky sent fewer. The explanation of this shift is not easily arrived at; probably it was partly due to the fact that, because so many migrants had previously departed from the Kentucky coal area, high rates of out-migration could not be maintained (though the out-migration from Ky. 9 to Cincinnati was still large in 1970). Employment opportunities in the West Virginia coal fields, on the other hand, decreased drastically because of mechanization of coal mining which came somewhat later there than in Eastern Kentucky; thus the area had its greatest migration losses later.

Dayton had a pattern similar to Cincinnati's, although the Kentucky Hills area's (Ky. 8) proportion of total out-migrants going to Dayton steadily decreased after 1950 (from 32 percent to 21 percent in 1970). On the other hand, the Eastern Kentucky Coal Fields (Ky. 9) contributed higher proportions of Dayton's in-migrants (increasing from 20 percent for 1949–50 to 31 percent for 1965–70). The importance of East Tennesseans to Dayton declined somewhat, but the southwestern section of Virginia increased its proportion.

Hamilton's pattern changed from one receiving very concentrated streams of migrants from Ky. 8 and Ky. 9 (a total of 82 percent of the total Appalachian migrants in 1949–50) to a pattern similar to Cincinnati's and Dayton's. The proportions coming from the two Kentucky SEAs declined a great deal while West Virginia's proportion increased considerably, along with significant increases from East Tennessee and Va. 1 (also a coal field area, contiguous to the Eastern Kentucky coal fields).

Cincinnati, Hamilton, and Dayton have been three midwestern metropolises most important to out-migrants from Eastern Kentucky. They are, of course, close to one another, and are the large industrialized cities nearest to Eastern Kentucky. They are closely bound by transportation routes (especially in recent years by Interstate 75) to Eastern Kentucky.

Columbus, Cleveland, Akron, and Canton—all east of Cincinnati, Hamilton, and Dayton—have been more strongly influenced by West Virginia; or, to put it another way, have been the most important destinations for West Virginia migrants. They are relatively close to each other and are linked by Interstates 71 and 77. Interstate 77 (part of which is the West Virginia Turnpike) is a direct route to Ohio from West Virginia. Like the first three metropolises, these four are also industrial manufacturing centers employing many unskilled and semi-skilled workers, as well as the typical lower-income white-collar employees (teachers, secretaries, clerks, waitresses, etc.).

Columbus received a heavy concentration of its Appalachian in-migrants from West Virginia in 1949–50 (58 percent), and even more, proportionately, in 1955–60 (59 percent) and 1965–70 (64 percent) (Table 3.5). The two largest contributors by specific SEAs were both coal-mining areas, W. Va. 4 and Ky. 9. Both Ky. 8 (a subsistence-farming area) and Ky. 9 were significant contributors to Columbus for all three decades. It is probably not incidental that U.S. Highway 23 is a readily accessible link between Eastern Kentucky and Columbus.

Cleveland attracted an even higher proportion of its Appalachian migrants from West Virginia than did Columbus, with the coal fields (W. Va. 4) its largest single Appalachian contributor. All the other Appalachian states which influenced the midwestern urban areas contributed 5 percent or more of their migrants to Cleveland, indicating that city's broad influence throughout Appalachia. East Tennessee, however, sent a much greater percentage of migrants to Cleveland in 1949–50 (22 percent) than in 1955–60 or 1965–70 (14 percent). Charleston (West Virginia C), one of the few metropolitan areas in the United States to have very heavy net losses through migration, became an important source of Cleveland's in-migrants in the 1965–70 period (16 percent). This was part of a recent general exodus from Charleston to all the Ohio metropolises. Charleston was the only Appalachian metropolis from which there was significant migration to a number of midwestern metropolitan areas, though one would expect much more intermetropolitan migration than there has been. This is still another indication of the lack of influence within Appalachia from its metropolises.

Akron and Canton had even more concentrated streams of migration from West Virginia than did Columbus and Cleveland. However, though W. Va. 4 (a coal-mining area in southern West Virginia) was the largest contributor to both Columbus and Cleveland, W. Va. 2 and W. Va. 3 (the Hills and Monongahela Valley areas) were the largest contributors to both Akron and Canton.

The patterns of migration streams to these seven Ohio metropolitan areas illustrate the great consistency and continuity over time in the

migratory-stream systems involving Appalachian SEAs. There has been
an obvious tendency for the streams to continue from the same places
to the same destinations once the streams have been initiated. If data
were available for smaller units, we would almost certainly see that migratory patterns were even more specific. Entire families from certain
hollows have migrated to the same neighborhoods, even to particular
streets, in the metropolitan areas, as did relatives and friends in the
past.

The next three metropolitan areas examined differed from the other
midwestern areas for the most part only in that their Appalachian migration streams were less concentrated.

Indianapolis, as expected, had a migratory-stream pattern similar
to that of Cincinnati, Dayton, and Hamilton except that it had fewer
in-migrants from Eastern Kentucky and more, in general, from Tennessee, West Virginia, and Virginia. But Ky. 8 and Ky. 9 contributed
the most, as they did in Cincinnati, Dayton, and Hamilton.

Detroit was influenced more by Eastern Kentucky, Ky. 9 in particular, and had significant numbers and proportions of Appalachian migrants from more areas of origin than had Indianapolis. The proportions of migrants from Kentucky and West Virginia increased over the
three decades, while the percentage from Tennessee steadily declined.
The major coal areas of Kentucky (Ky. 9), West Virginia (W. Va. 4),
and Virginia (Va. 1) all contributed large numbers of migrants to
Detroit. Automobile plants in midwestern cities employed thousands of
Appalachian migrants, and the auto industry, with related industries
such as the tire industry in Akron, was probably the single largest employer of Appalachians in urban areas of the Midwest.

Like Detroit, Chicago also received a substantial proportion of its
Appalachian migrants from the three principal coal-mining SEAs (Ky.
9, W. Va. 4, and Va. 1). The migrants from the coal areas formed
smaller proportions of Chicago's in-migrants in 1965–70 than in
1955–60, but much greater than in 1949–50. This pattern is a result of
the mass migration of the late 1940s and 1950s, when the employment
of miners declined so drastically because of technological changes in
coal mining. The 1950s, it is worth noting, were the time when
Chicago received its greatest number of Appalachian migrants. West
Virginia's migrants increased proportionately among Chicago's in-migrants, while East Tennessee became a somewhat less important source
of migrants. About the same proportion of Appalachian migrants to
Chicago came from Kentucky over the three decades, and the same is

true of Virginia, though the number of migrants from Virginia was much smaller.

In thinking of some of the implications of these variations, one would expect Appalachian migrants in Chicago to be of greater social and cultural diversity than those in Ohio metropolises, since they came from a less concentrated group of SEAs which (though this is not commonly understood) are very diverse socially and culturally though all are "Southern Appalachian." Appalachian migrants in Chicago, incidentally, were also forced to adjust to a more culturally differentiated population, since Chicago has drawn migrants from more cultural and ethnic origins than other midwestern cities. An additional adjustment, probably a considerable disadvantage in many ways, which Appalachian migrants faced especially in Chicago, was that they made up a much smaller minority of the migrants there than in most of the other midwestern cities.

A notable fact also is the high proportion of the migrants to the midwestern urban areas from the Appalachian coal fields of Kentucky (Ky. 9), West Virginia (W. Va. 4), and Virginia (Va. 1). This trend has been repeatedly emphasized in the preceding discussion, but it is worth stressing, for when the pattern of migration from all the Southern Appalachian SEAs is examined (Table 3.3), it is clear that the three major coal-mining areas *did not* contribute a disproportionate share of the total Appalachian migrants to all other SEAs in the United States. By contrast, to summarize, in every one of the midwestern metropolises examined, except Akron, the Appalachian coal mining SEAs were the most significant sources of migrants. For the three southwestern Ohio metropolises and for Indianapolis, Ky. 9 sent the most significant proportion; for Cleveland and Columbus, W. Va. 4 was the most important; Canton had significant numbers from both Ky. 9 and W. Va. 4; and Chicago and Detroit had significant proportions of their total Appalachian in-migrants from all these coal SEAs. These supermetropolises were obviously attracting migrants from very widely scattered origins. It should be obvious that persons and agencies concerned with Appalachian migrants need to know well the cultural and social characteristics of the coal-mining areas.

For contrast, we now want to compare the midwestern cities' selectivity of Appalachian migrants to that of Atlanta, a metropolis which belongs to a very different migratory-stream system, though of course not a totally distinct one, since all the great metropolitan areas of the country are interrelated in many ways, obvious and obscure.

Atlanta mainly attracted its Appalachian migrants from other parts of the Southern Appalachians than did the midwestern metropolises. Not surprisingly, Atlanta drew most of its migrants from Georgia and nearby Tennessee. Much of Atlanta's recent rapid growth has been due to Appalachia, though this seems not to be widely recognized, even in Atlanta, which has been (perhaps rightly) more concerned with the dominance of blacks in the central city than with the changing composition of the greater Appalachian metropolitan area. In fact, though Atlanta is an obvious and well known destination for blacks, it has been even more important for Southern Appalachian migrants. Less than 10 percent of all Atlanta's in-migrants from 1965 to 1970 were black, but almost 20 percent were from Appalachia. Black in-migrants and Appalachian in-migrants are not necessarily, of course, entirely separate. Some Appalachian migrants are black, but the black proportion of Atlanta's Appalachian in-migration is small. In the 1955–60 period an even greater proportion of its in-migrants were from Appalachia.

Because of our special interest in Appalachian migratory streams to midwestern metropolises, we have concentrated on demonstrating the importance of specific SEAs in Appalachia for the midwestern cities. Obviously Kentucky's and West Virginia's SEAs have been very important parts of the midwestern migratory-stream systems. For other migratory-stream systems of Appalachians, other areas of destination and other areas of origin would be stressed. For instance, in the Piedmont Crescent (extending from Raleigh-Durham, North Carolina, through western North and South Carolina, down to and for some researchers even including Atlanta), Appalachian SEAs in North Carolina and South Carolina have been predominant in the migration which is part of the development of metropolitan and other urban industrial centers.

Our discussion thus far has concentrated on migration to the midwestern metropolises from Appalachia. But how does Appalachian migration compare to migration from all other areas of the United States to these midwestern metropolises? To answer this question one must understand the total system of in-migration to each of the selected midwestern focal areas. Therefore, we tabulated data for all SEAs in the United States which contributed significant numbers of migrants to each of the midwestern focal areas (Table 3.6) in the three decades.

Component areas of the migratory-stream systems were chosen on the basis of two criteria: (1) All SEAs (of the 509 in the United States) which contributed 1 percent or more of the total in-migration to the

Table 3.6 Migratory-stream Systems to Selected Metropolitan Focal Areas, 1965-70

CINCINNATI

Total in-migrants: 96,937

SEA of origin	No. of migrants	% of focal area's total in-migrants
Mass C	1,063	1.10
NY G	2,135	2.21
Penn D	1,254	1.30
Ohio 3	2,490	2.57
Ohio 6	971	1.01
Ohio 7*	7,861	8.11
Ohio B	3,211	3.32
Ohio C	3,261	3.37
Ohio D*	4,102	4.24
Ohio E*	3,267	3.37
Ind 8	1,433	1.48
Ind D	1,392	1.44
Ill C	3,070	3.17
Mich F	1,593	1.65
Mo B	1,147	1.19
Ky 5*†	1,153	1.19
Ky 6	1,737	1.80
Ky 8**	1,006	1.04
Ky 9**	1,789	1.85
Ky A	1,039	1.08
Ky B*	4,494	4.64
Cal F	1,957	2.02
Total	51,425	53.15

5 percent of out-migrants from SEA migrated to focal area

SEA of origin	No. to focal area	Total out-migrants	%
Ohio 7	7,861	31,840	24.69
Ohio D	4,102	31,082	13.20
Ind 8	1,433	22,444	6.39
Ky 5†	1,153	19,034	6.06
Ky B	4,494	23,351	19.25

* SEA which contributed 5 percent or more of its out-migrants to the specified focal area and whose out-migrants to that focal area also constituted 1 percent or more of the focal area's total in-migration.

† Appalachian SEA (as defined in Delineation II; see note 1).

** Appalachian SEA (as defined in Delineations II and IV; see note 1).

DAYTON

Total in-migrants: 107,113

SEA of origin	No. of migrants	% of focal area;s total in-migrants
NY G	1,694	1.59
Penn D	1,418	1.33
Ohio 2	1,805	1.69
Ohio 3*	9,204	8.60
Ohio 6	1,104	1.03
Ohio 7*	1,751	1.64
Ohio 8	1,743	1.63
Ohio B	3,610	3.37
Ohio D*	2,213	2.07
Ohio E	2,549	2.38
Ohio K	3,748	3.50
Ohio N*	3,832	3.58
Ill C	2,300	2.15
Mich F	1,780	1.67
Ky 8*/**	1,640	1.54
Ky 9**	2,430	2.27
Cal F	2,567	2.40
Total	45,389	42.44

5 percent of out-migrants from SEA migrated to focal area

SEA of origin	No. to focal area	Total out-migrants	%
Ohio 3	9,204	62,947	14.63
Ohio 7	1,751	31,840	5.50
Ohio D	2,213	31,082	7.12
Ohio N	3,832	20,396	18.79
Ky 8**	1,640	28,852	5.69

HAMILTON

Total in-migrants: 35,488

SEA of origin	No. of migrants	% of focal area's total in-migrants
NY G	490	1.38
Ohio 1	357	1.01
Ohio 2	590	1.67
Ohio 3*	4,361	12.29
Ohio 4	441	1.25
Ohio 6	660	1.86
Ohio 7	515	1.46
Ohio B	1,018	2.87
Ohio C	2,140	6.03

(continued)

Table 3.6 (continued)

HAMILTON (*continued*):

SEA of origin	No. of migrants	% of focal area's total in-migrants
Ohio E	1,535	4.33
Ohio K	6,589	18.57
Ind 4	368	1.04
Ind 8	525	1.48
Ill C	727	2.05
Ky 8**	793	2.24
Ky 9**	523	1.48
Ky E	427	1.21
Cal F	364	1.03
Total	22,423	63.25

5 percent of out-migrants from SEA migrated to focal area

SEA of origin	No. to focal area	Total out-migrants	%
Ohio 3	4,361	62,947	6.93

COLUMBUS

Total in-migrants: 130,512

SEA of origin	No. of migrants	% of focal area's total in-migrants
NY G	2,502	1.92
Penn D	2,098	1.61
Ohio 1	2,198	1.69
Ohio 2*	3,983	3.06
Ohio 3*	7,072	5.42
Ohio 4*	4,024	3.09
Ohio 5*	1,431	1.10
Ohio 6*	10,156	7.79
Ohio 7*	1,872	1.44
Ohio 8*	6,710	5.15
Ohio A	1,757	1.35
Ohio C	4,886	3.75
Ohio E	7,252	5.56
Ohio F	2,173	1.67
Ohio G*	1,846	1.42
Ohio H	1,752	1.35
Ohio K	3,522	2.70
Ill C	2,459	1.89
Mich F	1,937	1.49
W.Va 4**	2,621	2.01
Cal F	1,940	1.49
Total	74,191	56.95

COLUMBUS (*continued*):

5 percent of out-migrants from SEA migrated to focal area

SEA of origin	No. to focal area	Total out-migrants	%
Ohio 2	3,983	50,395	7.91
Ohio 3	7,072	62,947	11.24
Ohio 4	4,024	59,023	6.82
Ohio 6	10,156	73,294	13.86
Ohio 7	1,872	31,840	5.88
Ohio 8	6,710	47,535	14.12
Ohio G	1,846	36,687	5.04
Ohio J	599	8,858	6.77
Ohio L	627	7,999	7.84
Ohio N	1,250	20,356	6.14

CLEVELAND

Total in-migrants: 149,712

SEA of origin	No. of migrants	% of focal area's total in-migrants
Mass C	1,729	1.16
NY A	1,996	1.34
NY G	4,810	3.22
Penn 1	1,512	1.01
Penn 4	2,030	1.36
Penn B	1,962	1.31
Penn D	5,434	3.63
Ohio 1	1,915	1.28
Ohio 4*	4,711	3.15
Ohio 5*	8,666	5.79
Ohio 6	2,027	1.36
Ohio 8	1,823	1.22
Ohio B	4,151	2.78
Ohio C	1,822	1.22
Ohio F*	5,546	3.71
Ohio G*	2,121	1.42
Ohio H*	3,064	2.05
Ohio K	2,092	1.40
Ohio M*	4,852	3.24
Ill C	4,878	3.26
Mich F	4,035	3.70
W.Va 4**	2,624	1.76
W.Va C**	1,603	1.07
Cal F	2,337	1.56
Total	77,740	53.00

(continued)

Table 3.6 (continued)

CLEVELAND (*continued*):

5 percent of out-migrants from SEA
migrated to focal area

SEA of origin	No. to focal area	Total out-migrants	%
Ohio 4	4,711	59,023	7.99
Ohio 5	8,666	52,807	16.41
Ohio F	5,546	67,517	8.22
Ohio G	2,121	36,687	5.79
Ohio H	3,064	43,236	7.09
Ohio M	4,852	30,477	15.92

AKRON

Total in-migrants: 57,713

SEA of origin	No. of migrants	% of focal area's total in-migrants
NY G	897	1.55
Penn D	1,220	2.11
Ohio 4*	3,108	5.39
Ohio 5*	4,994	8.65
Ohio 6	1,388	2.41
Ohio 8	580	1.00
Ohio E	10,125	17.54
Ohio G*	2,277	3.95
Ohio H	1,250	2.17
Ill C	1,428	2.47
Mich F	1,303	2.26
W.Va 2**	1,209	2.09
Cal F	1,313	2.28
Total	31,094	53.87

5 percent of out-migrants from SEA
migrated to focal area

SEA of origin	No. to focal area	Total out-migrants	%
Ohio 4	3,108	59,023	5.27
Ohio 5	4,994	52,807	9.46
Ohio G	2,277	36,687	6.21

CANTON

Total in-migrants: 37,664

SEA of origin	No. of migrants	% of focal area's total in-migrants
Penn D	776	2.06
Ohio 4	1,410	3.74

CANTON (*continued*):

SEA of origin	No. of migrants	% of focal area's total in-migrants
Ohio 5	2,290	6.08
Ohio 6*	4,294	11.40
Ohio E	1,990	4.28
Ohio F*	5,618	14.92
Ohio H	2,159	5.73
Ohio M	408	1.08
Ill C	605	1.61
Mich F	447	1.19
W.Va 2**	498	1.32
W.Va 3**	684	1.82
Cal F	760	2.02
Total	21,939	58.25

5 percent of out-migrants from SEA
migrated to focal area

SEA of origin	No. to focal area	Total out-migrants	%
Ohio 6	4,294	73,294	5.86
Ohio F	5,618	67,517	8.32

INDIANAPOLIS

Total in-migrants: 99,713

SEA of origin	No. of migrants	% of focal area's total in-migrants
NY G	1,248	1.25
Ohio J	1,594	1.60
Ind 4*	4,208	4.22
Ind 5*	13,277	13.32
Ind 6*	3,238	3.25
Ind 7*	3,703	3.71
Ind 8*	1,653	1.66
Ind 9*	3,652	3.66
Ind A	1,945	1.95
Ind B	1,024	1.03
Ind C	1,074	1.08
Ind E	1,098	1.10
Ind G*	1,708	1.71
Ind H*	1,229	1.23
Ill C	4,014	4.03
Mich F	1,682	1.69
Ky 5*†	1,024	1.03
Ky 9**	1,044	1.05
Ky A	1,017	1.02
Cal F	2,107	2.11
Total	51,539	51.70

(continued)

Table 3.6 (continued)

INDIANAPOLIS (*continued*):

5 percent of out-migrants from SEA migrated to focal area

SEA of origin	No. to focal area	Total out-migrants	%
Ind 4	4,208	61,836	6.81
Ind 5	13,277	59,592	22.39
Ind 6	3,238	35,418	9.14
Ind 7	3,703	40,194	9.21
Ind 8	1,653	22,444	7.36
Ind 9	3,652	64,172	5.69
Ind G	1,708	17,419	9.81
Ind H	1,229	20,339	6.04
Ky 5†	1,024	19,034	5.38

DETROIT

Total in-migrants: 282,185

SEA of origin	No. of migrants	% of focal area's total in-migrants
NY G	5,905	2.10
Penn D	4,124	1.47
Ohio B	3,290	1.17
Ohio E	6,013	2.13
Ill C	14,209	5.04
Mich 4*	5,483	1.94
Mich 5*	4,374	1.55
Mich 7*	3,757	1.33
Mich 8*	6,646	2.36
Mich 9*	3,761	1.33
Mich B	3,025	1.07
Mich D*	5,554	1.97
Mich E*	6,430	2.28
Mich G	2,834	1.00
Mich J*	9,473	3.36
Ky 9*/**	4,229	1.50
Ala A†	3,076	1.09
Cal F	8,835	3.13
Total	101,018	35.82

5 percent of out-migrants from SEA migrated to focal area

SEA of origin	No. to focal area	Total out-migrants	%
Ohio A	2,641	49,835	5.30
Mich 1	2,276	28,861	7.89
Mich 2	1,666	21,854	7.62
Mich 3	960	15,820	6.07
Mich 4	5,483	49,987	10.97

DETROIT (*continued*):

SEA of origin	No. to focal area	Total out-migrants	%
Mich 5	4,374	40,341	10.84
Mich 7	3,757	28,842	13.03
Mich 8	6,646	27,745	23.95
Mich 9	3,761	56,859	6.61
Mich A	1,693	21,728	7.79
Mich B	3,025	49,908	6.06
Mich C	1,175	12,848	9.15
Mich D	5,554	48,600	11.43
Mich E	6,450	55,381	11.65
Mich G	2,834	31,629	8.96
Mich H	1,418	17,377	8.16
Mich J	9,473	47,002	20.15
Ky 9**	4,229	52,767	8.01
Tenn 3	836	13,429	6.23

CHICAGO

Total in-migrants: 464,794

SEA of origin	No. of migrants	% of focal area's total in-migrants
Mass C	5,141	1.11
NY G	15,582	3.36
Penn B	5,125	1.11
Penn D	5,656	1.22
Ohio E	6,343	1.37
Ind A*	11,290	2.43
Ill 1*	6,884	1.49
Ill 5*	7,186	1.55
Ill 6*	13,851	2.98
Mich F	11,293	2.43
Wisc C*	7,782	1.68
Minn B	7,617	1.64
Mo B	7,831	1.69
Miss 1*	6,517	1.41
Cal A	5,987	1.29
Cal F	14,268	3.07
Total	138,353	29.83

5 percent of out-migrants from SEA migrated to focal area

SEA of origin	No. to focal area	Total out-migrants	%
Ind A	11,290	71,552	15.78
Ind B	2,580	36,893	7.00
Ill 1	6,884	40,894	16.84
Ill 2	556	4,094	13.58
Ill 3	3,701	37,913	9.77

(continued)

Table 3.6 (continued)

CHICAGO (*continued*):

SEA of origin	No. to focal area	Total out-migrants	%
Ill 4	1,970	32,623	6.04
Ill 5	7,186	32,276	22.27
Ill 6	13,851	110,281	12.56
Ill 7	959	17,607	5.45
Ill 8	1,109	16,881	6.57
Ill 10	1,885	17,641	10.69
Ill 11	2,501	21,343	11.72
Ill A	1,801	22,193	8.12
Ill B	3,105	32,004	9.71
Ill D	3,818	37,762	10.11
Ill E	1,889	22,491	8.40
Ill G	1,671	19,669	8.50
Wisc 8	2,959	58,095	5.10
Wisc B	3,081	51,568	5.98
Wisc C	7,782	145,017	5.37
Wisc D	1,234	20,394	6.05
Wisc E	1,822	34,010	5.36
Wisc F	2,106	16,416	12.83
Wisc G	855	15,878	5.39
Iowa D	1,346	21,656	6.22
Miss 1	6,517	44,190	14.75
Miss 2	2,149	29,711	7.24
Miss 4	1,017	19,494	5.22
Ark 8	3,178	55,854	5.09

ATLANTA

Total in-migrants: 238,050

SEA of origin	No. of migrants	% of focal area's total in-migrants
NY G	5,190	2.18
NY D	2,838	1.20
Ga 1*/**	4,895	2.06
Ga 3*†	9,041	3.80
Ga 4*	16,812	7.07
Ga 7*	5,277	2.22
Ga 8*	3,558	1.50
Ga C*	3,671	1.55
Ga E*	2,521	1.06

ATLANTA (*continued*):

SEA of origin	No. of migrants	% of focal area's total in-migrants
Ga F*	2,776	1.17
Fla 4	2,507	1.06
Fla A	4,438	1.87
Fla B	3,852	1.62
Fla C	5,576	2.35
Fla E	2,833	1.19
Tenn 8**	2,949	1.24
Tenn B	2,452	1.03
Tenn D**	2,935	1.24
Ala 3*†	2,615	1.10
Ala A*†	4,484	1.89
Cal F	3,577	1.51
Ill C	4,437	1.87
Total	99,234	41.78

5 percent of out-migrants from SEA migrated to focal area

SEA of origin	No. to focal area	Total out-migrants	%
NC D	2,838	49,013	5.79
Ga 1**	4,895	27,318	17.92
Ga 2**	2,279	10,202	22.34
Ga 3†	9,041	29,411	30.74
Ga 4	16,812	64,277	26.16
Ga 5	729	6,895	10.58
Ga 6	1,417	18,037	7.86
Ga 7	5,277	58,441	9.03
Ga 8	3,558	40,757	8.73
Ga 9	2,015	29,773	6.77
Ga C	3,671	59,546	6.17
Ga D	2,113	30,351	6.97
Ga E	2,521	32,257	7.82
Ga F	2,776	22,168	12.53
Ga G	924	14,527	6.36
Tenn C**	1,973	34,757	5.68
Tenn D**	2,935	49,226	5.97
Ala 3†	2,615	42,369	6.18
Ala 4†	1,738	24,911	6.98
Ala A†	4,484	76,475	5.87

specific metropolis were considered parts of that migratory-stream system. (Cincinnati, for example, had total in-migration of 96,937; twenty-two SEAs in the United States, each comprising 1 percent or more of this total, sent migrants totalling 51,425, or 53 percent. (2) All areas of origin which contributed 5 percent or more of their out-migrants to a specific metropolis were also considered parts of that area's system. With this delineation, one can see at a glance all the SEAs in the United States which made up the migration stream systems of any metropolis being considered.

From such delineations (Table 3.6), some patterns characteristic of almost all the systems emerge: Most migrants came from contiguous or nearby SEAs. A majority of the migrants moved from one metropolitan area to another, with an especially large exchange between metropolitan areas within a state and between supermetropolises such as Detroit, Pittsburgh, Chicago, New York, and Los Angeles. (Los Angeles, indeed, was the greatest migration center—of both in- and out-migration—of all American metropolises.) These national metropolises are significant in most of the migratory-stream systems in the United States.

Of those SEAs contributing significant numbers to midwestern migratory-stream systems which are not contiguous to them and are not focused on metropolitan areas within the same state or on national metropolitan areas, we found Appalachian SEAs to be *the most significant*, and in almost all cases, *the only significant* ones. If complete 1949–50 and 1955–60 data had been available, the Appalachian SEAs would probably have been found to be even more significant because the peak of Appalachian migration was during the 1950s and the movement had decreased greatly by 1965–70. But even with the data on hand, Southern Appalachia was clearly the major rural influence outside the immediate environs of the metropolises, except in the case of Chicago where, instead of Appalachian SEAs, the SEAs contributing the greatest numbers of migrants were the Mississippi and Arkansas Delta areas. Although no specific Appalachian SEAs were found by our criteria to be components of the Chicago system, all Appalachian researchers are aware of the thousands of Appalachians concentrated in certain areas of Chicago, such as Uptown. Chicago receives migrants from so many and such varied sources that no specific Appalachian streams are included, according to our criteria, in Chicago's enormous stream system. Nevertheless, accumulation of most Appalachians in a few areas in Chicago has resulted in a significant and visible concentration.

For comparative purposes we also delineated Atlanta's migratory-stream system. Atlanta was the largest single recipient of Appalachian migrants for 1960 and 1970 (Tables 3.8 and 3.9). Atlanta drew migrants from many Appalachian SEAs, although most Appalachian migrants were from contiguous Georgia and Tennessee SEAs and others in the southern part of Appalachia. This is to be expected since Atlanta is the largest and closest metropolis to these Appalachian SEAs. When the growing recognition of Atlanta as a supermetropolis is considered, the predominance of migrants from its own region rather than from areas across the nation (as is usually true of national metropolises) is perhaps indicative of a pattern which the other rapidly growing southern metropolises will follow.

These data emphasize again the great importance of Appalachian migrants to the midwestern metropolises, for the Appalachian SEAs are the only nonmetropolitan areas from a substantial distance which are influential in the migration streams to the Midwest. These data verify, too, the specific directions of migration; for example, Eastern Kentucky's SEAs, particularly Ky. 8 and Ky. 9, are important for southwestern Ohio, Indianapolis, and Detroit; West Virginia's SEAs are important for the north-central Ohio area.

The analysis presented above attempts to describe in some detail the role of Southern Appalachia in the migratory-stream systems of the midwestern metropolises. A summary of the types of streams which comprise each migratory stream system shows that Appalachia is included in each system except Chicago (Table 3.7). The data show conclusively that Appalachia has been important to all of the midwestern metropolises we considered and that this is a decades-long phenomenon with a cumulative, increasing importance. The 1970 pattern of migration began with the great migration of the forties and continued for three decades, with significant migration streams still linking the Midwest to Appalachia.

In order to see this Appalachian midwestern migratory-stream system in the context of total Appalachian migration to metropolitan areas, migratory streams were determined from all 43 Appalachian SEAs (this is approximately the southern part of the Appalachian Regional Commission's delineation of Appalachia by counties)[8] to all the 206 metropolitan SEAs in the United States for 1955–60 and 1965–70.

Table 3.7: Types of Migratory-stream Components
for Selected Midwestern Metropolitan Areas and Atlanta

| Metropolitan destination | Appalachia | Type of origin | | Interstate metro |
| | | Intra-state | | |
		Nonmetro	Metro	
Cincinnati	3	3	4	8
Dayton	2	4	5	5
Hamilton	2	6	4	3
Columbus	1	8	7	5
Cleveland	2	5	7	8
Akron	1	4	3	5
Canton	2	3	4	4
Indianapolis	2	6	6	5
Detroit	2	5 (3)*	5 (2)	6 (1)
Chicago	0	3 (7)	0 (5)	12 (7)
Atlanta	6 (2)	5 (4)	3 (2)	10 (1)

* Numbers in parentheses indicate the number which met the 5 percent criterion but not the 1 percent. This situation occurs only with metropolises which have migratory-stream systems that are more national in scope; see note 5.

To limit the system to more manageable proportions, all the metropolises were ranked by the number of Appalachian migrants received, and only the thirty attracting the greatest number of Appalachians for each period were listed. Percentages, based on total out-migration from Appalachia, are therefore indices of the importance of the metropolises for migratory streams from Appalachia (Tables 3.8 and 3.9). Indeed, examination of these two tables indicates immediately that these top thirty metropolises alone accounted for a third or more of all Appalachian out-migrants (for 1960, 36 percent; for 1970, 33 percent).

Only four metropolises were not in the top thirty for both 1955–60 and 1965–70. Although the rankings changed significantly for certain metropolitan areas between 1960 and 1970, there was still a great deal of consistency in the rankings (as indicated by a correlation of .87). The major shifts in rankings between the two decades involved an elevation in rank of those metropolises *nearer* the Southern Appalachian region, which experienced great overall population growth during the 1960s. All of the midwestern metropolises declined in rank from 1960 to 1970, except Detroit, which increased one rank.

The data for Atlanta clearly illustrate the decline of Appalachian migration relative to other migration by 1965–70. Although Atlanta at-

Table 3.8: Ranking of the 30 Metropolitan Destinations Receiving the Largest Number of Migrants from 43 Appalachian SEAs, 1955-60

Rank	Destination	Number	Appalachian migrants % of total in-migrants to specified area	% of total out-migrants from the 43 areas of origin
1	Atlanta	38,640	27.11	2.99
2	Washington	32,797	29.50	2.54
3	Chicago	26,859	6.04	2.08
4	Detroit	25,681	13.09	1.99
5	Birmingham	24,589	41.24	1.90
6	Cleveland	22,772	15.60	1.76
7	Los Angeles	19,195	1.83	1.48
8	Cincinnati	17,291	18.94	1.34
9	Baltimore	16,934	12.79	1.31
10	Knoxville	16,669	47.25	1.29
11	Tampa/ St.Petersburg	16,102	6.86	1.25
12	Columbus	14,941	13.71	1.16
13	Chattanooga	14,765	49.59	1.14
14	Charleston	13,697	55.87	1.06
15	Dayton	13,445	15.52	1.04
16	Nashville	12,807	21.43	.99
17	New York	12,025	3.27	.93
18	Miami	11,636	5.36	.90
19	Orlando	11,003	9.65	.85
20	Greenville	10,759	35.67	.83
21	Huntington	10,325	48.26	.80
22	Norfolk	10,109	7.85	.78
23	Philadelphia	10,044	2.50	.78
24	Richmond	10,002	18.01	.77
25	Roanoke	9,352	40.31	.72
26	Huntsville	9,205	31.33	.71
27	Pittsburgh	9,081	8.06	.70
28	Montgomery	8,636	24.33	.67
29	Columbia	8,380	15.62	.65
30	Jacksonville	8,336	8.84	.64
	Total	466,077		36.05

Source: U.S. Bureau of the Census, U.S. Census of Population: 1960, Subject Reports, Final Report PC(2)-2E, *Migration between State Economic Areas* (Washington, D.C.: G.P.O., 1967).

tracted an even larger number of Appalachians in the later period, its percentage of the total Appalachian out-migration and of Appalachian migration to the top thirty areas of destination both dropped. Atlanta was, it should be remembered, one of the fastest growing large metropolises in the United States during the 1960s. Its total in-migration increased phenomenally, from 142,534 to 238,345, with more Appalachians going to Atlanta in 1965-70 than in 1955-60.

Table 3.9: Ranking of the 30 Metropolitan Destinations Receiving the Largest Number of Migrants from 43 Appalachian SEAs, 1965-70

		Appalachian migrants		% of total out-migrants from the 43 areas of origin
Rank	Destination	Number	% of total in-migrants to specified area	
1	Atlanta	46,345	19.47	3.82
2	Washington	29,605	36.63	2.44
3	Detroit	24,387	11.57	2.01
4	Birmingham	22,633	38.81	1.86
5	Knoxville	16,680	35.86	1.37
6	Chicago	15,357	3.30	1.27
7	Chattanooga	13,606	43.20	1.12
8	Cleveland	13,154	8.79	1.08
9	Los Angeles	12,435	1.36	1.02
10	Nashville	12,087	19.04	1.00
11	Huntington	11,740	70.59	.98
12	Huntsville	11,118	30.06	.92
13	Baltimore	10,709	7.64	.88
14	Columbus	10,604	8.12	.87
15	Tuscaloosa	10,500	49.64	.87
16	Cincinnati	10,465	10.80	.86
17	Greenville	10,314	31.59	.85
18	Charlotte	10,301	15.92	.85
19	Charleston	10,299	46.64	.85
20	Columbia	9,732	14.98	.80
21	Tampa/St.Petersburg	9,701	4.26	.80
22	Dayton	9,601	8.96	.79
23	Norfolk	9,425	6.46	.78
24	Richmond	9,246	13.38	.76
25	New York	8,960	2.47	.74
26	Louisville	8,583	12.29	.71
27	Roanoke	8,528	32.68	.70
28	Winston-Salem/High Point/Greensboro	7,838	11.25	.65
29	Pittsburgh	7,736	5.60	.61
30	Philadelphia	7,443	3.21	.61
	Total	399,132		32.90

Source: U.S. Bureau of the Census, U.S. Census of Population: 1970, Subject Reports, Final Report PC(2)-2E, *Migration between State Economic Areas* (Washington, D.C.: G.P.O., 1972).

One of the exciting aspects of the above data is that they provide a partial answer to an often-asked question to which we formerly could give almost no answer: How many Appalachians are there in specific metropolitan areas—in Cincinnati or Columbus or Atlanta? Because the ethnic status of blacks is based on race and color, and because race and color have been included in the census, information on the number of blacks in any given metropolis has been available. The ethnic status of Appalachians, however, is based on a geographical culture and has not been determined by the census. So migratory-stream data furnish almost the only opportunity (except for special censuses or surveys) for even partially determining the Appalachian proportions in metropolitan populations.

Although there are difficulties inherent in the data, one can begin to appreciate from them the volume of Appalachian migrants in these metropolitan areas. The proportions of the total in-migration to each of these areas comprised by Appalachians for 1955–60 and 1965–70 are shown in Table 3.10. Since most people are aware of the magnitude and significance of the impact of black in-migration to these metropolises, we also compare Appalachian in-migration to black in-migration. Regretably, the information on blacks is available only for 1965–70.

The significance of Appalachian migration for these metropolitan areas is obvious. The large percentages for 1955–60 are striking. If similar data for 1949–50 were available, even greater percentages of the total in-migration would be Appalachian, we expect, since the peak of Appalachian migration was in the late 1940s and early 1950s. The decrease from 1955–60 to 1965–70 was dramatic only because the migration had been so great in previous decades. The figures even for the later periods indicate great streams of Appalachian migrants still moving to these metropolitan areas.

Even with decreases of Appalachian migrants during the 1965–70 period, the percentages of total in-migration which were Appalachian were still greater than those which were black in Cincinnati, Dayton, and Columbus, among other metropolises. Since migration to these urban areas has been so great for several decades, these midwestern cities have continued to have tremendous numbers of Appalachians living and working in them.

The specificity of direction and the large concentration of Appalachian migration in these thirty metropolitan areas cannot be presented here in great detail, but, to give some idea of these two dimensions, we determined the three largest streams of migration from Appalachia to each of the thirty metropolitan areas for 1955–60 and 1965–70 (Tables 3.11 and 3.12).

Although migratory streams from each of the forty-three Appalachian SEAs are the base for the total, the three largest streams account for a large proportion of Appalachian migration to almost all of the metropolises. For many of the metropolises, the three largest streams

Table 3.10: Percentage of Total In-migrants to
30 Metropolitan Areas Constituted by Appalachians,
1955-60 and 1965-70, and by Blacks, 1965-70

Rank, 1965-70	Destination	Appalachian in-migrants* 1955-60	Appalachian in-migrants* 1965-70	Black in-migrants 1965-70
1	Atlanta	27.11	19.47	9.65
2	Washington	29.50	36.63	39.87
3	Detroit	13.09	11.57	19.80
4	Birmingham	41.24	38.81	8.86
5	Knoxville	47.25	35.86	10.52
6	Chicago	6.04	3.30	10.72
7	Chattanooga	49.59	43.20	4.29
8	Cleveland	15.06	8.79	12.66
9	Los Angeles	1.83	1.36	8.07
10	Nashville	21.43	19.04	13.04
11	Huntington	48.26	70.59	N.A.
12	Huntsville	31.33	30.06	10.16
13	Baltimore	12.79	7.64	12.58
14	Columbus	13.71	8.12	6.98
15	Tuscaloosa	45.62	49.64	11.12
16	Cincinnati	18.94	10.80	7.57
17	Greenville	35.67	31.59	4.40
18	Charlotte	15.18	15.92	11.06
19	Charleston	55.87	46.65	N.A.
20	Columbia	15.62	14.98	11.56
21	Tampa/St.Petersburg	6.86	4.26	3.92
22	Dayton	15.52	8.96	7.08
23	Norfolk	7.85	6.46	7.69
24	Richmond	18.01	13.38	14.31
25	New York	3.27	2.47	15.34
26	Louisville	11.56	12.29	6.72
27	Roanoke	40.31	32.68	N.A.
28	Winston-Salem/High Point/Greensboro	14.87	11.25	12.58
29	Pittsburgh	8.60	5.60	4.45
30	Philadelphia	2.50	3.21	11.58

* Delineation II was followed in this table; see note 1.

Sources: U.S. Bureau of the Census, U.S. Census of Population: 1960, Subject Reports, Final Report PC(2)-2E, *Migration between State Economic Areas* (Washington, D.C.: G.P.O., 1967).
Idem, U.S. Census of Population: 1970, Subject Reports, Final Report PC(2)-2E, *Migration between State Economic Areas* (Washington, D.C.: G.P.O., 1972).

account for more than 50 percent of the total migration from Appalachia. The metropolises either within or closest to the Appalachian region had the largest percentages; particularly large, as a rule, was the primary stream from areas contiguous to the metropolis.

The consistency between the three largest streams in 1955–60 and

Table 3.11: Three Largest Appalachian SEA Migration Streams and Their Percentage of Total Appalachian Migration to Top-ranking Metropolitan Destinations, 1955-60

Rank	SMSA	(1) SEA	%	(2) SEA	%	(3) SEA	%	Three streams
1	Atlanta	(Ga 3)	24.75	(Ga 1)	16.08	(Ga 2)	7.97	48.80
2	Washington	(WV 4)	11.59	(Va 4)	9.95	(Va 3)	6.24	27.78
3	Chicago	(WV 4)	13.31	(Ky 9)	8.87	(Al A)	8.83	31.01
4	Detroit	(Ky 9)	17.70	(WV 4)	10.46	(Al A)	7.42	35.58
5	Birmingham	(Al 3)	34.33	(Al 5)	15.47	(Al 2)	14.22	64.02
6	Cleveland	(WV 4)	24.79	(WV C)	8.06	(WV 3)	7.58	40.43
7	Los Angeles	(Al A)	13.66	(Tn D)	7.46	(Tn B)	7.38	28.50
8	Cincinnati	(Ky 9)	33.00	(Ky 5)	16.11	(Ky 8)	15.02	64.13
9	Baltimore	(Md 1)	11.79	(WV 4)	9.93	(WV 3)	7.74	29.46
10	Knoxville	(Tn 8)	60.68	(Tn C)	6.78	(Tn 7)	5.27	72.73
11	Tampa	(Tn 8)	7.85	(Al A)	6.70	(WV C)	6.63	21.18
12	Columbus	(WV 4)	26.01	(Ky 9)	16.90	(Ky 8)	7.55	50.46
13	Chattanooga	(Ga 1)	18.35	(Tn C)	16.99	(Tn 8)	14.53	49.87
14	Charleston	(WV 4)	35.17	(WV 2)	34.03	(WV B)	7.05	76.25
15	Dayton	(Ky 9)	23.34	(Ky 8)	15.02	(Tn 8)	10.37	48.73
16	Nashville	(Tn 6)	29.48	(Tn D)	13.11	(Tn C)	1.51	44.10
17	New York	(WV 4)	11.67	(Al A)	10.74	(SC 2)	9.20	31.61
18	Miami	(Al A)	10.04	(Tn D)	8.85	(Tn B)	6.06	24.95
19	Orlando	(WV 4)	10.72	(Tn 8)	8.15	(Al A)	6.24	25.11
20	Greenville	(SC 2)	55.45	(SC 1)	18.88	(NC 1)	5.05	79.38
21	Huntington	(WV B)	42.46	(Ky 8)	25.87	(Ky 9)	9.08	77.41
22	Norfolk	(WV 4)	11.83	(Va 3)	7.00	(Va A)	6.64	25.47
23	Philadelphia	(WV 4)	11.69	(Tn 8)	9.50	(SC 2)	7.09	28.28
24	Richmond	(Va 3)	42.13	(Va 2)	13.68	(WV 4)	10.11	65.92
25	Roanoke	(Va 3)	45.06	(Va 2)	14.63	(WV 4)	10.82	70.51
26	Huntsville	(Al 1)	18.28	(Al A)	17.89	(Al 2)	15.43	51.60
27	Pittsburgh	(WV 3)	19.44	(WV 1)	14.28	(WV A)	11.77	45.49
28	Montgomery	(Al 5)	34.82	(Al A)	19.49	(Al 4)	11.50	65.81
29	Columbia	(SC 2)	28.79	(SC D)	14.99	(Tn 8)	6.29	50.07
30	Jacksonville	(Al A)	35.56	(Tn D)	8.50	(Al 1)	7.81	51.87

Source: U.S. Bureau of the Census, U.S. Census of Population: 1960, Subject Reports, Final Report PC(2)-2E, *Migration between State Economic Areas* (Washington, D.C.: G.P.O., 1967).

1965-70 is impressive. Twenty-six metropolises were in the top thirty in both periods; twenty-four had at least two streams which were among the largest three for that metropolis for both periods. (Ten had *the same three streams* for 1960 as for 1970.)

The discussion above has emphasized the three largest streams *from* Appalachia to metropolitan destinations. To assess better the concentration of the migration streams from the perspective of the areas of origin, we determined the three largest streams from each Appalachian

Table 3.12: Three Largest Appalachian SEA Migration Streams and Their Percentage of Total Appalachian Migration to Top-ranking Metropolitan Destinations, 1965-70

Rank	SMSA	(1) SEA	%	(2) SEA	%	(3) SEA	%	Three streams
1	Atlanta	(Ga 3)	19.51	(Ga 1)	10.56	(Al A)	9.68	39.75
2	Washington	(Va 4)	9.34	(WV 4)	9.23	(WV 3)	6.14	24.71
3	Detroit	(Ky 9)	17.34	(Al A)	12.61	(WV 4)	8.15	38.10
4	Birmingham	(Al 3)	33.83	(Al 2)	13.19	(Al E)	11.09	58.11
5	Knoxville	(Tn 8)	53.47	(Tn C)	12.82	(Tn 6)	4.23	70.52
6	Chicago	(Al A)	11.06	(WV 4)	10.43	(Ky 9)	8.54	30.03
7	Chattanooga	(Ga 1)	25.80	(Tn 8)	17.72	(Tn D)	11.08	54.60
8	Cleveland	(WV 4)	19.95	(WV C)	12.19	(WV 3)	8.28	40.42
9	Los Angeles	(Al A)	13.58	(Al F)	9.70	(Tn 8)	6.88	30.16
10	Nashville	(Tn 6)	25.76	(Tn D)	13.86	(Tn 8)	10.66	50.28
11	Huntington	(WV 4)	26.98	(Ky 8)	22.51	(WV 2)	20.41	69.90
12	Huntsville	(Al 1)	26.91	(Al 2)	17.96	(Al A)	15.29	60.16
13	Baltimore	(Md 1)	14.80	(WV B)	5.61	(WV 3)	5.66	25.97
14	Columbus	(WV 4)	25.09	(WV B)	11.60	(Ky 9)	10.75	47.44
15	Tuscaloosa	(Al A)	34.55	(Al 5)	16.59	(Al 3)	13.90	65.04
16	Cincinnati	(Ky 9)	25.45	(Ky 8)	15.59	(Ky 5)	12.06	53.10
17	Greenville	(SC 2)	49.54	(SC 1)	12.93	(NC 1)	6.02	68.49
18	Charlotte	(NC A)	12.66	(NC 1)	12.58	(NC 2)	9.77	35.01
19	Charleston	(WV 2)	29.55	(WV 4)	29.32	(WV 3)	8.69	67.56
20	Columbia	(SC 2)	27.52	(SC D)	24.86	(SC 1)	5.67	58.05
21	Tampa	(Al A)	10.25	(Tn 8)	9.61	(Tn D)	8.04	27.90
22	Dayton	(Ky 9)	25.31	(Ky 8)	17.08	(Tn 8)	6.97	49.36
23	Norfolk	(WV 4)	8.38	(Va 3)	8.21	(Va A)	6.83	23.42
24	Richmond	(Va 3)	17.92	(Va 4)	16.63	(Va A)	13.62	48.17
25	New York	(Al A)	15.02	(SC 2)	5.76	(WV C)	5.75	26.53
26	Louisville	(Ky 9)	23.33	(Ky 5)	18.83	(Ky 8)	10.17	51.33
27	Roanoke	(Va 3)	38.34	(Va 2)	14.46	(WV 4)	11.39	64.19
28	Winston-Salem/ High Point/ Greensboro	(NC 1)	18.09	(NC 2)	9.68	(NC A)	8.79	36.56
29	Pittsburgh	(WV 3)	18.99	(WV 1)	13.11	(WV A)	11.84	43.94
30	Philadelphia	(Al F)	7.00	(WV 3)	6.33	(Tn 8)	6.23	19.56

Source: U.S. Bureau of the Census, U.S. Census of Population: 1970, Subject Reports, Final Report PC(2)-2E, *Migration between State Economic Areas* (Washington, D.C.: G.P.O., 1972).

SEA, as well as the concentration in the 30 largest streams to the metropolises (Tables 3.13 and 3.14). The next twenty-seven ranking streams were, of course, not as concentrated as the three largest Appalachian streams to the urban areas, for when the streams to the thirty metropolises are included, there are few percentage gains beyond those accounted for by the three largest streams. Nevertheless, when one recognizes that from any specific origin 508 SEAs are possible destinations,

Table 3.13: Focal Areas of Migration from Southern Appalachia (43 SEAs), Total Numbers and Percentages for 3 and 30 Largest Metropolitan Streams, 1955-60

SEA	Metropolises	3 largest streams		30 largest streams	
		No. of out-migrants	% of total out-migration	No. of out-migrants	% of total out-migration
Md 1	*Baltimore, Washington, Pittsburgh	3,958	31.40	5,416	43.00
Va 1	Washington, Baltimore, Cleveland	2,737	9.01	9,188	30.26
Va 2	Washington, Roanoke, Winston-Salem	3,956	13.37	9,084	30.70
Va 3	*Roanoke, Washington, Richmond	7,598	27.35	12,268	44.17
Va 4	Washington, Richmond, Baltimore	4,984	24.19	8,337	40.46
Va A	*Washington, Richmond, Norfolk	3,396	16.22	7,036	33.61
WV 1	Pittsburgh, Cleveland, Los Angeles	1,950	8.48	5,851	25.43
WV 2	*Charleston, Huntington, Cleveland	7,880	19.59	13,517	33.61
WV 3	*Pittsburgh, Washington, Cleveland	5,228	14.19	12,138	32.94
WV 4	Cleveland, Charleston, Columbus	12,137	13.82	40,100	45.67
WV 5	Washington, Baltimore, Cleveland	3,718	14.10	8,286	31.42
WV 6	*Washington, Baltimore, Philadelphia	1,604	23.09	2,286	33.76
WV A	Pittsburgh, Cleveland, Los Angeles	1,814	13.87	4,256	32.54
WV B	Columbus, Charleston, Cleveland	2,193	9.41	7,069	30.33
WV C	Cleveland Huntington, Columbus	4,227	10.35	12,624	30.92

(continued)

Table 3.13 (continued)

SEA	Metropolises	3 largest streams		30 largest streams	
		No. of out-migrants	% of total out-migration	No. of out-migrants	% of total out-migration
NC 1	*Winston-Salem, Atlanta, Charleston	3,393	9.62	9,106	25.82
NC 2	*Winston-Salem, Charleston, Washington	2,932	15.11	5,259	27.11
NC A	Winston-Salem, Washington, Charleston	1,713	9.61	5,671	31.80
NC B	*Washington, Charleston, Atlanta	1,760	9.00	4,904	25.08
SC 1	*Greenville, Atlanta, Columbia	2,729	26.19	3,862	37.06
SC 2	*Greenville, Columbia, Atlanta	9,511	24.64	16,649	43.13
SC D	*Columbia, Atlanta, Charleston	3,033	9.95	7,719	25.33
Ga 1	*Atlanta, Chattanooga, Los Angeles	10,353	36.11	13,736	47.91
Ga 2	Atlanta, Detroit, Los Angeles	3,152	26.26	4,080	33.99
Ga 3	Atlanta, Greenville, Tampa	9,972	34.68	12,022	41.81
Ga A	Atlanta, Chicago, Los Angeles	409	5.80	891	12.64
Ky 5	Cincinnati, Louisville, Dayton	4,723	19.93	6,479	27.35
Ky 8	*Cincinnati, Huntington, Dayton	6,336	19.20	10,295	31.20
Ky 9	*Cincinnati, Detroit, Dayton	2,113	3.06	25,650	37.13
Ky C	Columbus, Cincinnati, Dayton	553	6.06	1,978	21.76

(continued)

Table 3.13 (continued)

SEA	Metropolises	3 largest streams		30 largest streams	
		No. of out-migrants	% of total out-migration	No. of out-migrants	% of total out-migration
Tn 6	Nashville, Cincinnati, Detroit	4,783	20.35	9,502	40.43
Tn 7	*Chattanooga, Knoxville, Nashville	3,197	47.73	6,578	95.24
Tn 8	*Knoxville, Chattanooga, Atlanta	14,783	19.28	31,826	41.50
Tn C	Atlanta, Nashville, Los Angeles	3,781	10.04	11,461	30.42
Tn D	Atlanta, Nashville, Los Angeles	4,343	7.77	16,687	29.86
Al 1	Huntsville, Birmingham, Chicago	3,574	15.36	8,285	35.61
Al 2	*Birmingham, Chattanooga, Huntsville	6,530	25.38	10,027	38.97
Al 3	Birmingham, Atlanta, Huntsville	11,240	20.98	20,173	37.65
Al 4	Birmingham, Atlanta, Huntsville	3,635	14.29	6,968	27.39
Al 5	Birmingham, Tuscaloosa, Chicago	6,165	18.20	11,668	34.45
Al A	Tuscaloosa, Atlanta, Los Angeles	6,739	9.30	21,943	30.27
Al E	Birmingham, Los Angeles, Chicago	2,277	16.89	4,241	31.46
Al F	Chicago, Los Angeles, Birmingham	699	5.87	3,182	26.73

* Same three cities 1960 and 1970.

Source: U.S. Bureau of the Census, U.S. Census of Population: 1960, Subject Reports, Final Report PC(2)-2E, *Migration between State Economic Areas* (Washington, D.C.: G.P.O., 1967).

(continued)

Table 3.14: Focal areas of Migration from Southern Appalachia (43 SEAs), Total Numbers and Percentages for 3 and 30 Largest Metropolitan Streams, 1965-70

SEA	Metropolises	3 largest streams		30 largest streams	
		No. of out-migrants	% of total out-migration	No. of out-migrants	% of total out-migration
Md 1	*Baltimore, Washington, Pittsburgh	4,102	29.94	5,752	41.99
Va 1	Washington, Detroit, Roanoke	2,639	11.65	6,537	28.87
Va 2	Roanoke, Washington, Richmond	2,759	12.16	6,035	20.60
Va 3	*Roanoke, Richmond, Washington	6,540	22.82	10,872	37.94
Va 4	Washington, Richmond, Norfolk	4,934	18.99	8,490	32.67
Va A	*Richmond, Washington, Norfolk	2,817	12.07	6,694	28.69
WV 1	Pittsburgh, Charleston, Huntington	2,038	8.83	5,686	24.63
WV 2	*Charleston, Huntington, Cleveland	6,106	18.08	10,447	30.93
WV 3	*Washington, Pittsburgh, Cleveland	4,376	13.86	10,331	32.73
WV 4	Charleston, Huntington, Washington	8,643	15.65	24,417	44.22
WV 5	Washington, Baltimore, Charleston	2,698	12.35	5,698	26.08
WV 6	*Washington, Baltimore, Philadelphia	1,288	19.64	1,904	29.03
WV A	Pittsburgh, Cleveland, Washington	1,641	12.70	3,900	30.18
WV B	Columbus, Charleston, Baltimore	2,722	12.61	7,309	33.85
WV C	Huntington, Cleveland, Washington	4,659	11.01	13,582	32.10

(continued)

Table 3.14 (continued)

SEA	Metropolises	3 largest streams		30 largest streams	
		No. of out-migrants	% of total out-migration	No. of out-migrants	% of total out-migration
NC 1	*Winston-Salem, Atlanta, Charleston	4,031	11.71	8,709	25.30
NC 2	*Charleston, Winston-Salem, Washington	2,021	11.84	3,610	21.15
NC A	Charleston, Atlanta, Winston-Salem	2,688	13.60	6,000	30.36
NC B	*Charleston, Washington, Atlanta	2,246	8.06	5,658	20.32
SC 1	*Greenville, Columbia, Atlanta	2,155	22.27	3,318	34.28
SC 2	*Greenville, Columbia, Atlanta	8,732	26.44	13,493	40.85
SC D	*Columbia, Atlanta, Charleston	4,539	15.56	8,047	27.58
Ga 1	*Atlanta, Chattanooga, Los Angeles	8,757	32.06	11,094	40.61
Ga 2	Atlanta, Knoxville, Charleston	2,428	23.80	2,974	29.15
Ga 3	Atlanta, Chattanooga, Tampa	9,551	32.47	11,247	38.24
Ga A	Atlanta, Knoxville, Los Angeles	515	6.35	1,093	13.49
Ky 5	Louisville, Cincinnati, Detroit	3,339	17.54	4,734	24.87
Ky 8	*Huntington, Dayton, Cincinnati	5,682	19.69	9,416	32.64
Ky 9	*Detroit, Cincinnati, Dayton	9,322	17.67	18,757	35.55
Ky C	Louisville, Columbus, Detroit	1,326	13.81	2,384	24.83

(continued)

Table 3.14 (continued)

SEA	Metropolises	3 largest streams		30 largest streams	
		No. of out-migrants	% of total out-migration	No. of out-migrants	% of total out-migration
Tn 6	Nashville, Knoxville, Detroit	4,398	18.57	7,668	32.37
Tn 7	*Chattanooga, Knoxville, Nashville	2,642	17.75	4,962	33.33
Tn 8	*Knoxville, Atlanta, Chattanooga	14,278	21.76	28,034	42.72
Tn C	Knoxville, Atlanta, Washington	5,279	13.28	10,757	27.06
Tn D	Atlanta, Nashville, Chattanooga	6,070	12.33	15,426	31.34
Al 1	Huntsville, Birmingham, Atlanta	5,396	19.79	9,863	36.17
Al 2	*Birmingham, Huntsville, Chattanooga	6,123	24.86	9,615	39.04
Al 3	Birmingham, Atlanta, Tuscaloosa	11,730	27.69	18,062	42.63
Al 4	Atlanta, Birmingham, Tuscaloosa	4,121	16.54	6,914	27.75
Al 5	Birmingham, Tuscaloosa, Atlanta	4,462	16.33	8,221	30.08
Al A	Atlanta, Tuscaloosa, Detroit	11,188	14.63	24,347	31.84
Al E	Birmingham, Atlanta, Huntsville	3,664	21.60	5,993	35.30
Al F	Birmingham, Washington, Atlanta	5,094	11.73	12,408	28.56

* Same three cities 1960 and 1970.

Source: U.S. Bureau of the Census, U.S. Census of Population: 1970, Subject Reports, Final Report PC(2)-2E, *Migration between State Economic Areas* (Washington, D.C.: G.P.O., 1972).

these data indicate that the streams were remarkably concentrated. Here, once again, the often-repeated patterns of consistency from one decade to the next are illustrated. For eighteen of the forty-three SEAs, for instance, the same three metropolises were the three largest recipients of migrants for both 1955–60 and 1965–70.

Another striking pattern found in these data is the presence of so few metropolitan destinations. There are a small number of "Appalachian-flavored" metropolises, then, which are favorite destinations for many Appalachian sending-areas. It is obvious that each section of Appalachia has formed different migratory linkages with specific metropolitan focal areas. The varying linkages of the different Appalachian SEAs with the Washington/Baltimore area, the Atlanta area, the Piedmont Crescent area, or the Birmingham area, for example, become evident.[9]

Another conclusion relevant to Appalachia's tie to midwestern metropolises is that comparison of the 1955–60 with the 1965–70 streams indicates some decline in the linkage between Appalachia and the southwestern Ohio focal area. Migratory streams seem to be focusing in larger volume, on the other hand, upon growth centers in the rapidly industrializing and growing South.

The systems we have delineated here we know to be more than just *demographic* systems (Brown, 1967; Brown, 1971). They are parts of much more inclusive metropolises and hinterlands. The migratory aspects of these broader migration systems have been neglected, however, and are worthy of much more intensive and careful analysis.

In the case of Eastern Kentucky migration, for example, we know that the demographic system is part of a broad social system. The kinship structure channels, stops, and starts migration to and from Eastern Kentucky, and greatly affects the clustering of migrants in certain cities and towns, even in specific factories. Furthermore, the kinship structure significantly influences the adjustment of Kentucky migrants. This broader system is also a communication system which is especially important in the diffusion of new knowledge, patterns, and beliefs (Schwarzweller et al., 1971).

Similar patterns no doubt characterize other migratory-stream systems involving Southern Appalachia, though we suspect there are significant variations among them, since kinship patterns, occupational experiences (e.g., coal mining as compared with subsistence farming), and other social and cultural aspects of the different parts of Appalachia, vary extensively. The migration of other populations such as blacks, we are sure, also varies in many ways from the patterns characteristic of Eastern Kentuckians, almost all of whom are white.

In general, larger proportions of the migrants from Appalachia are moving longer distances than formerly. As educational levels rise in the Appalachians, kinship ties will almost certainly have less influence on the destinations of migrants, for Appalachian migrants appear to be scattering more in response to other, nonkinship factors. But of course there are many other reasons, too, for the wider diffusion of migrants. There is little doubt, for instance, that the governmental programs already instituted—regional development, highways, and so forth—though of limited scope, have had some influence on both the volume and the direction of movement of Appalachian migration. These governmental programs could undoubtedly have been much more successful if our knowledge of the migratory-stream systems had been more precise and more available to the policy-makers.

One aspect of migratory-stream systems that has had great appeal is the need of metropolitan areas which serve as destination points for specific Appalachian areas to foster and encourage greater understanding of and contact with the "Appalachian culture" of the migants' areas of origin. Such knowledge, it is hoped, might even encourage urban populations to have greater concern for the education, health, and development of their future citizens in these specific Appalachian areas.

We hope it has become obvious that migratory-stream system analysis is applicable to the whole country, not just to Appalachia. These systems overlap; they are not discrete. Some systems dominate others, just as some metropolises dominate others. Finally, we hope we have shown that the study of migratory-stream systems is a promising approach for integrating the many complex facets of social, cultural, and economic conditions.

NOTES

Most of the data used in this paper were acquired by the University of Kentucky Agricultural Experiment Station, though supplemental support for the 1949-1950 material came from the Southern Appalachian Studies Group, Berea, Kentucky. Throughout the whole period, Gladys K. Bowles and Calvin L. Beale, both of the Research Division, Rural Development Service, U.S. Department of Agriculture, advised us about sources for data and on a number of occasions actually furnished data in advance of publication. The U.S.

Bureau of the Census (especially Henry Shyrock) has also been most cooperative.

This research is indeed a team project, and the authors are grateful to the following: Julie Penrod, Stephen Abney, Cornelia Morgan, Steven Murdock, Jerry Fly, William Lowrance, Robin Chisolm, and Lillian York Stafford. Special thanks are expressed to Sandra Young Penn and Beverly Penman, who have typed many drafts of this article.

1. Nearly every study made of Southern Appalachia delineates the area differently. This is not surprising since there are no sharp regional boundaries. In fact, a case may be made that "Southern Appalachia" is not a "region" at all; i.e., the various units included usually are not uniform and homogeneous in economic, social, and cultural characteristics (as the term "region" used to be defined). The various sections of the Southern Appalachians are so diverse and so varied that "region-wide" interpretations should be looked on generally with a good deal of skepticism. Furthermore, Southern Appalachia is not a "region" in the sense in which that term is often used today, i.e., an area the various parts of which are closely linked in such ways that they form a "system" of some sort. Obviously some parts of the Southern Appalachians are more closely tied together than others; for example, the coal mining areas of Kentucky, West Virginia (especially southern West Virginia) and Virginia have a good deal of social and economic interaction and also share many more cultural similarities than any of these parts has with, say, northern Georgia. One of the ways in which some areas function together, or are interrelated, is that they are parts of the same "migratory-stream system," to be discussed later in this paper.

In this paper, not surprisingly then, we use four different delineations, primarily because in previous articles each of these was used and because there is not enough time to reorder the data to conform to one delineation (certainly desirable). We have been careful to specify when we are using each of them. Since most of our discussion concerns individual state economic areas or limited groupings of SEAs, rather than Southern Appalachia as a whole, this is not, we believe, a serious handicap. Later we hope to revise the tables so that only one delineation is used; and because the Appalachian Regional Commission has compiled so much data using its own delineation, we will probably follow that, though in many ways it is a political definition, not a carefully worked out, more or less scientific delineation, such as, for example, the delineation by John C. Campbell (1921) or by the researchers who produced the U.S. Department of Agriculture's Miscellaneous Publication No. 205, *Economic and Social Problems and Conditions of the Southern Appalachians* (1935).

The four delineations we have used in this paper are as follows:

Delineation I (used in Table 3.1): The delineation by the Appalachian Regional Commission, modified, for our purposes, by excluding counties in New York, Ohio, and Pennsylvania (that is, "Northern Appalachia") to get

"Southern Appalachia." This delineation includes 303 counties and 5 independent cities (the latter all in Virginia) in 10 states (Alabama, Georgia, Kentucky, Maryland, Mississippi, North Carolina, South Carolina, Tennessee, Virginia, and West Virginia). For a list of the counties and cities included, see ARC's *Appalachian Data Book*, second edition, April 1970.

Delineation II: A delineation made by use of state economic areas which conforms as nearly as possible to our delineation of "Southern Appalachia," derived from the ARC's delineation of "Appalachia." For the counties included in the SEAs listed here (and in other delineations), see U.S. Bureau of the Census (1967 and 1972 b). For the names of each of the SEAs and excellent brief descriptions of them, see Donald J. Bogue and Calvin L. Beale (1961).

The SEAs included in Delineation II are:

Alabama: 1–Middle Tennessee Valley; 2*–Sand Mountain; 3–Alabama Ridge and Valley; 4–Alabama Piedmont; 5–Alabama Upper Coastal Plain; Met. A–Birmingham; Met. E–Tuscaloosa; Met. F–Huntsville.

Georgia: 1*–Northwest Georgia Ridge and Valley; 2*–Georgia Blue Ridge; 3–Georgia Upper Piedmont; Met. A*–Chattanooga (part in Georgia).

Kentucky: 5–South Central Kentucky Highland; 8*–Eastern Kentucky Hills; 9*–Eastern Kentucky Coal Fields; Met. C*–Huntington/Ashland (part in Kentucky).

Maryland: 1–Western Maryland.

Mississippi: 4–Mississippi Pine Hills; 5–Mississippi Black Prairie.

North Carolina: 1*–North Carolina Blue Ridge; 2*–Blue Ridge Slopes; Met. A*–Asheville; Met. B–Winston-Salem/High Point/Greensboro.

South Carolina: 1–South Carolina Blue Ridge-Piedmont Transition; 2–Northwestern South Carolina Piedmont; Met. D–Greenville SMA.

Tennessee: 6–Eastern Highland Rim; 7*–Tennessee Cumberland Plateau; 8*–Valley of Eastern Tennessee; Met. C*–Chattanooga SMA (part in Tennessee); Met. D*–Knoxville.

Virginia: 1*–Southwest Virginia Coal Fields; 2*–Valley of Virginia-Southwest; 3*–Valley of Virginia-Lower.

West Virginia: 1–Upper Ohio and Little Kanawah Valley; 2*–West Virginia Hills; 3*–Monongahela Valley and North Central West Virginia; 4*–West Virginia Southern Coal Fields; 5*–Allegheny Mountains-Greenbrier Valley; Met. A–Wheeling-Steubenville (part in West Virginia); Met. B–Huntington/Ashland (part in West Virginia); Met. C–Charleston.

*SEAs also included in Delineation IV used by the Southern Appalachian Studies Group (see below).

Delineation III (used in tables 3.2-3.5): A delineation used in an earlier paper by James S. Brown (see note 2 to this chapter) which is like Delineation II except that the two Mississippi SEAs are not included (at the time data for the earlier paper were collected the Mississippi areas were not considered "Appalachian") and that two Virginia SEAs (Va. 4 and Va. A-Roanoke) are included here; they were *not* included in ARC's delineation of Virginia's Appalachian counties but are included in the Southern Appalachian Studies Group's delineation (see Delineation IV below). Delineation III was used in the present article because extensive data were available for the earlier Delineation IV and could be used on a regional basis roughly approximating the ARC's delineation (of 303 counties and 5 independent cities) by adding to it additional SEAs.

Delineation IV: A delineation used by the Southern Appalachian Studies Group (see Ford, 1962), which included twenty-six state economic areas, twenty-four of which are included in Delineation II (only Va. 4 and Va. A-Roanoke are not included). These areas are indicated by an asterisk in Delineation II and together with Va. 4 and Va. A form the twenty-six-area delineation.

2. A "migratory-stream system" consists of a focal area, usually a metropolitan area or a cluster of metropolitan areas, which attracts migrants from outlying areas (in this study, state economic areas, both metropolitan and non-metropolitan) and which in turn sends out migrants to the outlying areas. The demographic relationship is one of many which tie certain metropolises and certain outlying areas into an interdependent system to form what Duncan and his colleagues have defined as a "region" (Duncan et al., 1960). For further discussion of southern Appalachian migratory-stream systems, see Brown (1970).

3. "Metropolitan areas" as used in this article refers to a "special class of state economic areas" as defined by Bogue and Beale (1961). For counties included in metropolitan and nonmetropolitan areas, and maps of these areas, see this work. These areas were the ones used by the Bureau of the Census in reporting much of the data on migration for the censuses of 1950, 1960, and 1970.

4. The sources of the migratory-stream data used in this article are as follows:

1949–50: Special tabulations from the U.S. Bureau of the Census purchased by the Department of Rural Sociology as part of a project of the Kentucky Agricultural Experiment Station, University of Kentucky, Lexington.

1955–60: U.S. Bureau of the Census, U.S. Census of Population, 1960, Subject Reports, Final Report PC(2)-2E, *Migration between State Economic Areas* (1967).

1965–70: U.S. Bureau of the Census, U.S. Census of Population: 1970, Subject Reports, Final Report PC(2)-2E, *Migration between State Economic Areas* (1972b).

5. The net migration data reported in Table 3.1 are estimates derived by the "residual method," i.e., by determining the excess of births over deaths, adding this to the population of the base year and subtracting the population of the last year of the decade.

Though this method has been found to be a reasonably accurate way of determining net change, it does not, of course, determine the total number of out-migrants or in-migrants during the decade, for the actual number of migrants is greater than the net figures shown in our tables. Even these indicate, however, that out-migration from Appalachia was tremendous during the three decades. It should be emphasized, nevertheless, that these data are great understatements of the actual number of migrants and this fact should be remembered in interpreting all the data given in this paper.

6. The report giving 1965–70 data explains that "Persons 5 years old and over who indicated they had moved into their present residence after April 1, 1965, but for whom sufficiently complete and consistent information regarding residence on April 1, 1965, was not collected, are included in the group 'moved, place of residence in 1965 not reported.' When no information was reported for the person himself, information for the other members of the family was used, if available. The category also includes persons who gave no information on residence on April 1, 1965, but were classified as having moved into their present house since that date on the basis of the final edited information reported for question 18, 'When did this person move into this house (or apartment)?' " (All nonresponses on the latter question were allocated.) (U.S. Bureau of the Census, 1972b.)

7. An important factor differentiating local, regional, and national migration systems is seen by comparing the 1 percent and 5 percent criteria. The more local migration systems are delineated more selectively by the 1 percent criterion. However, the opposite is true for the national migration centers like Chicago, for which the 5 percent criterion, based on origin, is more important in determining components of the total migration-stream system. Both criteria are about equally significant in determining stream components for regional metropolises like Atlanta. Put somewhat differently, the larger national migration centers such as Los Angeles and Chicago draw from many origins and therefore have smaller proportions of their total in-migration accounted for by areas contributing 1 percent or more. This means that many smaller streams are attracted to these national metropolises, whereas the local and regional metropolises draw much more concentrated streams from fewer areas, usually nearby. Even Atlanta is shown by the data to be mostly a regional migration center, and the 1 percent streams account for 42 percent of all its migrants, compared to Chicago, which has less than 30 percent of its in-migrants accountable by the 1 percent streams. However, the more local migration destinations such as Hamilton and Canton have about 60 percent of all their in-migrants accounted for by those areas contributing 1 percent or more.

8. For a list of the counties included, see *Annual Report of the Appalachian Regional Commission* (1975).

9. The authors are at present delineating more fully the migratory-stream systems involving other focal areas.

4 GARY L. FOWLER

The Residential Distribution
of Urban Appalachians

The majority of migrants from the Appalachian region are living in metropolitan areas. Cities such as Atlanta, Washington, Detroit, and Chicago have traditionally had large Appalachian minorities to which large numbers of newcomers are added annually. Appalachians are conveniently regarded as marginal people who impose significant social costs upon urban America. Recent studies, however, have challenged many of the casual assumptions about Appalachian migration, the adjustment of migrants, and their relationship to urban poverty and public welfare which are associated with the hillbilly stereotype.[1] The assumptions include the residential distribution of Appalachians in the city.

Classical models of urban ecology provide conventional explanations for the residential distribution of urban Appalachians. They predict that Appalachians will be concentrated in predominantly white, lower-class areas near the central part of the city, with a decline in the number of Appalachians at increased distance from the city center. The models also predict that Appalachians will concentrate in specific sectors of the city which generally exclude blacks and other ethnic groups. Distance and directional, or sectoral, bias assume that socioeconomic characteristics attributed to Appalachians restrict their housing choices in the city. Residential segregation assumes that Appalachians not only have residential preferences analogous to those of other groups, but also that they face discrimination in housing (Berry and Horton, 1970: 307–09).

The purpose of this paper is to compare the distribution of Appalachians in Cincinnati, Ohio, with theoretical settlement patterns derived from models of the internal structure of cities. Public elementary

school enrollments are used as indicators of the residential distribution
of Appalachians in the city.

Explanations of the settlement patterns of urban Appalachians are
deeply rooted in traditional sociological research on the adjustment of
white farm labor migrants from the rural South in northern cities. In
this research, conducted during the 1930s and 1940s, migrants were
generally found to occupy small areas of lower-class housing within
larger, stable, working-class communities, many of which were rem-
nants of urban villages created by earlier European immigrants. Southern whites in areas such as Chicago's ethnically heterogeneous Near
West Side were concentrated in cheap furnished flats with easy access
to industrial plants near the city center (Killian, 1970: 104–17). Kinship ties, dialect, and cultural characteristics distinguished them from
other groups in the community. Southerners reportedly lost status to
foreigners as well as to urban blacks; and established ethnic groups discriminated against them as unstable, marginal elements in the community. External pressures such as these contributed to the concentration
of southerners near friends and relatives who had migrated previously.
Leybourne (1937) described adjustment patterns among Appalachians
in Cincinnati which were similar to those of southern whites in
Chicago and Indianapolis (Smith, 1953; 1956). They were all considered "hillbillies," a generic term which people in the urban North re-
served for working-class whites from the South. Social class differences
as well as regional cultural origins were the criteria which defined
them as a distinct subgroup in the socioeconomic structure of the city.
Sections of the city which housed white migrants from the rural
South were considered marginal residential locations. Freedman
(1964: 178–200) explained the newcomers' distribution in Chicago as a
function of the social and economic disadvantages common to rural migrants and of the characteristics of the city's ecological structure. More
recently, Rainwater (1968: 251-53), in his report to the President's
Commission on Rural Poverty, generalized the functions of ports-of-
entry as places near the city center which could best accommodate the
migrants' needs.[2] He argued that the migrants' orientation to such
areas is temporary, since they see socioeconomic opportunities in other
parts of the city which are potentially available to them as members of
the urban majority. As their economic condition improves, they move
into better residential areas away from the city center.
Successful adjustment involves geographical as well as social and

economic mobility. Ports-of-entry may indeed have been the places in which poor white migrants traditionally began the rural-to-urban transition (Elgie, 1970). But where large concentrations of southern whites, or Appalachians, were visible, the residential areas were popularly known as the locations at which the hillbillies "invaded" the city (Banas, 1969; Votaw, 1958).

Places such as Cincinnati's Over-the-Rhine, Chicago's Uptown, and Dayton's East End are notorious in the folk geography of urban Appalachia. Huelsman (1969: 99), for example, writes that:

The migrant to Dayton usually gets here in a wheezing old car full of kids with hungry bellies and maybe a guitar. In the pocket of his faded blue work shirt is a letter from a second cousin or an uncle with an address near Fifth and Brown or Tecumseh St. in East Dayton. This is in the heart of Dayton's port-of-entry, a strange new style of life for the southern white migrant. He brings his wife, four, five, or six children and about eight years of grammar schooling because he's heard from his kinsman that "they're hirin' on at NCR" or something else. The southern mountain man in the port-of-entry is most likely to be from one of the mountain counties of Eastern Kentucky. His kinsman on Tecumseh or Brown St. has four or five young'uns of his own, but he'll not turn down Dayton's newest migrant. They will all pile into one big flat, sleeping on couches, on the floor, or, in nice weather, maybe some of the kids will sleep out in the car. The family baggage is meager . . . a few changes of old clothes, a toy or so, some snapshots, a few trinkets and souvenirs of life back in the hills and hollows of Eastern Kentucky. The family has brought the most important baggage of all of them . . . the culture of the southern mountaineer, unfamiliar with city life.

As this quotation illustrates, and contrary to popular impressions, migrants who settle in places such as East Dayton come in search of work. Most are successful in obtaining employment and make significant gains in personal income, as well. However, they depend upon the social support of kin and friends in the city to compensate initially for their meager economic resources. This dependence has a decisive influence upon their settlement patterns.

For most Appalachian migrants, primary group networks, especially kin, dominate the decision-making process.[3] The majority move directly to the city from the place in which they have spent practically all of their lives. The decision to move is made relatively quickly, and migrants go to places where they are aware of favorable opportunities. The availability of jobs and other economic considerations are most important. Although some harbor doubts that migration will lead to socioeconomic gain, most Appalachians who settle in low-income areas of the central city enter the labor force relatively quickly and, after some initial instability, realize considerable economic gain.[4] In the interim, they rely upon relatives and friends who have migrated previously to ease adjustment problems.

The migrants' use of their social networks restricts their choice of places to live in the city. Finding a "first night" location is relatively simple. The majority stay with relatives and friends while searching for a job and a place to live.[5] They also use relatives and friends more frequently than other methods in finding a permanent residence. They routinely face discrimination in housing because they are stereotyped as hillbillies, and they consider access to social networks an important criterion in evaluating known vacancies. They depend upon kin as their primary reference group and as buffers to an outside world which includes foreigners and blacks, neither of whom white Appalachians especially want as neighbors (Photiadis, 1970: 110-15). Even migrants with limited social networks may establish pseudo-kin relationships with people from their home area, state, or region, and live in proximity to them (Fowler and Davies, 1972).

The Appalachians' dependence upon social networks and a cultural preference for specific social structures in the face of uncertainty lead to their geographical concentration within central-city poverty areas. Their settlement pattern is more clustered than that of poor whites from other regions, and their orientation is away from predominantly black residential areas[6] (Fowler and Davies, 1972; Watkins, 1976). They may have little knowledge of people from other backgrounds who live near them, and their associations with groups and institutions in the community are few and ephemeral.[7] Contact with their place of origin is frequent, however, and temporary resettlement in Appalachia is a common part of adjustment (Photiadis, 1970: 105).

Conventional descriptions of the residential distribution of urban Appalachians assume that they initially settle as migrants in central-city ghettos. Consider, for example, Powles's model (1964: 273-74):

The Appalachian migrant is likely to make his first night nest in a slum where his folks may have arrived a short time before, where life is informal and housing cheap: tenements often charge rent weekly, an apparent economy to the untutored. Such districts in a Midwestern city (ghettos, they might be called) are unkempt and disorderly, not merely because of poverty and social instability, but because such city amenities as garbage collection are unknown and unpracticed "down home." The lucky or more enterprising migrants soon find a job. They move to a more settled lower-class district, renting an apartment, and hoping ultimately for something better. Migrants, if "successful," rise through apartment-renting to home owning in a lower-middle class section, still in the congenial neighborhood of other Appalachians but with an increasing participation in city middle-class ways, such as membership in a regular community organization or a formally structured church. The highest ambition of many is to own an acre or two of land in the suburbs or true farm country. . . . Some remain settled on the various rungs of this migratory "ladder." A few never even make it out of the slums.

Accordingly, the port-of-entry functions as the territorial base for an evolutionary settlement pattern in which Appalachians, like groups of migrants who have preceded them, follow an orderly progression of socioeconomic and geographical mobility through the residential areas of the city according to classical models of urban ecology (Berry and Horton, 1970: 307–08).

Empirical data from the Cleveland Southern In-migrant study support this model (Peterson, Sharp, and Drury, 1977: 207–11). The majority of Appalachians and southern whites made only one or two moves and remained within the low-income neighborhoods on the periphery of the city or in the suburbs, where they purchased homes. Those who remained in the city also would have preferred to move to the suburbs, although a large proportion of them were dissatisfied with the city and seriously entertained the possibility of returning home to Appalachia.

Other evidence, however, suggests that the traditional ports-of-entry no longer serve as staging areas for Appalachian newcomers to the city. In places such as central Cincinnati, the majority of the Appalachians are long-term residents of the city[8] (cf. Fowler, 1976a). This is a sharp reminder that Appalachians, like other urban migrants, may initially settle in a variety of residential locations. This was the case for Beech Creek migrants to southwestern Ohio (Schwarzweller, Brown, and Mangalam, 1971: 125): "Some, by reason of circumstance rather than choice, found themselves in an urban slum situation that was in sharp contrast to the rural (although also poverty-stricken) atmosphere of the mountain neighborhoods they had left. Some, through family ties, located in an enclave of mountain people near [Cincinnati] and the industrial heartland of Ohio—where community life was by and large 'Kentucky.' Others melted very quickly into the mainstream of suburban middle-class American society." The migrants' initial location depended upon their economic resources, social class origins, and the prior settlement of kinfolk. The use of kinship networks in the selection of a place to live in the city is not exclusive to poor migrants in the central city. Most Beech Creek migrants, in fact, were in "Little Kentuckies" on the periphery of the metropolitan area. Appalachians in Cleveland have similar locational patterns.[9]

The Cincinnati metropolitan area is the principal destination for Appalachians in southwestern Ohio (McCoy, Brown, and Watkins, 1975). Approximately 14,000 (22 percent) of the nearly 65,000 in-migrants to the Cincinnati area from 1955 to 1960 came from southern Appalachia; another 10,500 came between 1965 and 1970. The majority were from adjacent areas in southeastern Ohio and from Eastern Kentucky.[10] Although recent in-migration from the Appalachian region has declined, an estimated 14 percent of metropolitan Cincinnati's 1.38 million people in 1970 were born in Appalachian states (U.S. Bureau of the Census, 1972). The proportion is even higher in the city. Most Appalachians are white, but a small minority of the black population is also of Appalachian origin.

The residential areas of Cincinnati are grouped into forty-four statistical neighborhoods (Figure 4.1). Maloney's (1974) social area analysis of these neighborhoods describes them as relatively homogeneous areas distinguished from each other by income, occupational structure, educational status, family organization, and housing.

Enrollment in public elementary schools is one indicator of the residential distribution of Appalachians in Cincinnati. The Administrative Research Branch of the Cincinnati Public Schools conducted a special survey in October 1973 to determine the number of pupils of Appalachian origin in the school system.[11] A pupil was considered of Appalachian origin if either he or one of his parents was born in any of the 397 counties and five independent cities in the Appalachian Region (Appalachian Regional Commission, 1975: 7–8, 121). According to estimates from the survey, approximately 32 percent of the elementary school pupils were first- or second-generation Appalachian. They formed 28 percent of the total enrollment in junior high schools and 30 percent in senior high schools.

Public elementary school enrollments generally underestimate the population of city neighborhoods. The data are from a universe of families or households with at least one child of elementary school age. People with no children, as well as those with preschoolers, with chil-

Figure 4.1

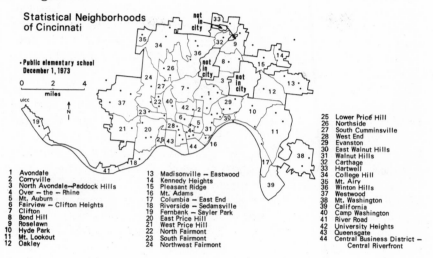

Statistical Neighborhoods
of Cincinnati

• Public elementary school
December 1, 1973

0   2   4
   miles

uicc

1	Avondale	13	Madisonville — Eastwood
2	Corryville	14	Kennedy Heights
3	North Avondale—Paddock Hills	15	Pleasant Ridge
4	Over — the — Rhine	16	Mt. Adams
5	Mt. Auburn	17	Columbia — East End
6	Fairview — Clifton Heights	18	Riverside — Sedamsville
7	Clifton	19	Fernbank — Sayler Park
8	Bond Hill	20	East Price Hill
9	Roselawn	21	West Price Hill
10	Hyde Park	22	North Fairmont
11	Mt. Lookout	23	South Fairmont
12	Oakley	24	Northwest Fairmont

25	Lower Price Hill
26	Northside
27	South Cumminsville
28	West End
29	Evanston
30	East Walnut Hills
31	Walnut Hills
32	Carthage
33	Hartwell
34	College Hill
35	Mt. Airy
36	Winton Hills
37	Westwood
38	Mt. Washington
39	California
40	Camp Washington
41	River Road
42	University Heights
43	Queensgate
44	Central Business District — Central Riverfront

dren who were in high school or had dropped out, and with high school graduates are excluded. Families with children in private schools also may not be represented. Problems of underestimation are more serious among Appalachians, especially recent migrants in the central city. Sharp and Peterson (1967: 24–27) reported that public school enrollments have the potential of identifying only 12 percent of recent southern white migrants in Cleveland's low-income areas. Residential instability and other adjustment problems are the principal sources of error.[12] These factors become less important, however, as length of residence in the city increases.

Underestimation and geographical bias limit the usefulness of public school enrollment as an indicator of the residential distribution of urban Appalachians. Inaccuracies are concentrated geographically in low-income areas of the central city, in districts in which Appalachians are a relatively small proportion of total enrollments, and among recent in-migrants. The advantages of using public school data, however, outweigh the disadvantages. Elementary school enrollments are the best indicator of population characteristics for small areas on a continuing (annual) basis which are also symptomatic of neighborhood change (U.S. Bureau of the Census, 1970b).[13]

Over-the-Rhine is one of the traditional ports-of-entry for Appalachian migrants in the central part of Cincinnati. The public school en-

Figure 4.2

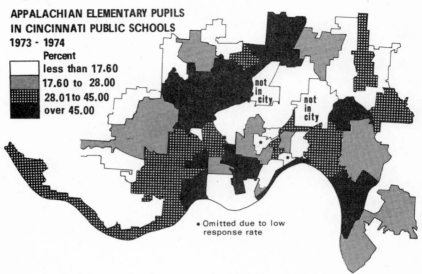

APPALACHIAN ELEMENTARY PUPILS
IN CINCINNATI PUBLIC SCHOOLS
1973 - 1974
Percent
less than 17.60
17.60 to 28.00
28.01 to 45.00
over 45.00

not in city

not in city

• Omitted due to low response rate

rollments reflect the neighborhood's function, as Appalachians were found to be in the majority in the western part of the area as well as in Mt. Auburn (Figure 4.2). They made up 69 percent in the predominantly white sections of Over-the-Rhine which focussed upon Washington Park School, and 74 percent of the enrollment in Mt. Auburn's Taft School. Recent Appalachian migrants settled by state-of-origin in areas which had large Appalachian populations. Migrants from Kentucky and Tennessee, for example (Watkins, 1976), settled almost exclusively in Over-the-Rhine. Although some lived in integrated neighborhoods, most migrants settled into the racially segregated residential pattern which dominates the city.

Elementary schools in the northern part of Over-the-Rhine and Mt. Auburn drew the majority of their students from predominantly black areas. In an earlier paper (Fowler, 1976) I estimated that four out of every ten Appalachians living in central-city neighborhoods were black people from the Southern Appalachian region who were long-term residents of Cincinnati. A large minority of elementary school students in the predominantly black neighborhoods were Appalachian, especially in Mt. Auburn.[14]

Racial and cultural diversity in Over-the-Rhine and Mt. Auburn are essential characteristics of the traditional ports-of-entry. Maloney (1972: 29) described the situation in Over-the-Rhine:

Most of the population is in the secondary labor market or is dependent and thus is part of the urban under-class. Culture conflicts and police occupation forces make life even harsher. Appalachians comprise about 65 percent of the population but control very little of the community. The economic system and property are largely in the hands of ethnic groups who have been in the city much longer. A growing black population controls the streets, schools, and social agencies for the most part. There is a lot of violence in the community and in the schools. The police patrol the streets as if they were a battlefield and thus add to the violence even as they try to control it. Most Appalachian youth do not survive in school through junior high school. As for their parents, they would move out of the neighborhood if their low wages or welfare checks could make it possible.

Ports-of-entry in other northern cities have been found to be similar. Appalachians shared space with older ethnic groups, blacks, and Puerto Ricans in Cleveland (Kunkin and Byrne, 1973: 7). In Chicago's Uptown, Chicanos, Native Americans, and South Asian immigrants provided additional competition for limited housing (cf. Gitlin and Hollander, 1970; Montgomery, 1968). However, the ports-of-entry are not primarily staging areas for upwardly mobile groups and in-migrants in the classical sense. The majority of the Appalachians in central Cincinnati were long-term residents of the city and its central neighborhoods (Fowler, 1976). In fact, the "newcomers" in central Cincinnati were more likely to be non-Appalachian whites than Appalachians.[15]

In western Cincinnati, Appalachians were concentrated in an arc that extended from Riverside and Lower Price Hill through Mill Creek Valley[16] to Carthage and Hartwell in the north. They were the majority population in three areas, two of which were predominantly white. Approximately 76 percent of the elementary school enrollments in Carthage and Hartwell, and 66 percent in Lower Price Hill and the eastern edge of East Price Hill were Appalachian. The eastern part of South Fairmont had similar characteristics. The other concentrations of Appalachians, however, were in predominantly black neighborhoods. The proportion of Appalachians was smaller and a minority were black (Figure 4.3). The black majorities in Queensgate and West End, and in Northside and North Fairmont, interrupted the continuity of Appalachian settlement. Elementary schools in neighborhoods in which blacks were a large proportion of the population had small white Appalachian

Figure 4.3

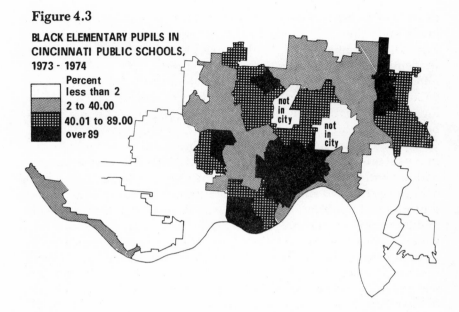

BLACK ELEMENTARY PUPILS IN
CINCINNATI PUBLIC SCHOOLS,
1973 - 1974

Percent
less than 2
2 to 40.00
40.01 to 89.00
over 89

minorities, and vice versa. Here as elsewhere in low-status areas, public housing was a significant factor in patterns of residential segregation.[17]

Lower Price Hill and the Mill Creek Valley neighborhoods are also traditional areas of Appalachian settlement. Leybourne's (1937) paper on the adjustment of Southern Appalachians in Cincinnati was based in part on rural migrants who had come to work in industries located in the Mill Creek Valley. Residential segregation in poor housing for the migrants was the result of real socioeconomic disadvantages, as well as discrimination against "hillbillies" by native Cincinnatians, especially German Catholics. Both factors, Leybourne reported, were prejudicial to the Appalachians' socioeconomic and geographical mobility in the city. In 1970, three of Cincinnati's five neighborhoods with lowest socioeconomic status—Lower Price Hill, North Fairmont, and Camp Washington—were Appalachian sections of the Mill Creek Valley (Maloney, 1974: 44). Each had experienced extensive public demolition, especially for highway construction, public housing development, and industrial expansion.

Elsewhere in western Cincinnati, Appalachians were a smaller proportion of the population at increased distance from the city center and in areas of higher socioeconomic status. They were large minorities in lower and upper middle-class neighborhoods such as East and West Price Hill and River Road. Within these, they reportedly clustered in residential areas that were geographically distinct from other ethnic minorities (Maloney, 1974: 28–30). Neighborhoods which had large white Appalachian minorities had few blacks. In Westwood and other high-status areas on the city's western periphery, all of the small numbers of Appalachians were white.

Appalachians in the eastern part of Cincinnati were concentrated in neighborhoods to the east and south of Norwood (a separate city within Cincinnati). They were in the majority in Oakley, which borders Norwood, and in Columbia-East End.[18] Except for Columbia-East End and California, the neighborhoods had either high or upper-middle socioeconomic status, and all of them were predominantly white. Conversely, the smallest proportions of white Appalachians were in predominantly black neighborhoods northeast of the Central Business District. The integration of blacks and white Appalachians was greatest in predominantly white Mt. Adams and Walnut Hills and in the relatively large upper-class black communities in the far northeastern part of the city.[19]

White Appalachians in northern cities do not, as a matter of preference, live in the same neighborhoods as blacks and other recent ethnic immigrants.[20] In Cincinnati, there was a strong negative correlation ($r = -.539$) between the proportion of Appalachians enrolled in a particular public elementary school and the proportion of blacks so enrolled. Integration was most characteristic of neighborhoods with low and lower-middle socioeconomic status, especially in the central part of the city, and of selected higher-status areas in the eastern and northeastern parts of the city. Segregation was most characteristic of predominantly white neighborhoods with large Appalachian minorities, and of predominantly black neighborhoods. However, Appalachian and black are not mutually exclusive terms; place-of-birth rather than race was the criterion used for identifying Appalachians.[21]

The geographical distribution of Appalachians in Cincinnati was found to be more complex than conventional stereotypes and classical models of urban ecology predict. The location of urban renewal and other public works projects in traditional areas of Appalachian settlement had significantly altered the residential structure of the city within which many newcomers competed with other low-income groups, especially blacks, for housing. The majority of Appalachians lived in predominantly white neighborhoods and a large proportion was concentrated on the west side of the city. Although the number of Appalachians declined with increased distance from the city center, they were large minorities and in some cases the majority population in neighborhoods elsewhere in the city. Their location was consistent with the residential distribution of other ethnic minorities.

Appalachians were also concentrated in areas with low and lower-middle socioeconomic status.[22] Forty percent of the Appalachians lived in lower class areas and 22 percent lived in lower-middle class areas, compared with 30 and 20 percent, respectively, of the total population of Cincinnati. This is a matter of concern for public policy. Segregation in poor areas of the city limited the Appalachians' accessibility to urban socioeconomic opportunities, and magnified the disadvantages they faced, which ranged from lack of employment and skills on the one hand to poor housing, inferior schools, and inadequate social services on the other (Watkins, 1976). The problems in Cincinnati are analogous to those facing Appalachians in poor areas of other midwestern cities.[23] So is their desire to move into better residential areas as their economic condition improves.

Black Appalachians were concentrated in other sections of the same areas as white Appalachians. An estimated 44 percent of the Appalachians in low-status areas, and 32 percent in lower-middle-class areas, were black. They were concentrated in Over-the-Rhine and Mt. Auburn, where black Appalachians ranged from 13 to 70 percent of the total elementary-school enrollments, and the predominantly black neighborhoods in Mill Creek. Black schools in lower-middle-class areas had Appalachian minorities of from 9 to 22 percent of total enrollments. Segregation by race and residence further fragmented the Appalachian community in Cincinnati.

The proportion of Appalachians in a neighborhood declined with increased social status. Twenty percent of the Appalachians lived in upper-middle class areas, and 18 percent lived in high status areas compared with 31 and 20 percent respectively of the total population of Cincinnati. Almost all of the Appalachians (97 percent) were white, and their visibility faded. Backes (1968: 33), for example, writes that when Appalachians move out of Chicago's Uptown

the trail becomes clouded, diffuse. It is a good bet that there are one-time [Appalachian] migrants living in every part of the city and in many of its suburbs, some of them holding good jobs, with long and faithful employment records and sons away at school. There might even be one right down the street. It isn't something you always know for sure.

After all, you don't stop an honest, hard-working neighbor on the street and ask him if he once was a hillbilly. You wouldn't be that crude.

Stereotypes of recent migrants and the assumption that Appalachians are concentrated in the central-city ports-of-entry have resulted in a large proportion of urban Appalachians remaining invisible (Killian, 1970: 113–17). Appalachians are a distinct ethnic group in Cincinnati and residential segregation is characteristic of their settlement pattern. Public school enrollments, however, do not explain whether they are segregated by migrant status, real socioeconomic differences, or discrimination which restricts their mobility in the city.

Classical models of urban ecology are adequate but incomplete descriptions of the residential distribution of Appalachians in cities such as Cincinnati. They emphasize central city port-of-entry locations to the exclusion of areas of higher socioeconomic status on the periphery of the city where Appalachians are large minorities, and sometimes the majority, of the population. Furthermore, urban renewal, model cities, and public works projects have directly changed some traditional Appalachian neighborhoods and affected others indirectly through changes in the housing market of the central city. Areas such as Over-the-Rhine may no longer serve exclusively as staging areas for new migrants. To the extent that distribution of Appalachians is dependent upon migrant settlement and mobility, changes in their location could alter significantly the future geography of urban Appalachians.

NOTES

The Urban Appalachian Council of Cincinnati gave valuable assistance in the preparation of this paper. I also appreciate Robert Wilburn's assistance in using data from the public school survey, which he supervised. The maps were produced by the Cartographic Laboratory, Department of Geography, University of Illinois at Chicago Circle.

1. Price and Sikes (1974), and Shannon and Shannon (1967) have critically reviewed the literature on rural-to-urban migration. Fowler (1976), Lex and Hartman (1974), and Maloney and Huelsman (1972) have reviewed selected research on Appalachian migration.

2. Rainwater states that lower-class whites do not create urban villages to protect a valued ethnic heritage, but move into parts of the city where ethnicity is not important. However, Appalachians may in fact develop ethnic,

place-based communities in the central city which are analogous to settlement patterns generally associated with European immigrants (Hyland, 1970; Hyland and Peet, 1973).

3. Choldin (1973), and Thompson (1974) describe the role of kinship in migration, while Schwarzweller, Brown, and Mangalam (1971) provide a detailed account of kinship systems and Appalachian migration. Fowler and Davies (1972, 1973) have analyzed the effect of kinship systems upon migrants' locational decisions.

4. Although they have some cause for concern about their immediate future, the majority of Appalachians receive significant economic benefits from urban migration (cf. Schwarzweller, Brown, and Mangalam, 1971; and Peterson, Sharp, and Drury, 1977). Empirical data fail to support the riff-raff theory of southern migration to which Appalachian people are commonly assigned (Fowler, 1976; Price and Sikes, 1974).

5. Among southern white migrants to Cleveland, for example, almost three-quarters of the men and the majority of the women first stayed with relatives, and half of each group remained from one to three weeks while searching for a permanent residence. They moved to a permanent residence when they found a job (Peterson, Sharp, and Drury, 1977: 107).

6. Black Appalachians, however, live in predominantly black residential areas (Fowler, 1976). The Appalachian community is segregated by race in the central city, a pattern which is even more sharply defined with length of residence in the city (Peterson, Sharp, and Drury, 1977: 207–08).

7. Appalachians in Cleveland's low-income areas often grieve for relatives and friends who live in Appalachia (Photiadis, 1970: 110–15). This is a common theme among recent, low-status migrants described by Coles (1971: 313-420) and Gitlin and Hollander (1970).

8. This is also true of the traditional ports-of-entry for Appalachian migrants in many large northern cities, including Chicago's Uptown. The relative numerical importance of Appalachian people in these communities has declined as the flow of migrants from Appalachia has decreased over the past decade.

9. Photiadis (1970: 95) also suggests a model of Appalachian resettlement. See chapter 9, below.

10. The Kentucky migrants were from coal-producing counties in the southeastern part of the state. Compared with migrants from Appalachian Kentucky who moved to Lexington, those who moved to Cincinnati were younger and less well educated, had larger families, had a higher rate of unemployment at the time of migration, and came from more distant, poorer counties (Morgan and Bordeaux, 1974a).

11. The survey (Cincinnati Public Schools, 1973) was designed and conducted in response to the Urban Appalachian Council's request for the numbers of first- and second-generation Appalachian pupils in the public schools.

Place-of-birth data for pupils and their parents, which is a permanent requirement of enrollment in the Cincinnati Public Schools, is entered into the permanent record of each pupil. The estimated number of Appalachian pupils for
1973–74 is based upon the response of 49.2 percent of the total pupil enrollment. (The elementary schools had a response of 48.1 percent, compared with
52.1 percent for the junior high schools and 49.2 percent for the senior high
schools.) Total pupil enrollment on October 1, 1973, was 70,263. Two elementary schools, Burdett and Columbia, are excluded from the analysis because of
low response rates.

12. The casual enrollment of Appalachian children in urban schools is frequently cited as a problem symptomatic of residential instability, poverty, and
alienation (Coles, 1971: 313–420; Dayton Human Relations Commission,
1966; Henderson, 1966; Kunkin and Byrne, 1973: 110–13; Morris, 1970). Appalachian communities in central city ports-of-entry have large proportions of
young, single people and large families (Photiadis, 1970: 67–69).

13. School enrollment data are most frequently used to monitor population
change and migration, as in the example for Oak Park, Illinois (Berry and Horton, 1970: 413–19). Griffin (1962) based his study of Appalachian migrants in
Cincinnati on a sample drawn from public school enrollments. Other methods
of locating migrants in cities are reviewed by Fowler (1973).

14. An estimated 95 percent of the Appalachians in Taft School, for example, were black; see footnote 20 below.

15. White Appalachians had relatively high rates of in-migration. They also
appeared to have high rates of residential mobility, although Varady (1975:
170–71) reports that Appalachians were actually less mobile than comparable
white families who lived in Cincinnati's Model Neighborhoods (West End,
Over-the-Rhine, and Mt. Auburn). Varady concludes that high rates of residential mobility are a function of class, not ethnicity.

16. The Mill Creek Valley includes the neighborhoods of Hartwell, Rose-
lawn, Carthage, Winton Hills, Northside, South Cumminsville, Camp Washington, West End, East Price Hill, and Lower Price Hill.

17. For example, West End was a predominantly (97 percent) black neighborhood with older, multi-family units, and with 2,700 units in three public
projects, whereas the 720-unit English Woods project in North Fairmont was
predominantly white and Appalachian (Maloney, 1974: 144).

18. Norwood traditionally has had a large Appalachian population (Leybourne, 1937; Miller, 1976). In both Norwood and St. Bernard (separate cities
within Cincinnati) less than 2 percent of the population was black.

19. Mt. Adams was a secondary center of settlement for white Appalachians
(Fowler, 1976).

20. The residential pattern is consistent from city to city (cf. Peterson,
Sharp, and Drury, 1977; Fowler, 1976; and Watkins, 1976).

21. Black Appalachians were identified for schools in which the number of

Appalachians was greater than the total white enrollment. The difference between the two was the estimated minimum black Appalachian enrollment. According to this measure, approximately 30 percent of the Appalachians in Cincinnati were black. By comparison, 40 percent of the Appalachians in central city neighborhoods were black (Fowler, 1976).

22. The distribution of Appalachians by social area class was based upon enrollment in schools which were located in the city of Cincinnati. Cheviot, Cloverdale, Losantiville, and Silverton elementary schools are excluded because they are located outside of the city. Because census tracts, statistical neighborhoods, and school district boundaries were often different, Appalachians were assigned to the social area class (quartile) in which the elementary school was located.

23. The disadvantages which face Appalachians living in low-income areas of northern cities are described by Coles (1971), Giffin (1957), Gitlin and Hollander (1970), Kunkin and Byrne (1973), Morris (1970), and Stekert (1971), among others.

5 JEROME B. PICKARD

Population Changes and Trends in Appalachia

The changes in Appalachia, as in any other area, can be partially understood by the dynamics taking place within the population. By observing the critical demographic events occurring within Appalachia, we can determine important patterns of change and the direction of change. The following discussion reveals recent trends in the population of Appalachia; specifically, fertility, mortality, migration (movement into and from Appalachia), and significant characteristics of its population such as the age structure.

Probably the factor having the most significant and extraordinary consequences for the Appalachian region has been the great out-migration. During the two decades from 1950 to 1970 the net outflow of migrants amounted to 3.3 million. In the decade of the 1950s, *net* out-migration numbered 2.2 million persons—an average rate of 12.5 percent of the mean population for that decade. One out of eight Appalachians moved out of the region without returning to live there during that single ten-year period. This huge outflow was 74 percent as large as the entire civilian in-migration into the United States during this decade. In the 1960s net out-migration from Appalachia dropped to 1.1 million (an average rate of 6.2 percent for the decade). The greatest number of out-migrants moved out of the northern subregion, but central Appalachia had the most severe rate of new out-migration (33 percent in the 1950s, 18 percent in the 1960s). The results were population losses in both decades.

One of the most significant facts in this great out-migration is that it is most selective of younger people. For the Appalachian Region in the 1960s, 38 percent of all net out-migration was concentrated in a

**Table 5.1: Distribution of Population by Age Group,
1970, United States and Appalachia**

| Age group (in years) | Percentage of total population | | Percentage of stable population |
	U.S.	Appalachia	
Under 5	8.4	8.2	6.8
5–14	20.0	19.5	13.5
15–19	9.4	9.6	6.7
20–24	8.1	7.5	6.7
25–44	23.6	22.9	26.4
45–64	20.6	21.9	23.9
65 and over	9.9	10.1	16.0
Median age	28.1 years	29.3 years	37.2 years

single five-year age group: those aged twenty through twenty-four years in 1970. The rate of out-movement was nearly twice as high for males as for females in this age group. One-third of all Appalachian males in this age group had left the region by 1970. Further indication of this youth movement outward is revealed by the fact that 95 percent of all net migration out of the region consisted of people under forty-five years of age in 1970.

One of the results of persistent and heavy out-migration of young persons is that the average age of the population remaining behind increases. Another important factor in increasing the average age of the population has been the drop in birth rates. This results partially from the great out-migration of the young. The drop in birth rates, in turn, means that the replacement of younger people is slowed down. Many areas within Appalachia have a markedly older population remaining, especially the rural counties in the northern and middle sections of Appalachia, the mountain counties of the Southern Blue Ridge, and those rural counties in the Deep South which have had heavy out-migration.[1]

The proportion of older population (sixty-five years of age and over) which resulted from this tremendous migration was more than 33 percent above the national proportion in 63 Appalachian counties in 1970; in 14 of these, the proportion was very high—50 percent or more above the national mean. In addition, 112 other counties had proportions of older people between 15 percent and 33 percent above the national norm. In sharp contrast, the counties with low shares of older people were few: in only 43 counties were the proportions of older persons less than 88 percent of the national average, and in only 13 of these were the proportions less than 75 percent of the national average. Most of these were areas which had had in-migration, were suburban in character, or had selective population movements (such as movement to universities and colleges).

Generally, young adults in the prime working-age group (twenty-five through thirty-four years in 1970) concentrated in areas having recent growth. Only one county in the entire Appalachian Region had a high concentration of this age group, Gwinnett County, Georgia, suburban to Atlanta. Five other counties in the region (four in Southern Appalachia and Clermont County, Ohio, suburban to Cincinnati) had between 15 and 33 percent more young adults than the national average. However, only 115 of the region's counties were above the United States average; 282 had deficiencies of young adults. Seventy percent of the region's counties in 1970 showed a "U-shaped" age profile, representing a deficiency of adults in the prime working ages, one reflection of the massive and persistent out-migration of the last decades.

The next younger group, aged fifteen through twenty-one years, which includes the high school, college, and prime military age groups, is revealed in any significant concentration (over 33 percent above the United States norm) in only thirteen counties in the region. Each of these counties contains a college or university; they are spread from Tompkins, N.Y. (Cornell University) to Oktibbeha, Mississippi (Mississippi State). The region also had a remarkably scarce military population in 1970 (only 23,000), about 1.5 percent of the national total, of which 13,000 were estimated to be under twenty-five years of age. The population eighteen through twenty-four years of age enrolled in school in the region numbered 616,000 in 1970, about 29,000 less than if the number had stood at the national average. Thus, out-migration primarily accounts for the deficits in this age group, although the absence of military camps and a lower proportion of college students also contributed to scarcities in the youth population.

Birth and fertility rates further affect the age distribution of the population in Appalachia, as well as being partially caused by the out-migration of the young. Fertility rates dropped sharply in the 1950s, with the result that in 1960 the Appalachian region's fertility (child–woman) ratio[2] at 529 was lower than the national ratio (563). Between 1960 and 1970, both the birth rates and the child–woman[3] ratios in Appalachia continued to drop, but not quite as rapidly as the U. S. average; the regional ratio fell to 396 while the United States ra-

.tio dropped to 404. The actual number of Appalachian children under five years of age counted in the censuses fell from 1,904,000 in 1960 to 1,486,000 in 1970.

In 1970 only 31 Appalachian counties had fertility ratios 20 percent or more above the U.S. average; eleven of these were in eastern Kentucky; others were in Mississippi (six); New York, Ohio, and Alabama (three each); Pennsylvania and West Virginia (two each); and Georgia (one). Twenty-eight of these counties were rural and three suburban. Average general fertility was below the national level in the Appalachian parts of Tennessee, North Carolina, Pennsylvania, West Virginia, and South Carolina.

Nationally, the birth rate has gone to a record low level (14.8 per 1,000 population in 1975); the Appalachian region likewise has hit a new low birthrate (estimated at 14.1 per 1,000), but a higher-than-average death rate (estimated at 9.9 per 1,000 in 1975). The resulting rate of natural increase is only about two-thirds the national rate. If this low rate of growth continues for a generation, both nation and region will approach a stable population that would look like this: persons sixty-five years of age and up would be one-sixth of the total population (10 percent in 1970); persons under eighteen years of age would be 24 percent of the population (in 1970, 33 percent); and the median age for the United States would be thirty-seven years (in 1970 it was 28 years). In 1970, the median age of the Appalachian population was 29.3 years, but the distribution was uneven, with more than the national average in ages fifteen to nineteen and ages forty-five and over, and lower proportions in the other age groups (the lowest in ages twenty through twenty-four years).

In addition to the dramatic changes in the population structure of Appalachia, there is evidence of some recent changes in the level of living. The Appalachian region has had low economic status in the postwar period. One reflection of this is per capita income levels well below the national average (80 percent of the United States average in 1969). In 1970, based upon 1969 incomes, only 4 of the region's 397 counties had per capita income levels higher than the national average. Three of these four were metropolitan counties, but none was as high as the U.S. metropolitan average. In contrast, the national and regional centers which surround Appalachia were major centers of attraction; in most of these areas (all of the national and large regional centers excepting some in the South) one or more of the major counties had per capita income above national levels. These centers in the aggregate had a 1970 population nearly four times that of the region. Not only is Appalachia at a lower economic level than the national average, but also it is ringed by dynamic competing centers which are at higher-than-average income levels. The few regional centers in the South which had lower incomes were lower basically because of two factors: a sizable lower-income black population or, in some areas, a relatively large lower-income military population.

Mean income levels were highest in the northern subregion as far south as central West Virginia; the lowest average levels are found in the middle of the region, with numerous counties in the South emerging with better income levels (with the exception of Appalachian Mississippi). Of the eighty counties which had 1969 per capita incomes better than the regional average, only three (all of which were metropolitan) were in Central Appalachia, while fifty-eight were in the northern subregion and nineteen were in Southern Appalachia. Southern Appalachia does better in the next category, with forty-eight counties having between 70 and 80 percent of the national per capita income level, while Northern Appalachia has forty-six counties and Central Appalachia, the most depressed subregion, only four counties in this category.

The population of the Appalachian region gained an estimated 977,000 persons between 1970 and mid-1976 (Table 5.2). Net in-migration contributed 380,000 (39 percent of the total population gain), while the excess of births over deaths was responsible for the remainder. Although representing 9 percent of the United States population, the region gained only 7 percent of the nation's natural increase. The difference in this natural increase can be understood by comparing the birth and death rates in the region to the national rates (1965–75). The Appalachian death rate is higher than the national rate for 1975 (9.9 vs. 8.9 per 1,000) whereas the birth rate is lower (14.1 vs. 14.8). As a result, the natural increase of population in Appalachia (4 per 1,000 per year in 1975) is significantly lower than the nation's (6 per 1,000).

However, a factor of growth other than natural increase is that of migration, which is estimated to be contributing a net increase to the population of Appalachia. Between 1970 and 1975, it is estimated that 1.7 million people migrated into the region, while 1.4 million left, for a net gain from migration of 300,000 persons. This indicates, of course, a sharp reversal from earlier periods, for as late as the 1965–70 period the

Table 5.2: Total Population, 1970, 1976, and 1977, and 1970-76 Estimated Components of Population Change, Appalachian Region and United States

Geographic division	Population (in 1,000s)			1970-76 estimated components of population change				
	April 1, 1970*	July 1, 1976†	July 1, 1977**	Births (in 1,000s)	Deaths (in 1,000s)	Net migration (in 1,000s)	Total change (in 1,000s)	Total change (%)
UNITED STATES	203,305	214,659	216,332	20,610	12,113	+2,857	11,354	+5.6
APPALACHIAN REGION	18,217.1	19,194.4	19,330	1,793.5	1,195.8	+379.6	977.3	+5.4
NORTHERN APPALACHIA								
Maryland	209.3	217.4	217	18.1	13.7	+3.7	8.1	+3.8
New York	1,056.6	1,089.8	1,086	95.9	65.8	+3.2	33.2	+3.1
Ohio	1,129.9	1,190.2	1,200	116.4	78.5	+22.4	60.4	+5.3
Pennsylvania	5,930.5	5,955.5	5,911	503.0	409.0	-69.1	25.0	+0.4
West Virginia	1,407.7	1,458.3	1,486	139.6	98.8	+9.9	50.6	+3.6
Total	9,734.0	9,911.3	9,900	873.0	665.7	-29.9	177.3	+1.8
CENTRAL APPALACHIA								
Kentucky	876.5	980.4	1,001	101.7	59.3	+61.5	103.9	+11.8
Tennessee	334.6	372.4	384	33.8	22.0	+26.0	37.8	+11.3
Virginia	197.3	224.3	232	22.6	13.4	+17.6	26.9	+13.7
West Virginia	336.5	362.4	373	40.4	25.0	+10.5	25.9	+7.7
Total	1,744.9	1,939.4	1,990	198.5	119.7	+115.7	194.5	+11.1
SOUTHERN APPALACHIA								
Alabama	2,137.4	2,273.2	2,282	226.2	131.6	+41.2	135.8	+6.4
Georgia	813.8	973.2	1,001	100.0	47.8	+107.1	159.3	+19.6
Mississippi	418.6	446.5	453	50.3	28.2	+5.8	27.8	+6.6
North Carolina	1,039.0	1,122.3	1,133	102.2	62.0	+43.1	83.3	+8.0
South Carolina	656.4	729.0	734	72.7	38.5	+38.4	72.6	+11.1
Tennessee	1,399.9	1,512.4	1,545	145.3	84.3	+51.6	112.5	+8.0
Virginia	273.0	287.1	292	25.4	18.0	+6.7	14.1	+5.2
Total	6,738.2	7,343.7	7,440	722.1	410.4	+293.8	605.5	+9.0
STATE PARTS††								
Tennessee	1,734.5	1,884.8	1,929	179.0	106.3	+77.6	150.3	+8.7
Virginia	470.3	511.3	524	48.1	31.4	+24.4	41.0	+8.7
West Virginia (entire state)	1,744.2	1,820.7	1,859	179.9	123.8	+20.4	76.5	+4.4

* Based on tabulations of the 1970 census prepared by ARC staff.
† July 1, 1976 data for Appalachian Region are provisional estimates. For this reason, single-year comparisons between 1976 and 1977 projected estimates should not be made.
** July 1, 1977 estimates projected by ARC staff based on provisional state estimates by U.S. Bureau of the Census (News Release CB78-13) and on ratio trend in Appalachian parts of states from 1970 through 1976.
†† Figures for the two subregional portions of these three states, the only states which fall in two subregions, are combined here.

region had an outflow of 1.6 million with an inflow of only 1.2 million, for a net loss of 400,000 persons.

Projected population estimates for 1977 (based on provisional state estimates by the Bureau of the Census) indicate that by mid-1977 the region's population had grown to 19.3 million, a gain of 1.1 million since the 1970 census. Appalachian population growth almost matched the national rate of increase in the 1970s, in sharp contrast to the two preceding decades.

Southern Appalachia has contributed the lion's share of regional growth, with 62 percent of total population gain. However, Central Appalachia represents the most rapid *rate of growth*, accounting for 20 percent of the increase in the Appalachian population. Northern Appalachia, while retaining the largest population total, had the smallest *net gain*, providing only 18 percent of Appalachia's population increase.

Appalachian population is projected to reach 19.7 million by 1980, representing a growth of 1.5 million in a single decade, or an 8 percent increase (compared with 2.7 percent for the 1960s), which approaches the decelerated rate of national increase. Paradoxically, this acceleration of Appalachian population growth is occurring in the same decade as the slowing down of national population increase to about 18 million (a gain of 9 percent), the lowest rate of increase in American history with the single exception of the depression decade of the 1930s.

Parallel to the increase in the population are indications of new growth in the level of income for the Appalachian region. Appalachian per capita income advanced from $2,505 in 1969, to $3,773 in 1974, rising from 80.3 percent to 82.5 percent of the United States average level in five years. Only 5 counties in the region had 1974 per capita income averages higher than the national average, while 392 counties were below it. A total of 190 counties had 1974 per capita incomes of less than 70 percent of the national average. Despite this continuing lag, the per capita income in the region over the five-year period increased at an annual rate of 2.4 percent, roughly one-third faster than the United States increase of 1.8 percent yearly. The difference was entirely due to the more rapid advances in income in Central and Southern Appalachia.

The 1970–75 period in the Appalachian region is best described as a period of accelerated economic and social development, with significant growth of both population and per capita income. Of the subregions, Central Appalachia had the most rapid development, but

Table 5.3: Per Capita Money Income, 1969 and 1974, Appalachian Region and United States (1969-74 Trends Adjusted for Inflation)

Geographic division	Population (in 1,000s)		Per capita money income			1969-74 income change*		1974 per capita income index (U.S.=100)
	April 1, 1970	July 1, 1975	1969 (in dollars)	1974 (in dollars)	1974* (in 1969 dollars)	Total change (%)	Annual rate (%)	
UNITED STATES	203,305	214,659	3,119	4,572	3,411	+9.4	+1.8	100
APPALACHIAN REGION	18,217	19,070	2,505	3,773	2,815	+12.4	+2.4	82.5
NORTHERN APPALACHIA								
Maryland	209	215	2,599	3,885	2,899	+11.5	+2.2	85
New York	1,057	1,081	2,845	3,912	2,919	+2.6	+0.5	86
Ohio	1,130	1,191	2,443	3,613	2,696	+10.4	+2.0	79
Pennsylvania	5,931	5,962	2,790	4,098	3,058	+9.6	+1.9	90
West Virginia	1,408	1,446	2,421	3,704	2,763	+14.2	+2.7	81
Total	9,734	8,896	2,698	3,957	2,953	+9.4	+1.8	86.5
CENTRAL APPALACHIA								
Kentucky	877	958	1,732	2,834	2,114	+22.0	+4.1	62
Tennessee	335	365	1,931	3,023	2,256	+16.8	+3.2	66
Virginia	197	220	1,807	3,220	2,402	+33.0	+5.9	70
West Virginia	336	354	1,966	3,265	2,436	+23.9	+4.4	71
Total	1,745	1,896	1,824	2,995	2,235	+22.5	+4.1	65.5
SOUTHERN APPALACHIA								
Alabama	2,137	2,241	2,430	3,787	2,826	+16.3	+3.1	83
Georgia	814	958	2,419	3,711	2,769	+14.5	+2.7	81
Mississippi	419	445	1,861	2,953	2,203	+18.4	+3.4	65
North Carolina	1,039	1,118	2,437	3,808	2,841	+16.6	+3.1	83
South Carolina	656	724	2,571	3,976	2,966	+15.4	+2.9	87
Tennessee	1,400	1,503	2,438	3,746	2,795	+14.6	+2.8	82
Virginia	273	289	2,250	3,439	2,566	+14.0	+2.7	75
Total	6,738	7,278	2,402	3,726	2,780	+15.7	+3.0	81.5
STATE PARTS†								
Tennessee	1,735	1,868	2,340	3,605	2,690	+14.9	+2.8	79
Virginia	470	509	2,064	3,344	2,495	+20.9	+3.9	73
West Virginia (entire state)	1,744	1,799	2,333	3,617	2,699	+15.7	+3.0	79

* 1974 income expressed in approximate 1969 dollars to eliminate inflation. The factor used is 1974/1969 = 1.3403 based on a weighted index composed of disposable personal income and cost of government purchases of goods and services used as a deflator of 1974 dollars. 1969-74 income change is measured after adjustment for inflation.

† Figures for the two subregional portions of these three states, the only states which fall in two subregions, are combined here.

Sources: U.S. Bureau of the Census, population and per capita income estimates for revenue sharing, published in "Current Population Estimates," Series P-25, *Economic Report of the President*, January 1978 (Washington, D.C.: G.P.O., 1978), Tables B-3 and B-22.

started from the lowest base (58.5 percent of U.S. per capita income in 1969). Southern Appalachia (in common with other developing areas of the South) combined an 8 percent increase in population with a gain in per capita income of from 77 to 81.5 percent of the national level. Although Northern Appalachia kept pace with the rest of the nation, it did not advance from its level of 1969 per capita income (86.5 percent), and its population increase (less than 2 percent) was far below the national rate.

Although it appears that the inequalities of income level in the region are diminishing more rapidly than in the nation generally, at least for Central and Southern Appalachia, there remain great differences between Appalachia and the national average as well as very wide variations in per capita incomes among the counties within the Appalachian Region.

The preliminary data presented above indicate that the 1970s have been years of change in the direction of reversing certain trends in Appalachia. In particular, certain areas show a trend toward reversal of the pattern of population loss through an excess of migration out of the region. And the economic level of Appalachia also shows some rebounding relative to the rest of the nation. Whether this reflects a trend that will eventuate in the renewal of Appalachia, or whether the region had suffered such great losses (demographically and economically) that the new growth can rise only to a certain level but will always remain below the national level, is one of the most important questions of the next decade for Appalachia. Are the reversals seen in the seventies mere reactions to the lessening of the economy nationally? And how long will the new growth, particularly the coal boom, last? Many such questions remain as to the permanence of these trends and the role of Appalachia in the national picture of growth and change.

NOTES

A portion of this chapter first appeared in *Appalachia* 11 (February-March 1978): 41-42.

1. In the 1970–1975 period, the number of people aged 65 years and older increased from 9.8 to 10.5 percent in the United States; for the Appalachian region, from 11.2 to 11.9 percent; in Northern Appalachia, from 10.5 to 11.2 percent; in Central Appalachia, from 10.7 to 11.0 percent; and in Southern Appalachia, from 9.4 to 10.3 percent. Thus, the *relative* aging rate has been most rapid in the southern portion, the heavy in-migration since 1970 has re-

duced the proportionate aging in Central Appalachia, and the northern portion remains high in proportion of older population, with the rate of change parallel to that of the nation and the region.

2. The child–woman ratio is the number of children under five years of age per 1,000 females aged fifteen through forty-four years of age.

3. These represent two possible measures of fertility; for a discussion of and data on fertility and its measurement, see Murdock and McCoy (1974).

6 CLYDE B. McCOY, JAMES S. BROWN & VIRGINIA McCOY WATKINS

Implications of Changes in Appalachia for Urban Areas

Any assessment of the many changes that have taken place within Appalachia in the past three decades needs to take into account the impact of the vast redistribution of the Appalachian population. These demographic factors have social consequences that reflect the many technological, economic, political, and environmental changes influencing the Appalachian regions. It is false to see these changes only within a regional context, however, for this region is a part of a total system of economies, technologies, energy resources, and policies. For example, approaches to solving future energy needs of the United States population must consider the role of coal, water, and timber resources in Appalachia. Attempts to restrict coal production or even to change techniques of mining have consequences, not only for the users of coal and other energy sources outside the Appalachian region, but for the total system of energy production and use. This means, of course, that forces outside Appalachia—economic, political, and technological—will influence Appalachia and its future, probably more than forces within Appalachia itself. But if Appalachia is affected, so are all the linkages with it.

One of the more important system consequences of changes within Appalachia is that of population redistribution. Technological, economic, political, and environmental changes have created new social conditions that have led to relocation of a great part of the Appalachian population. So much of the population has left that the human potential and resources of Appalachia have to be reevaluated with respect to the future of the region and other systems dependent upon it. Since loss of population has been very selective as to types of people (e.g., the young and more educated have left in greater numbers), an entirely different population structure is left behind. These changes have ramifications not only for the labor force but also for the types of public and private services needed by the population, such as schools, hospitals, geriatric facilities, and family planning agencies.

Population redistribution also affects the areas that attract the people forced to leave Appalachia. Our cities and metropolitan areas have been tremendously affected by the changes occurring in Appalachia. The reciprocal impacts of these events are felt within both the urban areas and Appalachia itself. But the kinds and rates of change are different for each.

At this point in history, it is too late to ask whether or not it is desirable to move large numbers of people from regions like Appalachia to urban environments. The people have migrated because there have been few or no alternatives for them. We too wish there had been alternatives so that more people could have made a choice of whether to leave for a new environment or to remain in the old one. (Probably more would still have chosen to migrate than we care to admit.) But there are many implications for the urban areas in the fact that hundreds of thousands of migrants from Appalachia reside within them. Although the streams have decreased considerably, the current migration is still significant, and it does not seem possible to supply the needed employment in Appalachia that would bring a sufficient level of living to reverse the trend of migration completely.

The Appalachians who have been attracted to employment in urban areas have carried with them a cultural heritage which, in many ways, is significantly different from those of other newcomers or of long-time urbanites. One cannot consider the effects upon the urban areas without considering the effects upon the migrants themselves. Too often the metropolitan areas and their majority citizenry have only viewed the migrants from one point of view: What are they costing us? Their perception is that they themselves are burdened with a great many costs because of large numbers of uneducated, inexperienced, nonskilled migrants. They see themselves being subjected to and paying for such urban maladies as high crime rates, poor housing, inferior sanitation, poor health, and the provision of total public assistance for those unable to sustain themselves in the urban environment. But is this an implication of fact for the urban areas, or do they actually enjoy net rewards and benefits from the migration from Appalachia? This will be a continual theme in our research on Appalachians in urban areas. Who shares a disproportionate amount of the cost of change in Appalachia? If it is found that either the migrants themselves or the urban areas have suffered disproportionate costs, will (or should) national, regional, and local policy attempt a balance of payments?

Ironically, or maybe it is more appropriate to say, tragically, the urban areas seem to have been twice victorious, while many migrants have been two-time losers. Have not the urban, industrial, "energized" metropolises gained the greater benefits from the resources extracted from Appalachia? And are they not, to some extent, responsible for the conditions forcing the Appalachian population to migrate to their area? Have not the migrants, once they have been forced to the city, become a very valuable urban resource as laborers—in most instances cheap laborers? The former environment of most Appalachians has not trained or educated them to receive high positions or great incomes for their labor in the city. Because of the industrial uses of coal and timber, the cities have exacted a heavy cost upon the people and environment of Appalachia. Not only has the beauty of its mountains and streams been disturbed, but the entire social system of Appalachia has been disrupted. Unemployment, lack of diversified technical and educational skills, inadequate health delivery and housing have been some of the results of changes—most of which were precipitated by policies formulated from the metropolitan areas to meet their own needs. With the collapse of the old systems of employment and with no new economic structures created to supply necessary supports, the only alternative has been to migrate. Having paid for the costs of technological, economic, and social changes in Appalachia, the migrants then must share another great cost in adjusting to the new urban environment.

Some of the heaviest costs of migration to the cities have accrued to the migrants themselves—the very ones from whom have been exacted very heavy (if not the heaviest) costs in Appalachia or similar areas they have been forced to leave. The Appalachian migrants are the persons who have served faithfully employers such as the coal companies, supplying energy for the nation and producing wealth for coal owners and investors, little of which has stayed in Appalachia to develop any future for the region or the people. The Appalachian migrants, by paying dearly for goods and services, have permitted the prosperity of local businesses and professionals. Although the coal miner works in one of the highest risk occupations (as regards health and facilities), his wages have never been sufficient to release him from dependency on the coal companies. These same companies have provided little protection to their employees as they have replaced them with new technologies and provided them with neither benefits nor skills with which to enter other occupations. Even the unions have offered little support to the miner for his many years of service and dues. Although their story is less dramatic and less rapid, Appalachians working in other economic systems, such as timber and subsistence farming, have been dealt similar fates.

Left with no alternatives in Appalachia, many persons have been pushed to find other economic support. Where should they go? Not unlike the millions of European, black, and Puerto Rican migrants before them, they have moved more often than not to one of the large metropolitan areas. Although more opportunities exist there than back home, the economic and political structure of the cities has changed from the time when earlier migrants were able to carve out their own identifiable niches that included specific job and political positions. The economic need for a more skilled labor force has left the Appalachian migrant ill prepared for the urban environment. Since they are no longer needed as employees in Appalachia, what need is there for them in the urban areas? Are they merely a burden to the cities?

It might be expected that where Appalachian migrants make up a large proportion of the population they would become a strong political block. But as yet it is notable that Appalachians have been neither recognized nor organized as a force. Neither have politicians in these cities succeeded in developing Appalachia as a constituency. Many people point to the Appalachians' abhorrence of any political system and their resistence to being organized. In some of the Appalachian areas, however, Appalachians have formed and participated in strong unions, such as the United Mine Workers. Appalachians have been much involved with their own "mountain" politics, which are usually very different from the urban political structures to which they migrate.

Much of the failure to seize upon the advantages of their great number is due to ignorance, even among Appalachians themselves, of just how many Appalachians there are in these urban areas. But also the urban political systems would seemingly have to change to accommodate the type of politics Appalachians would support, and Appalachians would need to adjust their mountain political style in order to influence urban politics. Is there a need to develop Appalachian leaders? Who is willing to be identified as an Appalachian leader of Appalachian people? How willing Appalachians are to be identified as Appalachians, or how beneficial or detrimental it would be, is not known. Since most images held about Appalachians by people in the cities to which they migrate seem to be negative caricatures of the poor, ignorant, home-sick home-crazed hillbilly, it is our impression that potential leaders are reluctant to identify themselves as Appalachians, preferring to blend into the more dominant non-Appalachian culture. People of Appalachian heritage who are successful as professionals or corporate personnel are accepted simply as part of the urban culture. Who bothers to remark that their next-door neighbor, who is a physician, is an Appalachian hillbilly?

The presence of large populations of Appalachian migrants in cities has major implications for all public agencies, especially because there seems to be some basis for the notion that Appalachians are resistent to and have some difficulties interacting with the large urban public institutions. Although no great difficulty seems to arise with large employers such as Fisher Body and General Motors, Appalachians do experience greater difficulties with such urban institutions as schools, medical services, and police. Central city schools with many Appalachian students show large drop-out rates; these same areas evidence high rates for certain crimes and there are frequent encounters between police and Appalachians. The urban areas provide less than adequate services and are not sensitive to the cultural needs of Appalachians. These are the areas where those Appalachians least successful in the job market must live.

There seems to be a much different and more positive participation in institutions in smaller urban areas and working-class suburbs, however, where Appalachians can behave in ways more consistent with the culture they know and appreciate best. These smaller urban and suburban areas undoubtedly have many more Appalachians as professionals, including teachers and police. Few Appalachian professionals choose to live or work in the central cities once they can move out, and most Appalachians seem to find it easy to move out once they are employed. They seem to make a much more satisfactory adjustment in areas other than the central cities, where they make up a larger proportion of the population and are thus not isolated as a distinct cultural group.

Many persons working with Appalachians, even those who are concerned, neither know nor appreciate the distinctiveness of Appalachian culture, and would probably prefer that Appalachians adjust to the urban environment using a cultural model that is known and recognized, such as the black cultural model, where black identity is strong. But one cannot apply an Appalachian model to blacks or vice versa. Appalachians form a sufficiently large proportion of the population (and the migration patterns are sufficiently specific so that one can know what Appalachian subculture should be understood), so that it does not seem unreasonable to expect public officials and employers to be knowledgeable about the specific cultural and social patterns of the Appalachian people with whom they deal. One of the more important aspects of this cultural sensitivity would be the reduction of negative responses to differences, even slight ones, in customs and mores. Another important response from these urban areas would be the development of programs aimed specifically at Appalachians. Different ethnic or cultural minority populations are often at different stages in their response to their dominant environment and their community development. Therefore it has often been necessary to establish new or culturally specific programs; e.g., for migrant farm workers, or for Cuban refugees in Miami. The established programs are often neither appropriate nor reformable. Can the Y.W.C.A, for example, meet the needs of first- and second-generation Appalachian girls? A positive example of meeting specific needs of Appalachians is the Black Lung Treatment Centers established in five Ohio cities by the Ohio Health Department and the Appalachian Regional Commission, although they also treat non-Appalachians and other respiratory diseases. The focus of such programs should be on the specific needs of the group, but the services should be available for *all* who possess the need, including other minorities. Most programs servicing the needs of one ethnic-racial group meet similar needs of others.

That there are many consequences of the fact that Appalachian migrants reside in metropolitan areas should be apparent, but how long will their migration from Appalachia continue? There have been some indications that Appalachian migration may be ceasing or even reversing itself, with some Appalachian areas gaining more migrants than they are losing. It is true that migration has slowed considerably, for several reasons. Among them are: (1) Migration from Appalachia was so enormous in the past that it was impossible for such great outpourings of people to continue; the decreases look more dramatic than they actually are because they are being compared to the tremendous rates in past decades. (2) Migration affects the age structure through the departure of greater numbers of young and productive persons than of the dependent ages (the very young and very old), thus prohibiting such high rates as were possible previously. Also the older people have less opportunity and/or desire to leave, and they are the population which returns to Appalachia more frequently. (3) The decline in Appalachian fertility, which is related to migration, the consequent age structure, and other factors, means there will be fewer people available to migrate. (4) Social and economic changes occurring in both metropolitan areas (where cycles of mild recessions are being experienced, particularly in automobile-related industries, in the 1970s) and in Appalachia itself (where some economic revival seems to be occurring) tend to reduce migration from Appalachia and increase migration into the region. This does not mean that out-migration from Appalachia will have ceased, but only that in-migration slightly exceeds out-migration.

Pickard's data have shown that practically every Appalachian area has evidenced some excess of in-migrants during 1970–76. He indicates that whereas 1.4 million left the region between 1970 and 1975, 1.7 million entered the region. It can be seen that areas like the Appalachian portions of Georgia and South Carolina are recognizing considerable growth due to the excess of in-migration over out-migration. No doubt much of this is due to the new industrial growth occurring in the new urbanizing areas, including those urban fringes of dominant metropolitan areas just outside the region. New population growth in other Appalachian areas can be attributed to the return of earlier migrants because of the recessive cycles of the cities and to increased economic growth in areas like the coal fields. The coal boom of the 1970s undoubtedly provided some jobs for returning migrants as well as for Appalachians who had remained. But who profited most from the new opportunity of the coal boom—Appalachians or newly arrived "outsiders"?

These implications are somewhat speculative and need to await assessment with the 1980 census data, whereby we can determine the overall extent of and address further implications of the so-called population turnaround. One of the important questions is whether the increased growth due to migration into Appalachia follows the same stream patterns as did the out-migration.

Four general policy implications should be stated concerning the demographic and social changes in Appalachia and the consequent migration to urban areas. First, there are such great numbers of Appalachians in specific urban areas that the cities can focus on the different cultures and subcultures of the new migrants. The implications for all the institutions—schools, police departments, health delivery systems, and employment centers—are enormous.

Second, the migration has been so specific as to direction that it is possible to know the particular subcultural areas of Appalachia which have sent most migrants to specific cities. This knowledge should allow public officials to acquaint themselves with the specific behavioral and cultural characteristics of their Appalachian migrants, the better to understand and serve them. For example, Cincinnati should be most concerned with migrants from Eastern Kentucky, whereas Atlanta does not need to address Eastern Kentucky migrants as much as the newcomers from nearby areas of Georgia.

Third, public officials now have the opportunity to know and be informed of the number of Appalachians in their areas. It behooves us to make them aware of these numbers, if for no other reason than to indicate to them the existence of a large potential voting base, and hence political influence.

Lastly, there is the need to develop an awareness in Appalachians of a common identity and the implications this has for achieving political and economic influence. Organizing around Appalachian identity is essential to political survival in the cities. Are there sufficient benefits in raising awareness of a unique identity to meet this challenge?

Part III

Attainments of Appalachians in Urban Areas

7 LARRY C. MORGAN

Economic Costs and Returns
of Appalachian Out-Migration

The Southern Appalachian Region experienced heavy net out-migration between 1940 and 1970 (Brown and Hillery, 1962). Although such contemporary problems as the energy crisis, rampant inflation, and ominous signs of a recession make it unusually difficult to predict the future course of population movements in Appalachia, there are several reasons for analyzing the region's migration experience during recent times.

First, Appalachian migrants are popularly believed to be net social costs in the urban point of destination. Unfortunately, few studies have dealt with this issue, primarily because of severe measurement problems. A correct determination of the Appalachian migrant's net economic impact in urban areas is needed so that urban growth policies and social welfare programs can be designed to meet community goals more nearly.

Second, the scope of migration studies is often restricted because of severe sampling problems. Residential location patterns of migrants are often completely unknown or based on rather dubious assumptions about the tendency of migrants to pool in ethnic, low-income ghettos. Unbiased surveys of migrant populations are necessary before the socioeconomic status of migrants can be accurately and comprehensively determined. The use of secondary data such as census and Social Security samples often provides valuable insights into the aggregate-migration situation, but it fails to provide much of the detailed information about household units that is necessary for fruitful analytical models of the migration process.

Finally, the Appalachian migration experience has undoubtedly been cited in many studies of human resource development. Since Appalachia is widely acknowledged as one of the poorest regions in the nation, a study of its migration experience should be helpful in evaluating public policies on out-migration from other depressed rural areas.

This paper summarizes selected results from a 1971 survey of Eastern Kentucky migrants who were living in Lexington, Kentucky, and Cincinnati, Ohio. The survey was part of research performed by the University of Kentucky's Center for Developmental Change.[1] The results presented here are based mainly on previous studies by Deaton (1972), Hanrahan (1973), and Morgan (1973). Much of the paper concentrates on the survey's unique sampling design and the private costs and benefits of Appalachian out-migration to urban destinations. Before discussing these topics, however, a brief effort should be made to relate the NICHD study to recent public policy developments.

If we did not personally witness the massive migrations that resulted from the Dust Bowl of the 1930s, we can at least read John Steinbeck's profound portrayal of that era in *The Grapes of Wrath*. World War II quickly obscured the plight of refugees from the Dust Bowl, and social awareness about migration declined throughout the 1950s. Concern over the large numbers of farm workers who were being displaced by agricultural mechanization prompted Maddox (1960) to develop an analytical framework for estimating the private and social costs associated with the movement of people out of agriculture. Wide public recognition of pronounced migration problems did not recur, however, until the advent of President Johnson's Great Society.

The emphasis on antipoverty programs took on new meaning when the President's National Advisory Commission on Rural Poverty (1968) issued its Rural Poverty Report. The report devotes a major section to mobility and migration aspects of rural people (pp. 149–308). Its recurring theme is that rural poverty ultimately compounds the already serious problems that confront the nation's cities. The report's celebrated article by Kain and Persky uses census data to show that large numbers of southern migrants in northern cities have poverty-level incomes. One of the report's general conclusions is that, although the migrant may reap great net private benefits by moving from a rural, low-income area to a large city, the net social costs of that move exceed the migrant's benefits.

It should be recalled that the Rural Poverty Report was issued during a period of great social unrest in most large cities. It is also important to note that the report, as its name denotes, deals solely with poverty. No analysis is offered of those migrants from rural areas who conquered poverty or continued to be successful in the city. Because of the report's exclusive concern with poverty, it is not surprising that many people arbitrarily connote "poor" when they speak of migrants, unless they have personal knowledge to the contrary. Too often, contemporary migration problems are generalized in a context more suitable to the viewpoint of *The Grapes of Wrath* than to the actual situation. Secretary of Agriculture Earl Butz made a similar generalization in 1972 when he testified in support of the Rural Development Act of 1972:

Rural outmigration, although less in absolute numbers, still continues—especially in the heartland areas. One of the great tragedies in the last 20 years of this country has been the outmigration of the population from the rural areas of our country to the ghettos of the downtown Baltimores, the downtown Philadelphias, and the Detroits, and the Chicagos, where [sic] they are not suited for, because they could not have the skills they need, they do not have the cultural background. While we obviously can't reverse that flow, I do hope that this proposal will slow it down, if not stop it. [U.S., Congress, House Committee on Agriculture, 1972: 9]

Yet Oscar Ornati (1968), an expert on urban poverty, argues that our knowledge about the composition and incidence of poverty in urban areas is inadequate because we have not ascertained which of the urban "newcomers" are poor and which of the urban poor are "newcomers." His distinctions are crucial to the growing question of a national population distribution policy.

Sunquist (1970) notes the Rural Poverty Report's concern with rural-to-urban migrants and asks, "Where shall those migrants live?" He argues forcefully that, for whatever reasons, large urban areas *are* experiencing increased traffic congestion, air pollution, and other phenomena that contribute to a deterioration of the quality of urban life. Whether all or only a select portion of rural-to-urban migrants are net urban social costs, he suggests that the nation will ultimately have to direct future migration consciously into smaller urban growth centers.

Meanwhile, we have a migration policy by default. If large cities decide to take the initiative in designing social welfare programs to aid poor migrants, or if the Department of Agriculture is successful in designing rural development programs that adequately support those rural people who are prone to be unsuccessful migrants or net social costs in urban areas, then the analysis of migration experiences will have to be performed with a scalpel, rather than a broadaxe. In this case, migrant populations must be unbiased if we are to be able to distinguish the "successful" from the "unsuccessful" migrants.[2]

Sample surveys of migrant populations are often immensely difficult. If the migrant population is only a small proportion of the total population in a given geographic area, and if the residential patterns of the migrant population are unknown, representative migrant samples cannot be drawn without incurring tremendous costs for location and interviewing. Since these conditions usually exist, and since migration researchers usually work with very limited budgets, sampling costs are often held low by sacrificing the representativeness of the sample. Samples drawn from low-income neighborhoods, based on the commonly voiced belief that most migrants are poor, often give grossly distorted descriptions of the true migrant situation. Effective migration policies must be based on accurate information about *all* relevant categories of migrants.

Schwarzweller (1963a; 1963b) developed a novel approach to many of these sampling problems during a study of both migrants and nonmigrants who were native Eastern Kentuckians. After developing a list of young men who were enrolled in the eighth grade in Eastern Kentucky in 1950, he methodically traced their movements until he located their places of residence in 1960, when he interviewed them and classified them as migrant or nonmigrant. Schwarzweller's sampling technique is admirable because it rigorously classifies the migrant with respect to geographic origin and it obtains the final sample without serious income biases. His approach involves great cost in locating the final respondents, but it has the advantages of a clearly defined sample and each potential respondent is identified and classified before the search procedure begins.

The NICHD sample survey was influenced by Schwarzweller's approach. The objective of the NICHD project was to analyze the economic effects of out-migration from Eastern Kentucky, one of the nation's most depressed rural areas, to two nearby urban growth centers, Lexington, Kentucky, and Cincinnati, Ohio. Because no reliable information was available on the geographic location of Eastern Kentucky migrants in either city, no attempt was made to draw the samples by trial-and-error methods. Instead, the Bureau of the Census contracted to draw the samples and interview the respondents by using questionnaires that were completed during the 1970 decennial census. All of the questionnaires in a random sample of enumeration districts were screened in each ciy in order to obtain a list of "potential migrants."[3] All persons who stated on the questionnaire that they were either born in Eastern Kentucky or were living in Eastern Kentucky on April 1, 1965 were considered "potential migrants."

In November 1971, census interviewers began locating the "potential migrants." In order to be classified as a migrant the respondent had to: (1) have been born in one of the forty-nine counties in Eastern Kentucky that are included in the Appalachian Regional Commission area; (2) have lived outside Eastern Kentucky less than five years prior to his sixteenth birthday; (3) have been at least sixteen years of age at the time of migration to either Lexington or Cincinnati; and (4) have moved to Lexington between April 1, 1965, and April 1, 1970, or to Cincinnati between April 1, 1965 and April 1, 1970. Also, Lexington migrants were not considered if they had commuted to jobs in the city for more than six months prior to establishing permanent residence there. If the individual fulfilled these criteria, a census interviewer administered a detailed questionnaire to the migrant household.[4]

This sampling procedure insured that the respondents were adults who were natives of the area of origin. It also included only those migrants who were deeply imbued with that area's culture at the time of migration. Finally, it avoided the tendency to sample urban neighborhoods that were not representative of the entire migrant population. The survey yielded 161 valid respondents in Lexington and 235 in Cincinnati. Various subsamples of migrants in both cities were used to analyze the costs and benefits of migration.

At the time of migration, during the period 1965–70, the typical migrant to Lexington or Cincinnati had approximately twelve years of education, was approximately twenty-six years of age, had slightly more than two persons in his household, and had had a total family earned income of about $4,000 (in 1971 dollars) during the last year of residence in Eastern Kentucky (Morgan, 1973: 237). Thus the migrant was approximately two years younger, had approximately four more years of education, and had approximately $2,200 less family earned income than the average for the total Eastern Kentucky population in the 1970 census (Morgan, 1973: 248–49).

Morgan (1973: 225–40) and Morgan and Bordeaux (1974a) used two-group discriminant analysis to identify the characteristics of migrants that most strongly determined their cities of destination. The analysis indicated that those migrants who had higher educational levels or who were employed in Eastern Kentucky immediately prior to migration were more likely to migrate to Lexington. Migrants were more likely to move to Cincinnati if their home county was more distant from Lexington or if they had larger families.[5]

The major categories of family migration costs are cash costs for transporting the migrant, his family, and their furnishings; other cash incurred while settling after moving, such as housing cost differentials while unemployed, job search expenses, and employment service fees; and foregone income which the migrant would have earned in Eastern Kentucky but did not because he was unemployed during the migration process. These costs are influenced by many factors, including migration distance, family size, and job search methods.

Although Cincinnati migrants had an average migration distance of more than twice that for Lexington migrants, transportation costs to both cities averaged about $55 per family (Table 7.1). The main reason for the similarity was that the Lexington migrant, being located nearer the city of destination, tended to make more than twice as many job-search trips to the city as the Cincinnati migrant.[6]

Research by Schwarzweller (1963b) indicates a strong stem-family relationship among Appalachian migrants in the industrial North. His findings, along with evidence from the NICHD study, reveal a highly developed communication system that operates through close friends and relatives to transmit important information on employment conditions, wage rates, housing costs, and general living conditions between Appalachia and the major Appalachian urban migration centers (Bordeaux and Morgan, 1973). Although other cash migration costs did not differ significantly for the two migrant groups, the slightly lower cost for the Cincinnati migrant ($32 per family, compared to $35 per family in Lexington) was influenced by the stronger stem-family relations among Cincinnati migrants (Morgan, 1973: 236–39). These lower costs were mainly due to savings in housing and job-search costs. Close friends and relatives of the migrant who already lived in the city played an important role in providing the migrant family free or relatively inexpensive temporary housing until more permanent quarters were found. Likewise, close friends and relatives were a valuable source of information about the availability of jobs and the initial wage rates that the migrant could expect. Consequently, a

Table 7.1: Summary of Selected Migrant Characteristics
and Migration Costs

	City of destination	
	Lexington*	Cincinnati†
Migrant characteristic at time of migration		
Age (in years)	26.4	27.4
Education (years completed)	12.7	10.3
Family size	2.2	2.5
Percent married	51	49
Days out of work during migration process		
Pre-move	22.9	19.5
Post-move	11.0	12.3
Number of job search trips to the city	1.2	0.5
Migration distance (miles)	86	182
Cash migration costs (in dollars)		
Transportation costs	55	54
Other cash costs	35	32
Total	90	86
Foregone earnings	199	199
Total family migration costs**	289	285

* Adapted from Morgan (1973: 67–103).
† Adapted from Deaton (1972: 49–98).
** All migration costs are in 1971 dollars.

strong stem-family relationship tended to save the migrant both time and money in finding the first job in the city.

It is noteworthy that the typical migrant to both cities spent $90 or less in cash during the migration process. In 1960, Maddox concluded that "many farm people can travel as far as 500 miles from their homes, take ten days to find a non-farm job, and wait a week for their first paycheck after they start work with a nest-egg of no more than $100 per person" (Maddox, 1960: 395).

While the typical migrant family in both Lexington and Cincinnati incurred foregone earnings of about $199 (Table 7.1) during the migration process, that figure is misleading. It is highly right-skewed, since approximately 56 percent of the migrants in both cities incurred no earnings losses during migration (Morgan, 1973: 95; Deaton, 1972: 82).

Although the relationship between foregone earnings and stem-family is not clear, stem-family ties do provide the migrant an important source of information about the first job in the city. In the NICHD study, 45 percent of the migrants obtained their initial job information through friends and relatives (Bordeaux and Morgan, 1973: 212). Less than 5 percent of the migrants used state-federal employment services.

The amount of foregone earnings varied directly with the number of days that the migrant was unemployed during the migration process (Morgan, 1973: 97–98), the average unemployment period being about thirty-three days. About two-thirds of this unemployment occurred in Eastern Kentucky, prior to the move, suggesting a reluctance to leave the area. Those migrants who found their first jobs in the city through information from friends and relatives incurred shorter unemployment and less foregone earnings during the migration process.

In a study of rural-to-urban migration in North Carolina in 1965, Osburn (1966: 85) found that total family migration costs averaged almost $500, in sharp contrast to total average migration costs of about $290 (Table 7.1) in the NICHD study. Although the NICHD results apply directly to only a small proportion of total Appalachian out-migration, the migration costs and moving patterns of Cincinnati migrants are more applicable to other Appalachian migration streams to the North than those of Lexington migrants. Since stem-family ties seem to be stronger among Cincinnati migrants, their job search methods, moving patterns, and unemployment experiences are more likely to be similar to those of Appalachian migrants in other northern cities. Cincinnati migrant families incurred transportation costs of approximately 30 cents per mile for an average migration distance of 182 miles. For longer migration distances, the transportation cost per mile would likely decline, primarily because of fewer job-search trips during the migration process.

In order to make more meaningful comparisons between the two cities, my analysis of migration benefits is restricted to the 1965–1970 period. Sample sizes for Lexington and Cincinnati during this period were 161 and 126, respectively.

In this analysis, a net family migration benefit is the change in family earned income due to migration. More specifically, it is the difference between the migrant family's earned income and its opportunity income. While it is easy to estimate the migrant family's actual income for a particular year by using personal interview techniques, the estimation of opportunity income is considerably more difficult, mainly because opportunity income is the income it is presumed the migrant family would have earned during a particular time if it had not migrated.

The NICHD survey was able to obtain detailed information on the migrant family's earned income during three distinct time periods: the last year of residence in Eastern Kentucky, the first year of residence in the city, and the last year of residence in the city, 1971. According to secondary data sources, per capita income in Eastern Kentucky increased at an annual rate of 6.5 percent during the 1965–1969 period (Morgan, 1973: 54–55). The opportunity income for a migrant family at the end of year T would be:

$$Y_{opp.} = (Y_{ek})(1.065)^T$$

where $Y_{opp.}$ is opportunity income; Y_{ek} is migrant family earned income during the last year of residence in Eastern Kentucky; and T is the number of years elapsed since migration.

This method of estimating opportunity income is unsatisfactory for cases where the income during the last year of residence in Eastern Kentucky is not representative of the family's long-run income experience. The most common example of this case is the migrant who was a student during the last year in Eastern Kentucky. Since approximately one-fourth of all migrants in the study were students immediately prior to migration, their income experiences were not used to estimate migration benefits. All migrants who were retired at the time of migration, or who retired after migration, were also excluded from the analysis. Migrants who were unemployed during the last year of residence in Eastern Kentucky but were actively seeking employment were included. These restrictions resulted in Lexington and Cincinnati sample sizes of 112 and 86, respectively. The average length of residence in both cities during the 1965–70 period was 4.3 years (Table 7.2).

The income experiences of Lexington and Cincinnati migrants appear to have been dramatically different during the crucial transition from Eastern Kentucky to the respective city. Although Lexington migrants had an average family earned income of almost $1,100 more than Cincinnati migrants during the last year of residence in Eastern Kentucky, by the end of the first year of residence in the city, the Cincinnati migrant's income exceeded the Lexington migrant's income by about $100 (Table 7.2). For both cities, family earned income in-

Table 7.2: Migrant Family Income and Migration Benefits, 1965-70 (in 1971 Dollars)

| | City of destination | | |
	Lexington	Cincinnati	Average
Total family earned income			
Last year in E. Kentucky	$5,436	$4,355	$4,976
First year in city	$6,942	$7,053	$6,991
Last year in city (1971)	$8,676	$8,681	$8,678
Family opportunity income*			
First year in city	$5,790	$4,638	$5,289
Last year in city (1971)	$7,069	$5,881	$6,553
Net family migration benefit†			
First year in city	$458	$1,710	$1,002
Last year in city (1971)	$740	$1,931	$1,257
Years of residence in city	4.0	4.6	4.3

* It is assumed that migrants' family incomes would have increased at 6.5 percent per annum in Eastern Kentucky if they had remained there.

† The cost of living in the city is estimated to be 10 percent higher than in Eastern Kentucky. Family opportunity income is subtracted from the deflated city income to obtain an estimate of net migration benefits that is adjusted for cost-of-living differences.

Source: "An Economic Analysis of Migration from Rural Eastern Kentucky to Selected Urban Centers," University of Kentucky Contract No. NIH-70-2198 with the National Institutes of Health.

creased by 41 percent between the last year of residence in Eastern Kentucky and the first year of residence in the cities.

After migration, family incomes increased at similar, though slower, rates. Between the first and last year of residence in the city, family earned incomes in both cities increased by 24 percent. At the end of the last year in the city, the incomes of the two migrant groups were approximately the same: $8,680.

Before subtracting the opportunity income from the appropriate city income, a cost-of-living adjustment was made so that net migration benefits are not only shown in 1971 dollars but also reflect purchasing power from the standpoint of Eastern Kentucky. It is estimated that the cost of living was 10 percent higher in the two cities than in Eastern Kentucky (Morgan, 1973: 56), so city income was deflated by 10 percent to neutralize the loss of purchasing power due to migration. In spite of the cost-of-living adjustment, net migration benefits appear

Table 7.3: Rates of Return and Value of Investment in Migration from Eastern Kentucky to Lexington and Cincinnati, 1965-70 (in 1971 Dollars)

	Lexington	Cincinnati	Both cities
Family migration cost	$378	$427	$399
Benefits			
First year after migration	$458	$1,710	$1,002
Last year after migration*	$740	$1,931	$1,257
Investment period (in years)†	4.0	4.6	4.3
Internal rate of return (percent)	132	404	260
Present value of cost-benefit stream for 4 years @ 10 percent discount rate*	$1,487	$5,267	$3,122
Sample size	112	86	198

* Migration benefits are assumed to change at a constant annual rate between the first and last years of residence in the city.

† The investment period is the mean length of residence in the city after migration for the respective sample.

Source: "An Economic Analysis of Migration from Rural Eastern Kentucky to Selected Urban Centers," University of Kentucky Contract No. NIH-70-2198 with the National Institutes of Health.

to be substantial, especially in the case of Cincinnati migrants. Average first-year net family migration benefits in Lexington were $458, about one-fourth of the Cincinnati average benefits (Table 7.2). At the end of the last year of residence in the city, the average net family migration benefit was $740 in Lexington, but over $1900 in Cincinnati.

These benefits can be placed in proper economic perspective by comparing them with their respective migration costs. In a human capital investment framework, it is assumed that investments that improve a person's labor productivity or that permit him to obtain a better-paying job become fundamental components of his human capital stock. The decision to invest in migration must therefore be considered as an alternative to other investments, such as the purchase of bonds. But which is the "best" investment? The two most common investment decision rules are: choose the investment that has the highest internal rate of return, or choose the investment that yields the highest present value for a specified interest rate.[7]

The internal rates of return are so high that there is no doubt that out-migration from Eastern Kentucky yields a higher rate of return than stocks, bonds, or bank loans (Table 7.3).[8] When the migration costs for the families with measurable benefits are compared with the

appropriate benefit streams, it is obvious that all migration costs are re-
covered during the first year of residence in the city. However, the
rates of return for the two migration streams cannot be used as a direct
measure of the difference in profitability. Although the internal rate of
return for Cincinnati migrants is 3.1 times greater than the Lexington
rate, it cannot be said that the returns or profitability of migration to
Cincinnati is 3.1 times greater than for Lexington migration.

A more acceptable method of comparing the financial attractive-
ness of the two migration streams is to compare the present values of
their cost-benefit streams over the same time period at the same interest
rate. Using a 10 percent interest or discount rate for four years still
shows a greater return to Cincinnati migration, with a cost-benefit
stream present value 3.6 times greater than the Lexington present
value.

Why are migration returns so much higher for Cincinnati migrants
than for Lexington migrants? Migration costs are similar for both
groups, but Cincinnati migrants have much lower premigration incomes. Morgan and Bordeaux (1974a) indicate that the two migration
streams have educational backgrounds compatible with the labor mar-
kets in the respective cities. Lexington migrants, with higher educational levels, tend to find approximately the same proportion of technical, professional, and administrative jobs as the entire labor market,
which is oriented toward service and light manufacturing industries.
The Cincinnati labor market has a strong demand for craftsmen and
operatives. Again, the Cincinnati migrants tend to be represented in
these occupations at about the same frequency as the entire labor market. In both cities, the migrants with the lower premigration incomes
have received the largest net migration benefits. These migrants with
high premigration incomes tend to have approximately the same income at the end of the last year of residence in the city, which means
that they actually incurred negative benefits due to migration (Morgan, 1973: 127).

Due to severe data problems, no analysis of migrant public service
costs could be made in Cincinnati. In Lexington, it was found that Appalachian migrant families paid average city taxes of $203, approxi-
mately equal to the value of city expenditure benefits received, $198
(Morgan, 1973: 175–94; Morgan and Bordeaux, 1974b). For local
school services, however, the typical Lexington migrant family im-

posed an annual net tax burden or net social cost (family school expenditure benefits exceeded family school taxes) of about $32 on the greater urban community. This finding cannot be interpreted as evidence that Appalachian migrants are net social costs to the cities until there is conclusive evidence on the incidence of local school tax burdens among all urban residents.

The results of the NICHD study confirm the earlier findings of Osburn (1966) and Wertheimer (1970) that there are substantial private returns to migration out of rural areas. Although the study could not analyze social costs of out-migration that fall on the Appalachian and national economies, it does offer compelling evidence about the two major focuses of migration policy: the costs and benefits of migration to the migrant family and the net tax burden of migrants in urban areas.

The results of the study of Appalachian out-migration suggest that private net migration benefits are so high and net social costs of urban public services for migrants are so low as to bring into question the justifications for reducing rural-to-urban migration. Although most of the migrants in the NICHD study can be classified as "successful," or more successful than if they had remained in Eastern Kentucky, there is a strong need for detailed information about those migrants who continued to earn poverty-level incomes, or whose incomes fell to poverty levels, after migration. This information would also complement the research of Deaton (1972: 144–66) and Deaton and Anschel (1974) on return migration. Based on data from the NICHD study and other studies at the University of Kentucky, they conclude the migrants are more likely to return to Eastern Kentucky if they: (1) do not own a home in the city, (2) have relatively lower levels of education, (3) own property in Eastern Kentucky, (4) have relatively low family incomes in the city, (5) are relatively old at the time of out-migration, or (6) did not expect the tenure in the city to be permanent.

Finally, we should not minimize the diligence of Appalachian people. We should compare cold statistics in the NICHD study with Coles's monumental studies of Appalachians. He argues quite effectively that Appalachian people are fully capable of taking advantage of opportunities that come their way. Unfortunately, Appalachia has a dreary history of being mined of its natural resources while its human resources have been and are being ignored. Out-migration has filled the void created by the absence of timely, efficient public policies to reduce Appalachian poverty. We should recognize that most migrants have improved personal and social welfare by leaving the region.

The major task that lies ahead is to refine our tools of observation and analysis so that we can identify those individuals who need assistance. Policymakers should then design programs to aid these people, instead of relegating them to the status of political pawns with rhetoric more akin to *The Grapes of Wrath* than the 1980s.

NOTES

1. The research was performed under the University of Kentucky contract No. NIH-70-2198 with the National Institute of Child Health and Development, Bethesda, Maryland.

2. If we follow the analytical framework of Morgan (1973), "successful" migrants should not be net social costs if they enjoy large private net benefits from migration but impose net tax burdens on the urban areas of destination.

3. In Cincinnati, both the 5 percent and the 15 percent samples of the 1970 census were screened. In Lexington, only the 15 percent sample was screened.

4. In accordance with the strict Census rules on confidentiality, no member of the NICHD project was allowed to learn the identity of any respondent or any member of the respondent's household.

5. Approximately 66 percent of the Lexington migrants were employed at the time of migration, but only 59 percent of the Cincinnati migrants were employed. It should also be noted that approximately 24 percent of the migrants (25 percent of Lexington migrants and 22 percent of Cincinnati migrants) were students immediately prior to leaving Eastern Kentucky.

Lexington-Fayette County borders the Eastern Kentucky area included in the NICHD project. It is a strong attractant to potential migrants in nearby counties. The Lexington migrants' native county seats were an average of approximately eighty-six miles from Lexington, but the Cincinnati migrants' county seats were an average of about 105 miles from Lexington (182 miles from Cincinnati).

6. The migration process includes all job-search activity in the city before and after migration, plus all migration activities and costs, such as foregone income, that occur between the time the migrant ceases full-time employment in Eastern Kentucky and the time the migrant begins full-time employment in the city. If the migrant traveled by private auto, travel costs were computed at the rate of ten cents a mile. Rates on rental trucks and trailers were obtained from local rental agencies. Travel costs by bus were estimated from prevailing local bus fare schedules for 1971.

7. The internal rate-of-return rule for a migration investment consists of

selecting the migration stream or the nonmigration investment that has the highest rate of return for the equation:

$$O = C_O^M + \sum_{t=1}^{T} \frac{B_t}{(1 + p)^t}$$

where C_O^M is the migration cost (investment) in time period T; B_t is the net migration benefit; and p is the implicitly determined internal rate of return.

The present-value rule is a simple modification of the internal-rate rule. The present-value equation is:

$$W_O = C_O^M + \sum_{t=1}^{T} \frac{B_t}{(1 + r)^t}$$

where W_O is present value of the cost-benefit stream, and r is a predetermined interest rate.

8. The migration costs for the migrants with measurable benefits are considerably higher than for the entire migrant sample (Table 7.1) because migrants who were students just prior to migrating generally had very low migration costs.

8 HARRY K. SCHWARZWELLER

Occupational Patterns
of Appalachian Migrants

Each year thousands of young men and women migrate from the rural neighborhoods and towns of Appalachia to industrial areas elsewhere. They are ambitious and generally rather optimistic. Through migration they seek to enhance their economic lot in life, for the holding power of Appalachia—a region long characterized by underemployment, relatively low wages, and widespread rural poverty—cannot complete with the "pull" of other, relatively more prosperous regions. Like the earlier European immigrants who turned to America, they look toward the promise of work opportunities in the Ohio Valley and in the teeming metropolises of the North and East.

Some migrants are married and move with their families, but most are single. Some have been to college, but most have terminated their education with high school graduation and many, even before. Some have acquired work experiences in the mountains that prepare them for the kinds of jobs available in the industrial areas of destination, but most have not. Many will "make it" as many before them have made it, but some will fail, drifting into a life of routinized frustration in the congested ghettos of our inner cities. And, of course, some will return to the mountains to work in the mines, on the roads, in the rapidly growing industries of the region, or simply to survive from day to day as best they can.

The complex and extremely varied phenomena of Appalachian migration (in certain respects, each individual migrant is a unique and interesting case) and, in particular, the dynamics of transition adjustment associated with the migration process, were the focuses of inquiry of the Beech Creek Project (Schwarzweller, Brown, and Mangalam, 1971) and a number of other researches with which I have been affiliated.[1] Although it would be relevant here to summarize our observations and to interpret our approach to the study of migration and its social, psychological, and structural ramifications, practical considerations demand a limitation of topic.[2] Consequently, my aim in this brief paper is to provide an overview, based upon insights gleaned from a variety of sources, of the occupational and work-related patterns of Appalachian migrants and, wherever possible, to relate these patterns to issues that have plagued the Appalachian people for too long. Attention is focused primarily on the rural low-income segment of the migrant population and the discussion is limited to male migrants. (There have been very few empirical studies dealing with the work patterns and adjustments of female migrants from Appalachia and most of these have treated the topic rather superficially.)

It should be clearly noted at the outset that migration is an integral part of the social organization of Appalachian communities, woven into the very fabric of the mountain way of life. By this I mean that families and institutions have accommodated to large-scale out-migration (despite the fact that, in the long run, the exodus may contribute to an erosion of these institutions) and that socialization practices tend to reinforce an expectation of eventual out-migration. In a recent study of high school seniors in Eastern Kentucky and Mingo County, West Virginia, for example, we found that over two-thirds of the boys definitely planned on moving out of the region after graduation (Marra, 1971: 41–44). Indeed, over half of the Mingo County seniors were oriented specifically toward Columbus, Ohio, a place they knew about from conversations and visits with kinsfolk and friends who had settled there earlier.

Information about jobs available in the areas of destination and about work expectations connected with these industrial occupation roles flows back into the Appalachian communities from various sources but especially from significant kin-group members who return home on visits. In this way, the potential migrant is aided in formulating an image of work requisites in the factory as compared with the kinds of jobs available at home. On occasion, he may visit friends and relatives in the city. Indeed, if the situation warrants, he may go to Ohio on what is perhaps more appropriately called a "work visit" (Schwarzweller, et al., 1971: 101). A work visit is a temporary migration, with little if any expectation of "permanency." It may be for a few months or even a year; the migrant normally lives with kinsfolk,

picks up a transitory job, and has no intention of remaining. It is usually made in the spirit of an exploratory venture that does not involve a
meaningful separation of the migrant from his family homestead. To
be sure, a work visit may eventually lead to permanent residence, but
that depends upon the socioeconomic circumstances the potential migrant encounters. (I should point out here that many of the statistics on
return migration are exaggerated because of a failure to distinguish between work visits and permanent migrations.)

Few, if any, Appalachian migrants have kinfolk in the area of destination who are in a position to actually hire them. Kinfolk, however,
are often able to supply potential migrants in the mountains with de-
tails about job openings. Indeed, employers in Ohio not only seem to
recognize the importance of kin ties among Appalachian migrants but,
at least in the past, have utilized the migrant kin network in securing
an adequate labor supply, especially for unskilled job levels. When job
vacancies occur, the word is passed along within the shop and, via the
kin network, soon becomes common knowledge in the migrant community, quickly trickling down to families in the coves and hollows of Appalachia. Such personalized appeals are far more effective than mass
media forms of communication or even, according to reports I have
read, job placement centers (Edwards and Krislov, 1971) for drawing
out job applicants from the mountain labor pool.

A small proportion of Appalachian migrants, mainly from relatively "upper class" families, have had the opportunity and advantage of
going to college. Their career patterns are in most respects not unlike
those of college students in other parts of America and, consequently,
the comments I make here do not apply to them.

The vast majority of Appalachian migrants enter the urban labor
market with no more than a basic high school education, often with
less, and rarely with any specialized vocational training. According to
our own survey findings, more than two-thirds of the rural Appalachian youngsters nowadays do not go beyond the high school level
(Schwarzweller, 1973); not long ago, the proportion was far greater
and dropout rates much higher.[3] As young, rural migrants, they frequently find initial jobs in factories that may not require at the time of
hiring any previous industrial experience or a high school diploma.
They are generally asked to perform simple assembly-line tasks that are
quickly learned with a minimal amount of on-the-job training. One of
our Beech Creekers, for example, recalled that "the boss took me to the

place where I'd work and told a guy there to explain what I'd do—he did—it took about ten minutes." Nevertheless, the work they are expected to perform and the job context itself invariably constitute a new experience for most of them. The formal schedule and rigid authority system of the factory, for example, may be particularly irksome, and working with and around complicated machines is for many quite confusing and perhaps even frightening at first.

Then, too, it takes some time for newcomers to become familiar with and accustomed to the tempo and tone of industrial life. This may be more true for migrants reared in the subsistence agricultural areas of Appalachia, where the rhythm of life is to some degree organized around and tempered by the seasonal demands of farming, than it is for those who come from coal field counties. For the social organization of coal communities tends to have an industrial character; they are "rural," to be sure, but not "agriculturally rural." Hence, work experiences and work role "models" acquired in the coal field communities are more compatible with the circumstances a migrant encounters in the northern industrial communities.

At least until recently, Appalachian migrants who had graduated from high school did not enjoy any immediate advantage in their initial patterns of job placement over those who had dropped out. They are started at or near the bottom regardless of level of schooling. This generalization, substantiated by one of our earlier follow-up studies (Schwarzweller, 1964) is consistent with the so-called "Lipset hypothesis," namely, that rural-reared workers enter the urban labor market at the lower end of the occupational hierarchy, replacing urban-reared natives who tend to move upward. Both groups gain, of course, as a result of status inflation (i.e., relative to their social class origins) and, since each is better off than before, both should feel satisfied.[4] In the Appalachian case, however, as suggested by our data and findings from other studies, migrants were absorbed into the industrial work force as an undifferentiated pool of workers, serving industry's enormous appetite and indiscriminate need for unskilled, fairly stable, and relatively cheap labor, much like "Gastarbeiter" (guest workers) in Germany. High school drop-outs, if they were willing to work hard, could become as good assembly-line workers as those migrants who had completed high school. This situation, to be sure, is changing rapidly as more and more employers are requiring at least a high school diploma and as more and more industries demand specialized skills. High school drop-outs everywhere, regardless of their residential origins (whether urban-reared or migrant), are finding it increasingly difficult to be considered even for semiskilled industrial work. Then, too, level of educational attainment has long served as a necessary credential for future advancement within the industrial context.

After initial entree into the industrial work situation, and after acquiring some basic technical skills, a degree of sophistication in dealing with the norms and demands of the industrial order, and greater self-confidence, the ambitious migrant invariably begins to look around for more rewarding jobs. Some are encouraged to rise up through the ranks within the factory where they have started. Seniority rules, however, and other constraints associated with a particular firm's organization of manpower make such intra-plant mobility rather difficult and certainly very slow. For the most part, and especially in the case of those who begin as unskilled laborers, upward mobility toward skilled levels and the better paid jobs generally means seeking out new employers. The relatively high rate of job turnover by Appalachian migrants in Ohio and elsewhere, therefore, should not be interpreted as a sign of occupational insecurity or instability per se. That may be so, to some extent. But it is also a manifestation of the Appalachian migrant's desire to get ahead—an indication that these workers are adapting to the demands and opportunities of the industrial labor market. Occupational "restlessness" and job changes occur most frequently and appear to be the norm during the early phase of a migrant's work career; the latter period, we have found, is markedly stable. As a matter of fact, the Appalachian migrant is rather reluctant to change jobs because it not only entails moving into an unfamiliar situation but it also means that he must give up the security of accrued seniority rights.

Longitudinal data on the general advancement in occupational status by Appalachian migrants are not readily available and normally we must infer these patterns from information collected through cross-section surveys and comparative analyses. A study that Photiadis made of West Virginia migrants in Cleveland, for example, provides some useful insights. He found that the employment status of male migrants had improved noticeably through migration and that these men and their families were markedly better off than a comparable cohort of West Virginians who had never migrated.[5]

In the Beech Creek case, we observed that male migrants had generally entered the Ohio labor market at unskilled levels. Over the years, however, they exhibited a pattern of gradual upward mobility.

Some men had availed themselves of opportunities to attend trade schools in the urban area or to acquire on-the-job industrial training, and a few had taken night school courses. About 18 percent eventually achieved skilled, clerical, or professional status (e.g., as school teachers), and only about 19 percent were still at unskilled levels after ten or more years in Ohio. Although advancement was not dramatic, it is clear that an up-grading occurred. In his study of a selected segment of male migrants from the Beech Creek area, few of whom had been fortunate enough to get beyond the eighth grade in school, Crowe (1964) found that the proportion who were able to command more skilled jobs had tripled during their years in Ohio and that their increased wages and standards of living reflected this advancement. When one takes into consideration the enormously difficult circumstances Appalachian migrants have had to overcome, their record of upward mobility in the urban areas is impressive.

The process of adaptation to industrial work roles invariably produces some tension and stress, and Appalachian migrants generally are not well prepared for this experience and its various immediate and long-range consequences. We have observed, however, that supportive functions performed by the kin network, which tend to reinforce the migrant's values, his feelings of integrity and self-confidence, his sense of wholeness, have much to do with keeping resultant tensions within manageable bounds.

The threat of being "laid off," for example, is an ever-present fact of life among manual workers, especially those employed in the large manufacturing and construction industries. Lay-off periods are normally associated with production change-overs and reentry operations that occur periodically in the automobile industry, but they may also be brought on by economic recessions and by situations such as the current energy crisis. Appalachian migrants, we have found, generally accept the threat of being laid off as one of those annoying conditions of industrial work, like punching a timeclock and working indoors, that has to be tolerated (Schwarzweller and Crowe, 1969). For those with seniority, of course, the threat is reduced, but even they are attitudinally prepared for the eventuality. Like other industrial workers, they feel fairly secure in the knowledge that unemployment compensation will hold them over. But more important, Appalachian migrants also figure that if a lay-off period turns into a long siege or into chronic unemployment, they can rely on kinfolk for help and, if things really get bad, they can return to the family homestead in the mountains to wait out the crisis. The kin network plays an important role, both socially and psychologically, in cushioning the disturbing effects of a lay-off period and, indeed, many migrants seem almost to welcome it (provided it doesn't last too long) as a chance to visit kinfolk and to make a trip back to the mountains.

In this and many other ways, the kinship network serves to stabilize the migrant's social world external to the factory and consequently helps to keep "on-the-job" problems and difficulties from becoming unmanageable and personally destructive anxieties.

On the other hand, the close-knit kinship network characteristic of the rural Appalachian subculture, and the particularistic orientations associated with it, while performing very important supportive functions during crisis periods and during various phases of the transitional adjustment process, also serve to "hold back" the migrant from active engagement with the sociopolitical forces that shape the limits of his opportunities. The Appalachian migrants' involvements with industrial unions, for example, are a case in point.

Like most other rank and file union members in American industry, Appalachian migrants focus their attitudinal support of unions on the practical functions of unionism, i.e., "bread and butter unionism." They are especially concerned with the union's role in resolving interpersonal difficulties that arise among work crew members and with the boss. To the highly individualistic, personalistically-oriented mountaineer, social relationships with fellow workers and immediate supervisors are a major source of potential strain and it is here that the union's efforts, through an understanding shop steward, become visible. But Appalachian people just aren't good joiners (Schwarzweller and Brown, 1962: 361). They feel uncomfortable in formal gatherings and their participation in union activities is in most cases minimal. A general behavioral apathy prevails. Participation in union meetings and activities outside of the immediate job situation are seen as interfering with home life and most migrants are unwilling to allow this to happen. They accept union membership in much the same way as they accept the other, more discomforting aspects of factory work life, and they obey union dictums in much the same way that they obey shop regulations or the orders of a foreman. Further involvement demands a social commitment over and above that for which the familistically-oriented mountaineer is prepared. A parallel example could be drawn in terms of the Appalachian migrant's political behavior.[6]

It also may be that the close-knit kinship system characteristic of the rural Appalachian subculture tends to slow down the occupational advancement and social mobility of migrants relative to their innate capabilities and potentials. In the setting of career goals and in the evaluation of career attainments, the Appalachian migrant may have as his reference those primary groups with which he was associated back in the old home neighborhoods; from this perspective he is doing well if, by simply drawing good wages from a semiskilled job, he can acquire the material amenities that are so scarce back home. We explored this possibility in an earlier study (Schwarzweller, 1964), but were unable to discern any differences in level of achievements between those who were more involved and those who were less involved with kinfolk; education was controlled. Further research, however, is necessary before we are willing to put the hypothesis aside.

From an historical perspective, nevertheless, it appears clear that if the Appalachian kin system had been a more nucleated form, migrant workers in the past would have experienced greater difficulty in adapting to the industrial work situation, and, as a consequence, factory managers in the receiving areas would have experienced many more labor problems and far greater labor costs. The contribution of Appalachian mountain families to the economy of Ohio, other states, *and* the nation that resulted from extended family normative obligations "to take care of their own," if it could be measured, would undoubtedly stagger the imagination of many government officials.

Migrants themselves appear to be rather optimistic about their own situations. Few feel "trapped" or "held down"; few feel that their job is a "dead-end." In general they seem aware of existing opportunities. This basic satisfaction with job and work situation is further reinforced by their favorable attitudes toward management (a naive trust whose roots, perhaps, are to be found in the puritanistic, patriarchical tendencies of mountain society) and by their conviction that employers are quite satisfied with the work performance of Appalachian people. Personnel managers and foremen whom we interviewed in Ohio (Crowe, 1964) tend to validate the migrant's self-image vis-a-vis hard work; but they add, often in the same breath, that the mountaineer appears to be a bit too docile for his own good in the industrial labor market.

"Ambition" is a relative thing. It refers to the desire for personal advancement, whether this be rank, fame, power, wealth, or some other preferment such as a reasonable level of living. Appalachian migrants,

I submit, are an ambitious people. This is evidenced not only by the fact of their rural-to-urban migration—a socially disruptive experience in many respects—but also by their occupational career patterns which reveal a remarkable tenacity in coping with the demands of the industrial labor market, a willingness to work hard, and a record of gradual upward social mobility. One must take into account, of course, that the socioeconomic constraints imposed upon them by conditions and circumstances over which they have had very little or no control creates a situation that is less than favorable. In thinking about future generations of Appalachian migrants, we should consider how those conditions could be bent, in a more equitable manner, toward the advantage of potential migrants, so that their lives can be more meaningful and their work careers more productive and satisfying. An obvious place to begin is with the improvement of primary and secondary school education in the Appalachian mountains. It is my belief that states receiving large influxes of migrants, such as Ohio, should share some of these costs.

In the past, the rural low-income areas of Appalachia produced a large, steady, relatively undifferentiated supply of labor which, as long as the industrial development of the great metropolitan centers in the North was still booming, could be readily absorbed, thereby contributing to that industrial development. Industry had little reason to press for an improvement in the level of skills and general education that workers brought with them into the receiving areas; factories were organized to use unskilled labor and Appalachia did a good job of producing what was needed. A similar situation existed in the mountains. Coal companies did little to encourage the improvement of educational facilities and other community services which would have created more options for those seeking jobs but also would have exerted some pressure to drive up wages for unskilled work. In the areas of both origin and destination of Appalachian migrants, there were few advocates of educational reform among those in positions of economic power. Quality of schooling suffered (Schrag, 1972). While other economically depressed rural areas of America, such as the northern cut-over region of the Great Lakes,[7] increasingly emphasized the improvement of educational facilities in remote communities, Appalachian migrants continued to arrive in urban industrial centers relatively less prepared to compete for skilled jobs with their counterparts from elsewhere.

The situation, however, has changed dramatically in recent years. As manufacturing firms have been forced to cut back in response to the energy crisis, there has been a sharp reduction in the capacity and eagerness of northern industrial states to absorb unskilled laborers from the mountains. Furthermore, for this and other reasons, net out-migration from Appalachia has been reduced and in some cases, most notably in the booming coal counties, actually reversed. Yet despite the coal boom, there are still relatively few good opportunities for unskilled, untrained workers in the region. Modern coal operations (both deep and surface) and their supportive industries also require and seek a skilled work force. Jobs that promise a reasonable degree of upward social mobility over time are becoming ever more selective at the point of entree.

In the future, I expect, much will depend upon the degree to which the school systems of Appalachia can be organized to respond to the growing demand of industries, both within and outside the region, for a well-educated, functionally literate, technically skilled labor supply.

NOTES

1. I especially wish to acknowledge the contributions of my colleagues on the Beech Creek Project, James S. Brown and J. J. Mangalam. Also, I am heavily indebted to the work of M. J. Crowe (1964) for much of the information and many of the insights dealing with the patterns of adaptation of Appalachian migrants to the industrial work situation.

2. For an outline of our theoretical perspectives on the sociology of migration, see Mangalam (1969).

3. Dropout rates are very difficult to determine, particularly in areas with high out-migration and frequent residential movements. Some observers, however, report rather startling figures. Branscome (1972), for example, suggests that "sixty-five percent of the Region's students still do not graduate from high school." Although I am certain that Branscome's statistics are grossly exaggerated, I agree with his concern about the relevance of education in the region.

4. Blevins (1971) reports an interesting study on the socioeconomic differences between migrants and nonmigrants. His data provide additional support for the perspective suggested here.

5. This segment of the Photiadis study is reported by Schweiker (1968).

6. Structural circumstances and the relative isolation of mountain neighborhoods, of course, have had an enormously influential "conditioning" effect on the political behavior of Appalachian people (Ball, 1971). For a very blunt description of the political process in Mingo County, West Virginia, see Lee (1972).

7. For comparative information on the occupational patterns of rural migrants from the Upper Peninsula of Michigan see Rieger et al. (1973).

9 JOHN D. PHOTIADIS
in cooperation with LEONARD SIZER & JAMES WAY

Occupational Adjustment of Appalachians in Cleveland

During the 1940s isolation of the rural Appalachian social system decreased rapidly, while the important processes of interaction and communication with the outside increased in intensity. Those first few who out-migrated—especially during and immediately after the war years—contributed to the intensity of these two social processes through visitations and other contacts, either by visits "down home" or by relatives visiting them in the city. A crucial indirect result of the availability of jobs in cities such as Cleveland was the weakening of the boundary maintenance mechanisms of the rural social system. Regardless of physical, cultural, or mental preparation for city employment, within less than two decades almost all young adult men and women left rural Appalachia. The purpose of this paper is to describe the occupational patterns of West Virginians who migrated to Cleveland, Ohio, and to compare their attainments with those of West Virginians who remained in their home state or returned there after migrating.

The data presented here were secured in 1967 by a survey of West Virginians living in the so-called Appalachian ghetto and the suburbs of Cleveland, Ohio. These data are compared with similar types of information collected from persons living in West Virginia and are supplemented by data from a survey of Southern migrants in Cleveland conducted at about the same time by the Bureau of Social Science Research.[1]

The sample of West Virginians in Cleveland included approximately 170 respondents from the so-called ghetto and 370 from the suburbs. In the ghetto, blocks were selected randomly and every male West Virginian in the block was interviewed. The suburban sample involved a stratified sample of communities in the area west of the Appalachian ghetto. Within these communities, respondents were secured from a list provided by the West Virginia Extension Service, by interviews with ministers, school principals, and employers, and finally, by the snowballing technique. The sample from the state of West Virginia is a cluster random sample of approximately 1,300 males. The sample of the Bureau of Social Science Research includes 1,300 black and white southern migrants (Peterson and Sharp, 1969).

The data from the West Virginia study are analyzed in terms of four groups: West Virginians living in the suburbs of Cleveland, those living in the ghetto of Cleveland, migrants who have returned to West Virginia, and West Virginians who never migrated. Throughout the analysis, the four groups are also matched in terms of age and education.

Probably excluding white collar workers and the few professionals, the bulk of the West Virginia migrants came from rural areas and, at least during the first years of the "Great Migration," went first to the Appalachian ghetto of Cleveland. As they secured new skills, in terms of both occupations and understanding of the urban culture, more and more moved to the suburbs and the so-called interstitial area between the ghetto and the suburbs of the west side of Cleveland. But as the years went by, more and more new migrants moved directly to where their relatives were living, which included places other than the ghetto area. At the same time, more and more Puerto Ricans, who first appeared in the early 1960s, moved into this area.

Health, Age, and Education: At least during the year the survey was conducted, ghetto residents were much younger than suburbanites; for instance, about 51 percent of the ghetto residents and only about 21 percent of the suburbanites were under thirty years of age (Photiadis, 1975: 240). But even suburbanites were younger than returned migrants or people who never migrated. Thirteen percent of the returned migrants were less than thirty years of age.[2] Cleveland migrants were not only younger but perceived themselves as considerably healthier physically than respondents from the two West Virginia samples. The differences remained when the four groups used in the analysis were controlled in terms of age and education (Photiadis, 1975: 230).

Migrants in Cleveland also differed in terms of education, with more people in the middle categories—seven to twelve years of schooling completed. But again, suburbanites had a higher proportion (47%) than ghetto residents (30%) of respondents who either had finished

142   JOHN D. PHOTIADIS

Table 9.1: Occupational Distribution for Nonmigrants, Returned Migrants, Ghetto, and Suburbs

	Total groups (percent)				Matched groups (percent)			
	Non-migrant	Returned migrant	Ghetto	Suburbs	Non-migrant	Returned migrant	Ghetto	Suburbs
Unskilled	47.5	44.6	20.4	24.8	51.3	52.9	20.3	20.2
Semiskilled	32.5	36.6	67.6	36.6	33.1	37.2	65.6	39.5
Skilled	20.0	18.8	12.0	38.6	15.6	9.9	14.1	40.3
Total number of cases	(360)	(112)	(142)	(314)	(109)	(51)	(64)	(139)

|____| Differences significant at the .01 level

high school or were close to it (Photiadis, 1975: 52–54). In general, three years of difference in education was associated with a whole array of economic, social, and sociopsychological factors. This does not necessarily mean that the three extra years of education were the cause of better adjustment. These findings do not seem to agree with the report of the Survey of Southern Migrants (Peterson and Sharp, 1969: 110), which states that "As far as the relative skill level of entry jobs in Cleveland is concerned, previous investment in education appears to make little difference."

West Virginian suburbanites in Cleveland also had more technical training than ghetto residents, but less than the returned migrants. The latter fact indicates that some West Virginia migrants acquired skills in the city and then returned home. Close to 5 percent of the suburbanites and 6 percent of the ghetto residents had at least one year of technical training.

Occupational Patterns: Probably more than any other variable, technical skill differentiated our four groups, particularly the three groups of migrants. Returned migrants had the largest proportion of unskilled workers; the ghetto residents had the largest proportion of semiskilled, two or three times as many as the other groups; and the suburbanites had the largest proportion of skilled workers, about twice as many as any of the other three groups (Table 9.1). Returned migrants, compared to the other two migrant groups, had by far the largest proportion of professionals (11%); the corresponding proportions for ghetto and suburbs were about 1 percent and 4 percent respectively. Thus professionals tended either to return to West Virginia or to re-

Table 9.2: Occupation in West Virginia for Ghetto and Suburbs

	Total groups (%)		Matched groups (%)	
	Ghetto	Suburbs	Ghetto	Suburbs
Coal miner	24.6	32.4	20.3	24.1
Unskilled	21.6	21.6	22.6	24.7
Semiskilled	15.0	17.6	7.2	6.6
Skilled	4.2	5.4	9.0	7.8
White collar	0.6	0.0	2.6	3.0
Managerial	1.2	0.0	1.0	0.0
Businessman	0.6	0.0	1.0	1.2
Farmer	0.0	0.0	4.6	5.4
Professional	0.6	0.0	0.8	0.0
Other	31.6	23.0	30.9	27.2
Total number of cases	(167)	(390)	(74)	(166)

side in areas other than those having high concentration of West Virginians included in our population universe.

The predominant occupation of the migrants before coming to Cleveland was coal mining; about 32 percent of the suburbanites and about 25 percent of the ghetto residents were so employed before coming to Cleveland (Table 9.2). On the other hand, only about 5 percent of the suburbanites and 4 percent of the ghetto residents had a skill before they left West Virginia; the proportions of skilled workers at the time of the survey were about 39 percent for suburbanites and about 12 percent for ghetto residents. It appears that a large proportion of the skills which suburbanites came to possess were acquired in the city.

In the case of returned migrants, less than a third of them held their first job less than six months; another third, seven months to three years; and the last third, more than three years. In general, about one-third of the returned migrants had spent less than a year outside Appalachia at the time of the survey; another third, two to four years; and only about 12 percent had spent more than ten years. In addition, about 62 percent of the returned migrants had worked outside West Virginia only once. By comparison, more than half of the suburbanites had the same jobs as when they first came to Cleveland (Table 9.3). Matched in terms of education and age, twice as many suburbanites as ghetto residents had kept the same job since they came to Cleveland; furthermore, close to 38 percent of the ghetto residents had moved to their current jobs in the previous six months, while only a little over 7

**Table 9.3: Number of Jobs Held since First Coming
to Cleveland, for Ghetto and Suburbs**

Number of Jobs	Total groups* (%)		Matched groups† (%)	
	Ghetto	Suburbs	Ghetto	Suburbs
One	29.6	52.5	27.1	55.4
Two	26.4	20.5	23.1	16.9
Three or more	44.0	27.0	49.8	27.7
Total number of cases	(167)	(387)	(74)	(166)

* x^2 = 26.17 ρ < .05
† x^2 = 17.18 ρ < .05

percent of the suburbanites had jobs acquired recently. About 45 percent of the suburbanites and 8 percent of the ghetto residents had held their jobs ten or more years. In summary, suburbanites, because they had either acquired a skill or possessed certain personality attributes, tended to be more stable in their jobs.

Suburbanites, in spite of having fewer job changes, had been in Cleveland much longer. About 24 percent of the ghetto migrants and only 2 percent of the suburbanites had been in Cleveland for less than a year at the time of the survey. A little more than half of the ghetto residents had been in Cleveland over six years and about a fourth over ten years. About 60 percent of the suburbanites had been in Cleveland more than ten years at the time of the survey.

As might be expected, data on southern migrants in Cleveland show that those who had prearranged jobs found work sooner than those who did not. Those slowest to find work were individuals, such as retired persons, who had no intention of working when they came to Cleveland. The data show that men who were urged to move by relatives or friends were twice as likely to have prearranged jobs as those who were not (Peterson and Sharp, 1969: 89). Otherwise, among the aids used in finding a first job, friends and relatives ranked first, then going around to prospective employers, then newspaper ads, and then the State Employment Service. According to the Survey of Southern Migrants, however, most migrants believed that going around to the prospective employer was the best method of securing a job (Peterson and Sharp, 1969: 93). A certain amount of selective recruitment was also reported by that survey, but such recruitment did not seem to be based on skill or experience. "For male white migrants there is a strong urge toward initial employment as operatives [jobs requiring a moderate level of skill]. One measure of the kind of people that move into the operative occupations is to note that from each category of usual premigration occupations, more white men began work in Cleveland as operatives than continued in a line of work akin to their usual occupation" (Peterson and Sharp, 1969: 101). Exceptions to this were craftsmen and foremen, who moved into their own occupations in the same proportion as those who became operatives. Among black males, "three in ten began work in service jobs, about the same number started in Cleveland as operatives, while a fifth found jobs as laborers. . . . In short, while previous experience was second to the demand for operatives among white males, among the male Negro migrants prior experience was more important" (Peterson and Sharp, 1969: 101).

Concerning occupational stability, figures on southern migrants showed that, counting only workers with previous experience, two-thirds of the black men, about three-fifths of the white migrants, and just over two-fifths of the black women changed occupations sufficiently to be classed in a wholly different occupational category when they began work in Cleveland (Peterson and Sharp, 1969: 105).

Occupational Mobility: According to data from Peterson and Sharp (1969), there was a great amount of turnover between the migrant's occupation before migration and his first Cleveland job. Three-fifths of the white migrants had to be classified in a different job category in Cleveland than what they had been in previously. When grouping the data in terms of functional divisions, Peterson and Sharp (1969: 108) found that three-quarters of the white male migrants remained in blue-collar occupations after migration. When grouping the data into three skill levels, they found that half of the males remained in occupations with the same level of skill as their premigration occupations. A quarter of the migrant males found jobs with a higher skill level, while a quarter found jobs of a lower skill level. Overall, therefore, there was a "standoff in net gains or losses in skill" (Peterson and Sharp, 1969: 110).

Those most interested in job training were persons who had worked in the past but were currently out of work. Next in interest were those who had never worked in Cleveland, and following these were persons holding jobs in Cleveland at the time of the survey. "Among job holders, persons whose current or most recent employment was in a skilled occupation were, understandably, less often interested in job training than the persons with semi- or unskilled jobs" (Peterson and Sharp, 1969: 93).

Unemployment and Assistance: As compared to nonmigrants and returned migrants, West Virginia migrants in Cleveland had a lower proportion of unemployed and retired: 27 percent for returned migrants, 25 percent for nonmigrants, 9 percent for ghetto residents, and 2 percent for suburbanites. About two-thirds of the unemployed in the two West Virginia groups were retired, but there were very few retired people in the ghetto and few in the suburbs. Of those who were unemployed and not retired, about three-fourths in the three migrant groups received some sort of assistance, but only one in ten was on welfare. We did not find any welfare cases in the suburban sample.

Peterson and Sharp found that migrants were more likely to have lost working time due to "disruptions of the job market system" (difficulty in finding work, plant shutdowns, strikes, or layoffs) than were long-term residents. The respondents were questioned about their employment situation over the previous two years, however. The recent migrants included within their unemployed time the time they spent searching for their first job in Cleveland while, of course, the long-term residents were not including this within their unemployed time. One-quarter of the long-term residents had lost work time involuntarily, while between half and three-fifths of the white migrants had lost time due to "disruptions of the job market system." The migrants said that the greatest part of their lost time was because no work was available to them, and when the migrants were out of work they tended to be out for some time (Peterson and Sharp, 1969: 147). According to Peterson and Sharp, 10 percent of the respondents were not working or looking for work. Six out of ten of these had worked at some point during their residence in Cleveland. Male migrants cited waiting to start a new job or hoping to return to an old job as reasons for not seeking work.

Job Appraisals: Three-fifths of the white migrants to Cleveland felt they had obtained a job "as good as they hoped to get" while one-half or more of the black migrants felt they had obtained a job "worse than they had expected" (Peterson and Sharp, 1969: 121). Consistent with these findings, Peterson and Sharp discovered within their sample that as the hourly wage rates rose the proportion of migrants who were satisfied with their first job also rose. There was a significant increase in satisfaction only after the wage levels reached $2.00 an hour for women and $3.00 an hour for men.

Table 9.4: Weekly Wages for Ghetto and Suburbs

Weekly wages	Total groups (%)		Matched groups (%)	
	Ghetto	Suburbs	Ghetto	Suburbs
$90 or less	3.4	13.1	3.6	6.6
$91 to $120	11.0	35.7	9.8	44.0
$121 or more	85.6	51.2	86.6	49.4
Total number of cases	(387)	(168)	(103)	(75)

Income and Level of Living: Excluding the over $14,000 income category, which at the time of the survey included professionals and large property owners, Cleveland migrants, particularly suburbanites, had a considerably higher income than either nonmigrants or returned migrants. Income differences became more pronounced when the four groups were matched in terms of age and education, so that even in the over $14,000 income category there were proportionately more suburbanites than nonmigrants. The $9,000 to $14,000 income category had about three times as many suburbanites (25%) as the other three groups. In the $5,000 to $9,000 category the percentages were 61 for suburbanites, 50 for ghetto residents, 37 for returned migrants, and 34 for nonmigrants.

Table 9.4 shows the weekly wages of the Cleveland migrants for the year 1965, indicating that about three-fourths of the respondents in the ghetto and half of the respondents in the suburbs were earning more than $120 weekly. These figures contrast with figures on annual income, which show that suburbanites had the highest annual incomes. Possible reasons for this discrepancy could be: (1) ghetto residents earned higher wages but not as many had steady jobs, at least as compared to the suburbanities; (2) more of the ghetto residents were new in Cleveland and therefore had not spent the entire year there, even in cases where they had steady jobs; and (3) many suburbanites worked in industries such as the automobile industry which often offer overtime work.

Empirical evidence and informal discussions with Cleveland migrants indicate that both steady jobs and longer stays in Cleveland were associated with the desire to settle in the suburbs and buy a house. At least in the earlier years of the flight to the suburbs, migrants were quite hesitant about going into debt in order to buy a home, even when its cost was less than twice their annual income. It is possible that economic deprivation and lack of security in early life had created some fear syndromes. However, such syndromes often were found to be in conflict with tendencies to spend for immediate gratification and with relative lack of interest in saving.

If one considers that a large proportion of migrants in Cleveland came from rural areas with average incomes of $5,000 or less, it becomes apparent that migration offered some very good opportunities for economic achievement. This, of course, should be examined along with the fact that migrants had to go through considerable difficulties to reach the economic level they were at during the time of the survey.[3] Furthermore, even today some migrants are forced to remain in the ghetto in order to cope with city life, and some cannot cope with the city at all and are forced to return to West Virginia. But one should also consider the societal pressures and, in turn, the undesirable psychological conditions these pressures may have brought about in those who had the qualifications to migrate out but lacked the opportunity and had to stay in the hollows of Appalachia. Television and other contacts with the outside world have encouraged in them a desire for the income and level of living of the urban lower class, levels unavailable for many in West Virginia. As a consequence, low morale, anomie, or some other form of alienation or deviance may be the result.

The Returned Migrant: Approximately one-third of the total group of migrants who had returned to West Virginia from Cleveland had spent one year or less outside the Appalachian Region, while another third had spent from two to four years outside the region; the remaining third had spent five or more years. The last group probably in large part includes those who had worked outside the region until they reached retirement age and then returned to retire.

The majority of the total group of returned migrants from Cleveland, 62 percent, worked only once outside the state, while 32.7 percent worked outside of the state two or three times. The remaining portion, 5.3 percent, worked four or more times out of the state. These data reflect the repeated attempts of some to make a successful go of it outside the state and show that some were satisfied after one attempt. Within these data are also those who were sucessful and returned to the state after retirement.

Among the total group of returned migrants 15.7 percent first worked outside of West Virginia between 1960 and 1965, 17.8 percent between 1953 and 1959, 19.1 percent between 1945 and 1952, and 47.4 percent before 1945.

Alienation of Migrants: Although the literature describes rural migrants in the city as alienated, unhappy, and withdrawing into sectarian churches and cultural ghettos, our data do not support this proposition. At the time of our survey (1967) there were considerably more West Virginians in the suburbs than in the ghetto of Cleveland. This was not the case fifteen or twenty years before. Likewise, alienation may have been more prevalent in the past, but in 1967 there was less alienation—measured in terms of bewilderment and confusion—among respondents of the Cleveland sample than among the West Virginia sample. Differences, although reduced, remain when age and education are matched (Photiadis, 1975: 207–15).

To an extent, the same is true of the tendency to join sectarian churches. There were fewer members of sectarian churches in the suburbs than in the other three groups. When age and education are matched, ghetto residents and returned migrants had the highest proportion of members of sectarian churches; nonmigrants came second, and suburbanites last (Photiadis, 1975: 144–48). As compared to suburbanites, ghetto residents were much stronger believers but participated in church much less frequently (Photiadis, 1975: 151–54).

Life Style Preferences and Attitudes: Nine different preferences as to style of life, which could imply value orientations, were used to compare the four groups. The profiles of the ranking of these nine preferences indicate similar overall patterns, although there were some distinct differences among the four groups. In all four, religious and family orientation were the two styles of life checked most often as primary preferences. Although religion ranked first for the two West Virginia groups, for the two Cleveland groups family ranked first and religion second. Education ranked third for all groups except suburbanites, who placed work in third place (Photiadis, 1975: 125–43). When age and education were controlled, differences with regard to work appeared, as shown in Table 9.5. Work as a desirable part of life was much more important for suburbanites who, more than ghetto residents, usually had skilled jobs that were more interesting than the mining work they had done before migrating. As Table 9.6 shows, although suburbanites valued work more highly, their attitudes toward achievement, progress, and education were less favorable than those of the other three groups (Photiadis, 1975: 115–19).

Finally, the proportions of those who indicated high satisfaction with their work were about the same for all four groups: 79 percent for nonmigrants, 71 percent for returned migrants, 78 percent for ghetto residents, and 78 percent for suburbanites. These percentages are sim-

Table 9.5: Preference for a Life Style Where Work Is Important, for Nonmigrants, Returned Migrants, Ghetto, and Suburbs

	Total groups (percent)				Matched groups (percent)			
	Non-migrant	Returned migrant	Ghetto	Suburbs	Non-migrant	Returned migrant	Ghetto	Suburbs
High (22–27)	25.0	18.4	10.8	21.0	13.3	12.5	6.1	22.2
Medium (12–21)	45.3	46.0	70.1	60.2	64.7	72.2	71.2	61.7
Low (3–11)	29.7	35.6	19.1	18.8	22.0	15.3	22.7	16.1
Total number of cases	(899)	(238)	(165)	(383)	(166)	(75)	(75)	(166)

|_____| Differences significant at the .01 level

ilar to those of the 1969 Gallup Poll which asked the same question about one's job.

The New Returned Migrants to West Virginia: A considerable proportion of the early returned migrants of the 1950s and 1960s were older people who had had difficulty adjusting to city life, had been unemployed, and had had lower incomes and levels of living than the other three groups. When they returned to West Virginia they often retreated into fundamentalist churches and welfare roles. The newer group of returned migrants, in particular those returning to West Virginia since the beginning of the energy crisis, were younger, skilled, had a higher income level, tended to be conservative, and valued economic achievement highly. Many of these newer returned migrants lived in trailers and worked in the mines, often as heavy equipment operators in strip mines. In contrast to the early migrants, they placed little value on sectarian fundamentalist religion. In other words, they did not return to retreat from the larger society but simply to fulfill its expectations, particularly in terms of economic achievement, which is the larger society's theme. As a matter of fact, because they subscribed to these expectations they often became impatient with the rate of development in the old community and thus came in conflict with the people who had stayed there. Their loyalties now were often divided, belonging to both the city and the old community.

Data presented here support the proposition that in order to satisfy societal expectations in terms of income and level of living, people often, regardless of fitness, move to the city, where they hope to implement such expectations. In this light migration is seen not as an undesirable phenomenon but as an equilibrating process or an outlet used to

Table 9.6: Proportion of Respondents with High Scores in Attitudes toward Achievement, Progress, and Education, for Nonmigrants, Returned Migrants, Ghetto, and Suburbs

	Total groups (percent)				Matched groups (percent)			
	Non-migrant	Returned migrant	Ghetto	Suburbs	Non-migrant	Returned migrant	Ghetto	Suburbs
Achievement	33.0	37.0	32.0	23.0	34.0	42.0	35.0	23.0
Progress	39.0	29.2	33.1	21.3	26.6	28.2	35.2	16.2
Education	56.8	59.0	55.7	41.5	52.5	58.3	56.9	31.9

|_____| Differences significant at the .01 level
|_ _ _| Differences significant at the .05 level

fulfill societal expectations and thus to assure self-satisfaction. After they are mobilized by societal pressures, those who feel happier in Cleveland remain there and (depending on their readiness and in turn expectations) stay in the ghetto or move to the suburbs. Others, with different potentials for adjustment and different expectations, return to West Virginia. Still others of similar age and education do not migrate at all. In more general terms, migration can be seen in this light as adjustment to the larger society. It is a vital process aiming to reestablish the equilibrium between the individual and his socioeconomic environment that modern technological changes have upset.

In Cleveland, at least during the first years of migration (the 1940s), people moved first to the ghetto. As they secured new skills in both occupation and understanding of the urban culture, they moved to the suburbs in large numbers. Direct movement to the suburbs increased in later years.

Suburbanites, who were physically healthier, slightly older, and more educated and skilled, and who valued family life more than those who remained in the ghetto, saw society as more orderly and felt more part of it than people in the other three groups. In fact, suburbanites not only identified themselves psychologically with the larger society, but tended also to behave and possess those attributes (such as level of living, income, church participation, and attitudes toward urbanites and toward certain social issues) which fit the urban middle class, and especially lower-middle class, stereotype. This group had entered the larger society with relatively full credentials.

Those who remained in the ghetto seemed to be not only different in a number of ways from those in the suburbs, but also different from those (at least of similar age and education) back home. They tended to be younger, predominantly semiskilled, often newer in Cleveland, and less stable in holding jobs than suburbanites. They had relatively high incomes but low levels of living. Moreover, they valued material comfort and recreation less than the other groups and family life more than the West Virginia groups. In addition, they had stronger religious beliefs than the other three groups but participated less in church. In fact they felt much less part of the community in Cleveland and used it less as a reference group than the suburbanites did. Similarly, although they had considerable contacts with West Virginia and large proportions of their relatives were still there, they did not like the Appalachian style of life as much as the two West Virginia groups did. The ghetto residents' orientation was neither toward West Virginia nor toward their community as much as was true of the other groups; in certain respects they were more oriented to the larger society. Probably because orientation toward the larger society did not relieve anxiety as much as community and church did, ghetto residents had more need than the other groups to become attached to something; thus they tended to be slightly stronger believers, although not as sectarian as returned migrants.

Different attributes characterized those who could not adjust to city life and returned to Appalachia. These people tended to be older, unskilled, and with lower incomes and levels of living than members of the other three groups. Although returned migrants rated achievement higher than the other groups, they primarily preferred a life in line with religion and tended to be more sectarian. Still, among returned migrants there were a considerable number of professionals (11 percent of the present sample) and a number of skilled workers who probably had attributes different from the rest of the sample of returned migrants.

The newer returned migrants, those who had returned since the beginning of the energy crisis, were very different. They were younger and skilled and did not return to their communities or elsewhere in West Virginia to retreat from society but to secure the higher income jobs that mining (strip-mining in particular) were providing.

In general, the two groups in Cleveland had higher incomes, were physically healthier, had more technical skills, liked Appalachian life less, were more oriented toward the larger society, and—in spite of commonly held beliefs about the alienation of migrants—felt themselves to be more a part of society than the groups in West Virginia. However, it should be added here that the opposite might be true for places having better employment opportunities and less social disorganization than Appalachia. As compared to those in West Virginia, the migrants preferred family life to religious life and felt more need of family life in order to alleviate the anxieties produced by societal changes.

NOTES

1. The Bureau of Social Science Research survey deals with occupational and social adjustment of southern migrants to Cleveland; it was conducted among residents of low-income neighborhoods in Cleveland between May 1967 and March 1968.

2. Some of these people had left West Virginia more than once.

3. Some of the early migrants complained bitterly because no one gave them simple instructions as to how they should go about moving to the city and settling there. For suggestions of old migrants to the newcomers, see Photiadis (1975: 205).

10 WILLIAM W. PHILLIBER

Accounting for the Occupational Placements of Appalachian Migrants

The post-World War II period has been a time of heavy migration from rural Appalachian communities to urban areas in the North. Many have migrated to the city because of the excitement it is thought to offer, but most probably have come in search of work (Photiadis, 1965). Although no national survey has been made of the occupational achievements of Appalachian migrants, the findings of local studies indicate that these migrants, in general, fare worse than other residents in urban areas. John D. Photiadis (1970) has documented the experiences of male West Virginia migrants to Cleveland, Ohio. At the time of his survey, 82 percent of the Appalachians living in the ghetto areas and 51 percent living in suburbs held either unskilled or semiskilled jobs, while only 36 percent of the total male labor force in that city were unskilled or semiskilled (U.S. Bureau of the Census, 1972a). Bill Montgomery (1968) described the situations of Appalachians in the Uptown ghetto of Chicago. Here twenty day-pay agencies provided jobs for migrants. These agencies located unskilled jobs which they in turn offered to applicants for a fee. In return for the work, persons had to agree not to accept permanent employment with the company where they were placed, so that the Appalachian migrants were prevented from developing more permanent jobs with some future. In Cincinnati, Ohio, Michael E. Maloney (1974) estimated the achievement levels of Appalachians there. Using social area analysis, he found that four of the five neighborhoods ranked lowest in socioeconomic status were heavily or predominantly Appalachian.

While data have accumulated to document the lower occupational achievements of Appalachian migrants, little attempt has been made to study the cause of this pattern. The purpose of this study is to analyze the explanations which have been proposed and to assess the importance of each in accounting for the lower attainments.

The most obvious factor which may account for the occupational placements of Appalachians is their low level of education. Forty-eight percent of the Cleveland migrants in Photiadis's (1970) study failed to go beyond the tenth grade. Maloney (1974) found that every census tract in Cincinnati with dropout rates higher than 40 percent was inhabited predominantly by Appalachians. In industrial urban areas where most jobs require technical skills, this lack of formal education may effectively close the door to higher occupational achievement. In many cases knowledge acquired through formal education is applied directly in the job, as in the professions and many of the managerial and white-collar positions. As society becomes increasingly mechanized, educational skills are probably used in higher numbers of operative, craft, and service occupations, as well. Even when the knowledge necessary to perform a job is acquired through direct experience, schooling may remain a prerequisite for employment. The amount of schooling an individual obtains is taken as an indication of both his level of ability and his motivation. Anyone who fails to complete high school may be seen by potential employers as either stupid or lazy. Consequently, the low educational achievements of Appalachian migrants may block occupational opportunities either because they do not have the necessary skills or because they are perceived as unable to acquire them.

The second reason Appalachian migrants may achieve lower occupational success is their dependence upon family and close friends for jobs. According to James S. Brown (1968) and Harry Schwarzweller (1964), Appalachians depend upon their contacts with family in the city to tell them when jobs become available, and employers may use this network to secure an adequate labor supply for their companies. This pattern of acquiring jobs, while it may insure the migrant employment, sets a ceiling on the level of occupation he can obtain. The best job a relative or friend can help a migrant acquire is at or below the level of work he himself does. If the relative knew of a better job, he would take that opportunity himself. This effectively places the migrant in lower-level occupations unless he is fortunate enough to have a relative or friend who has attained high success.

Because they have lived in the urban area a shorter length of time, migrants may not have the opportunities available to natives. People who grow up in the city or who live there a large number of years may know where to look for jobs. Through a wider range of contacts than just relatives or close friends they may learn what companies pay better wages, offer advancement, or have good positions available. Even if migrants and natives start at the same place in the occupational structure, natives will probably eventually obtain better jobs because they have lived in the area longer. A worker seldom spends his career in the initial job he takes. Instead, he often changes jobs as better opportunities become available. A worker who has been in the area longer is likely to be ahead of a recent migrant because he has had time to make more changes to take advantage of opportunities for advancement.

Better jobs are frequently obtained through promotion. Companies evaluate the performance of employees and keep notice of the number of years a person has worked for them. As better positions become vacant, workers who have a good record and years of seniority are promoted. Appalachian migrants may miss these promotions because they have not been with the company long enough. This is so for two reasons. First, migrants may have come to the city only recently, having tried to work in the area where they were raised and migrating when they discovered they could earn more money in the city. Second, migrants may possibly move back and forth between the city and the place they consider home. If their desire is to live in Appalachia, they may stay in the city only long enough to save some money, then return home for as long as it lasts. Either of these factors shortens the time a migrant has held a job and consequently reduces his chances for advancement within the company.

Most Appalachians have migrated to urban areas from farms and small towns. In the city this background may be a liability to getting good jobs. The types of work available down home do not always have counterparts in urban areas. The economy of Appalachia is heavily dependent upon farming and mining. Cities provide jobs in construction, factories, and offices. Although the migrant may have developed occupational skills through years of employment, those skills become irrelevant where they are not needed. This forces the Appalachian to take unskilled jobs with little prerequisite knowledge but also with little pay.

A rural background may further lower the level of achievement among Appalachians in urban areas by failing to develop in them an adequate frame of reference. Compared to the money they could earn on worn-out farms or from road work, migrants, even in unskilled jobs, are probably doing pretty well. When the migrant considers his previous situation and the situation of those who have stayed behind, he is fairly successful. It is only when he is compared to other urban residents that his disadvantaged state becomes apparent. This implies that the reference groups of rural Appalachian migrants may retard their occupational advancement.

Because of the difference between jobs in Appalachia and jobs in urban areas the migrant may not know what kinds of occupations are available to him. He may accept unskilled jobs because he does not know that he can qualify for better work. On-the-job training is provided to people in many types of semiskilled, skilled, and lower white-collar occupations. Yet the migrant may not know this. His familiarity with urban ways may be too limited for him to compete successfully with others.

Data to test the effects of the factors discussed above on the occupational achievements of Appalachian migrants come from a survey of 506 residents drawn as a multi-stage probability sample of adults who were living in the inner city area of Cincinnati, Ohio, during July, August, and September of 1971. The primary purpose of the survey was to evaluate the standard of living of residents in the area designated to receive federal funds under the Model Cities program. The research was conducted by the Institute for Metropolitan Studies at the University of Cincinnati.

The decision was made to limit analysis to the 151 respondents who were white. While race remains one of the most important variables affecting occupational achievement in our society, a large majority of Appalachian migrants are white. If blacks were included in the analysis, it would confound the results by depressing the average achievements of Cincinnati natives and migrants from areas other than Appalachia without affecting the average for Appalachians. Thus, the conclusion could be reached that Appalachian migrants were as successful as or even more successful than other people when in fact they might be less successful. Because too few black Appalachian migrants were interviewed to make analysis by race possible, they were omitted altogether.

Migration status was determined by asking respondents where they had lived before moving to the Cincinnati area. Those who had lived in counties defined as Appalachia by the Appalachian Regional Commission were classified as Appalachian migrants. People who had lived in Cincinnati all their lives were considered natives. Those who were neither Appalachian migrants nor Cincinnati natives were classified as "other migrants." This system underestimates the number of migrants from Appalachia. Anyone who first migrated from Appalachia to an area outside of Cincinnati was classified as an "other migrant." The frequency of this two-stage pattern of migration is probably low, however.

Occupational status was measured by the type of work done by the head of household. Males and unmarried females were asked the type of work they were currently doing if they were employed, or the type of work they did on their last job if they were laid off, unemployed, retired, or disabled. Married females were asked similar questions about their husbands' jobs. Responses were coded into the three-digit codes of the U.S. Bureau of the Census, *1960 Census of the Population, Alphabetical Index of Occupations and Industries* and grouped into five categories: white-collar workers, craftsmen, operatives, service workers, and laborers. Numbers from one through five were assigned to the categories with laborers assigned one for lowest status and white collar workers five for highest status.

To determine education, respondents were asked the highest grade in school they had completed. Answers were placed in one of two categories: less than high school graduate, or high school graduate and above.

Respondents who were currently employed were asked how they found their jobs. Those who did not have a job were asked how they got the last job they had. People who had obtained their last jobs through a relative or a friend were grouped into one category and everyone else was placed in a second group.

Males and unmarried females were asked either how long they had held their present job or how long they held the last job they had had, depending upon whether they were employed at the time of the interview. Married females were asked for similar information about their husbands' jobs. The actual number of years the respondent had held his job was recorded, with responses ranging from less than one year through fifty-six years.

All respondents, including natives, were asked how long they had lived in the Cincinnati area. Again, the number of years was recorded

Table 10.1: Distribution of Occupational Status by Migrant Status

| Occupation | Migrant status (percent) | | |
	Appalachian migrant	Other migrant	Cincinnati native
White-collar worker	8.9	24.4	23.8
Craftsman	13.3	20.0	26.2
Operative	31.1	26.7	31.0
Service worker	28.9	20.0	9.5
Laborer	17.7	8.9	9.5
Mean occupational status score	2.67	3.31	3.45
Number	49	46	44

without further grouping, producing a range from less than one year through eighty-four years.

Migrants to the area were also asked if their former place of residence was in a large city (over 100,000 population), a small city (2,500 to 100,000 people), a town, or a farm. Categories were ranked in terms of increasing size of population, and numbers were assigned. Cincinnati natives were grouped with migrants from large cities.

The first step in the analysis was to determine the effect of migrant status on occupational achievement. Table 10.1 shows the occupational distribution and mean status score for Appalachian migrants, other migrants, and Cincinnati natives. Little difference existed between "other migrants" and Cincinnati natives; approximately one-fourth of each group were in white-collar positions while the bulk of the remainder were either skilled craftsmen or semiskilled operatives. It was the Appalachian migrants who differed. Here less than 9 percent held white-collar jobs and only 13 percent were skilled craftsmen. Over three-fourths of the group were employed in semiskilled or unskilled jobs. While the typical Cincinnati native or migrant from areas outside Appalachia was employed either as an operative or in a higher status position, the average Appalachian migrant could expect no better job than an operative and had a good chance of ending up with lower-status employment. These findings conform to the results of earlier studies and give support to the reliability of these data.

The size of the effect of migrant status on occupational achievement was determined by calculating the proportionate reduction in variation (N^2). The variation of all cases around the mean occupational status score for the total sample was first measured. This constituted the amount of variation which existed before the effect of migrant status was introduced. Second, the variation in occupational status was calculated within each migrant category, using the mean occupational status of that category as the reference point. The variations for the three categories were then added together. Third, the variation about the subcategory means was subtracted from the variation about the mean of the total. The difference between the two numbers was due to the effect of migrant status. Dividing this difference by the variation about the mean for the total gave the proportionate reduction in variation.

For this sample, migrant status accounted for 7.26 percent of the variation in occupational status. While this amount is not high, it is more than would be expected by chance alone. This means that there is reason for some confidence in the conclusion that Appalachian migrants had lower occupational achievements than other residents.

To estimate the importance of each of the explanations for the lower occupational achievements of Appalachian migrants, the control variables were introduced one at a time. In an analysis of covariance procedure, each control was first correlated with occupational status to remove its effect from the variation. Both migrant status and the control variable were then introduced and the reduction in total variation was determined. The difference between the reduction in total variation using only the control variable and the reduction using both the control variable and migrant status was the effect of migrant status on occupational status which remained after the control. This controlled effect, divided by the effect of migrant status alone, revealed the proportion of the effect of migrant status which remained after the control. One minus this proportion is the percentage of the effect of migrant status on occupational status which was explained by the control. This procedure was carried out for each of the five explanations.

Only two variables actually were found to have an effect on the relationship between migrant status and occupational status: education and rural background. It is not at all surprising that education has such an effect. Taken alone it explains 44 percent of the original effect of migrant status. Because a high school diploma is a prerequisite for so many positions, a person who drops out before graduation never has a chance to get these jobs. Less than 19 percent of the Appalachian migrants in this study had graduated from high school, compared to 47 percent of the migrants from other areas and 38 percent of the Cincinnati natives. Even among the inner-city population, Appalachians are at a disadvantage. Before these people can compete for better jobs in urban areas the number of years of schooling they complete must be increased.

Rural background appears to have been an even greater factor in accounting for the lower occupational status of Appalachian migrants. Taken alone it reduced the effect of migrant status by 74 percent. This seems to document the fact that rural areas and small towns do not prepare migrants to live in urban areas. How this occurs is not fully understood but explanations were proposed in the earlier part of this paper. It remains the task of subsequent research to discover their validity.

Three explanations proposed to account for the lower occupational achievements of Appalachian migrants have little, if any, observable influence. The first of these is source of employment. Past literature, some of which has already been cited, has stressed the role of family and friends in obtaining jobs for migrants. The data here support that argument, with 37 percent of Appalachian migrants holding jobs they got through family or close friends. In addition, the data support the argument that people who obtain their jobs through family and close friends have lower-status jobs than those who secure employment through other means. The error occurs in underestimating the importance of family and friends in securing jobs for people who are not Appalachian migrants. In this study, 45 percent of the Cincinnati natives and 50 percent of the migrants from areas outside Appalachia used family and friends to find a job. In both cases this percentage is actually higher than that observed for Appalachian migrants. The importance of family and friends is not a characteristic unique to Appalachians. It is at least as strong in other groups.

The second factor which failed to account for the occupational status of Appalachian migrants is length of time on the job. Appalachian migrants were predicted to have held their present jobs a shorter length of time, either because they had come to the area more recently or because they had moved back and forth between Appalachia and Cincinnati. The data indicate that this is not the case. Appalachians had held their jobs about the same length of time as Cincinnati natives or migrants from other areas, an average of thirteen years compared to fourteen and fifteen years, respectively.

Length of time in the area also explained little of the effect migration had on employment status. This appears to be because the migration from Appalachia began some years ago, with the result that many Appalachians had been in Cincinnati most of their lives. Instead of staying in the place in which they were raised, many had probably migrated as soon as they got out of school. The average number of years an Appalachian had lived in Cincinnati was twenty. Consequently, they could not be considered newcomers to the city.

The only two factors which accounted for the lower occupational status of Appalachian migrants in this study were their less frequent completion of high school and their migration from rural areas and small towns. These two variables were intercorrelated; that is, people from rural areas and small towns had completed fewer years of schooling than people living in cities. Formal education may have been seen as less important in those areas. Most jobs there could be done by people with little schooling since they required little instruction but perhaps years of experience. As long as a person could read and write he could get by with little difficulty. Consequently, Appalachians who came from rural backgrounds may not have valued education as much as people raised in urban settings.

Education and rural-to-urban background were simultaneously included as controls to test their combined effect upon the relationship between migrant status and occupational status. Together these variables accounted for 87 percent of the effect. This, then, substantially explains almost all the observed effect that Appalachian migration had on occupational placement.

In summary, the findings of this survey indicate that Appalachian migrants do achieve less occupational success than other groups; that failure to complete high school, and migration from rural areas or small towns effectively account for the lower average occupational status of Appalachian migrants; and that source of job, number of years employed on the job, and number of years in the area do not explain the lower occupational achievements of Appalachian migrants.

Conclusion   MICHAEL E. MALONEY

The Prospects for
Urban Appalachians

The preceding articles collectively represent the greatest step yet taken toward understanding Appalachian Mountain people now living outside their native region. Prior to this publication the most important work was *Mountain Families in Transition* (Schwarzweller, Brown, and Mangalam, 1971), which described both the premigration and the postmigration cultural and socioeconomic situation of Eastern Kentucky mountaineers. Its chief limitation, attributable to sample limitations, was that it did not adequately describe social conditions in inner-city Appalachian neighborhoods. The primary contribution of this work was that the authors described the rural Appalachian cultural system without reverting to either romanticism or the pathology (cultural deficit) model. The authors of this book made an important methodological contribution to studies of rural-to-urban migrants by distinguishing three distinct socioeconomic strata among the migrants and by demonstrating the role of kinship networks in the migration process and in postmigration adjustment.

In other studies, James Brown and Clyde McCoy documented the existence and function of migration streams (chapter 3, above). By 1974, Brown, his associates, and their former students had developed detailed information on the scale and destination of Appalachian migration, premigration socioeconomic and cultural conditions, the emergence of a stem-and-branch family system, and occupational adjustment and residential location patterns within metropolitan areas. Also by this time, Cunningham (1962) and Wagner (1974) had completed studies, respectively, of the religious attitudes and problems faced by Appalachian children in urban schools.

Coordination of research on Appalachian migrants was advanced in 1972 by the formation of the Research Committee of the Urban Appalachian Council (then the Appalachian Committee). This group brought together some of the leading experts in the field, including James Brown, Clyde McCoy, and Gary Fowler, with researchers from Cincinnati area colleges and universities and the social activists involved in founding the Urban Appalachian Council. This collective effort stimulated some new research, created a dialogue among researchers, and led to the first national conference on Appalachian migrants, which was held in Columbus, Ohio, in March 1974. Most of the articles included in the present volume were presented at that conference, which was organized by the Appalachian Committee and hosted by the Academy for Contemporary Problems.

The major aim of the research presented in this volume is to document the socioeconomic and cultural conditions of Appalachians in midwestern and mid-Atlantic metropolitan areas. It is a matter of some urgency that statistics be collected on population, unemployment, education, and health conditions for each major receiving center. Also needed are ethnographies and sociological studies on attitudes, social structure, and political participation. This information needs to be collected at the level of the neighborhood as well as for more macro-level municipal and metropolitan units. Studies by Fowler (Chapter 4, above), Maloney (1974), and McKee (1978) are a step in this direction. Pickard has noted that Appalachian migrants and their immediate descendants probably comprise at least 15 percent of the population of the metropolitan centers in zones bordering on Appalachia and thus comprise one of the major population groups in the eastern United States. As Larry Morgan has pointed out, we need to know what part of this population has real unmet needs in order not to apply *Grapes of Wrath* stereotypes to the entire group.

That more information is available about Appalachians in Cincinnati and Cleveland is attributable in part to the fact that these areas are major receiving areas, respectively, for migrants from Eastern Kentucky and West Virginia. This, in turn, has caused the state universities in Kentucky and West Virginia to focus research attention on these cities. The presence of the Urban Appalachian Council in Cincinnati and its role in delineating the needs of Appalachian communities has added another incentive for focusing on these cities. Not enough is known about cities like Atlanta, Chicago, Pittsburgh, Detroit, and Washington where Appalachians have apparently settled largely in the suburban ring. It is important to find out, for example, whether the kinds of social problems present among Cincinnati and Cleveland migrants are emerging in any part of the Atlanta SMSA. Atlanta has been the primary receiving area for Appalachian migrants for nearly three decades.

In considering the prospects for Appalachian migrants, it is important to keep in mind the social-class distinctions developed by Schwarzweller, Brown, and Mangalam. They distinguish between high, intermediate, and low-class families and conclude that "an individual migrant's social class origins influenced, to some extent, not only when he left the mountains, but also his economic success in the area of destination. . . . Even for a rural low-income population, therefore, social class origin seems to have validity in predicting a migrant's abilities to cope with the external environment, and consequently, his chances of enhancing his own and his family's economic well-being in an urban area" (Schwarzweller et al., 1971: 174–75).

Inseparable from the concept of social class is the stem-family hypothesis. The social-class origins of the family and the strength of stem-and-branch family networks help to determine both economic success and the migrant's ability to resolve other problems associated with urban adjustment, such as stress and anomie. Especially less affluent migrants and recent migrants find involvement with their kin network a great help in reducing the stress associated with urban adjustment (Schwarzweller et al., 1971: 192–95).

Another distinction which is made in Schwarzweller's article on occupational adjustment (Chapter 8, above) is between inner-city and suburban migrants. Unemployment rates and occupational skill levels differ greatly between these two groups in Photiadis's Cleveland studies. Fowler's Cincinnati study also documents the existence of vastly different social indicators for different types of neighborhoods even within the central city. I am convinced that survey research of an entire SMSA would reveal enclaves of poverty in the suburban fringe. Considering the relationship between social class and residential settlement patterns, one can hypothesize that currently low-status migrants move to low-status areas within the metropolitan area, that intermediate-status migrants move to intermediate-status areas, and that high-status migrants move to stable blue-collar areas throughout the SMSA. The Urban Appalachian Council's preliminary analysis of special tabulations of census data on recent Appalachian migrants in the Cincinnati SMSA (1965–70) lends support to this theory (Watkins, 1976; Waites, 1976).

The remainder of this essay will consider the future prospects for urban Appalachians with regard to assimilation, return migration, and industrial decline in the Midwest, the crisis in education for inner-city youth, the viability of urban ethnic neighborhoods, and the need for the emergence of a social movement.

The assimilation[1] of low- and intermediate-class urban Appalachians will not be rapid. It is popularly believed, even by government and social welfare officials, that the "adjustment" of Appalachians to urban life is a temporary phase in the life of first-generation migrants. This belief has been placed in serious doubt by the research of Brown, Fowler, Philliber, and McKee.[2] Several reasons can be posited for a slower rate of assimilation. Large numbers of culturally different people cluster in specific areas of the SMSA. These areas can be slums, "urban villages,"[3] blue-collar enclaves, or even pockets in middle-class neighborhoods. These ethnic enclaves are maintained over time, even in the face of population loss through return migration or interneighborhood movement, by the migratory-stream systems.[4] The migration process does not destroy Appalachian kin networks but rather expands them over a larger geographic area. Appalachian migration is thus to a great degree "system maintaining." Rather than creating total cultural shock and social network breakdown (except for some in the slums), migration represents a transplanted subcultural system (Schwarzweller et al., 1971: 257). Limited opportunities for upward social mobility and for some limited expectations or aspirations also prolong the time required for breaking out of the ethnic enclave (Gans, 1962; Cloward and Ohlin, 1960). Urban Appalachian neighborhoods are thus not primarily "ports-of-entry" for new migrants but rather multigenerational ethnic neighborhoods whose population is maintained by both natural increase and new migrants from the mountains.

Return migration of Appalachians to the region may be detrimental to northern cities. Even if, for reasons cited above, return migration is partially counterbalanced by continuing in-migration, it could be substantial enough in the years ahead to weaken the social and economic base of northern cities. This will occur if large numbers of return migrants are in the nineteen to thirty-five year age group. Substantial amounts of return migration by this age group would increase the dependent population (both old and young) and weaken the tax base in affected cities. If many return migrants are skilled workers, the competitive position of northern cities in attracting or holding industries could be weakened. Thus the narrowing of the income gap between, for example, Kentucky and Ohio could ultimately weaken the economy of Ohio. Urban Appalachian community structure would also be weakened if a substantial loss of young workers began to create the kind of "hourglass" age structure which out-migration in the 1940–70 period created in many Appalachian counties. As Miernyk (1975) has pointed out the actual number of jobs created in the coal industry will vary greatly depending on the rate of automation. A shift in concentration of coal production to western fields could also have an impact.

Morgan (in this volume) has stated that the social costs to receiving cities of Appalachian migration are not great enough to justify a policy of discouraging further migration. If his analysis is accurate, it would also be ill-advised for midwestern public officials and news media to continue rejoicing in the thought that all the "hillbillies" might pack up and go home.[5]

It is important to realize that Appalachian out-migration has by no means come to a grinding halt. Movement within the migratory streams has always been a back-and-forth phenomenon. As Schwarzweller notes in his article here, many young people in Central Appalachia intend to migrate. Now that the boundary mechanisms of Appalachian society have been expanded to include urban enclaves of kin and friends, substantial out-migration will continue, regardless of a narrowing income differential between rural Appalachia and northern urban centers.

The actual pace of the narrowing of income differential between midwestern states and Central Appalachia is partially dependent on the severity of the trend toward fewer manufacturing jobs in the industrial heartland. Appalachians in cities are heavily dependent on employment in manufacturing. Conversion to service jobs is problematic for two reasons. Workers in manufacturing jobs may not have the skills and attitudes required for service work, and wages are generally 25 percent lower in service jobs. There are perhaps three major components to loss of industrial jobs in northern central-city areas: relocation of industry in the "sunbelt" region, overseas production of goods by multinational corporations, and the tendency for new plants to locate in the suburban fringe. These job losses to central cities are partially replaced by lower paying service jobs. The shift to more service jobs and fewer industrial jobs results in higher rates of underemployment and unemployment, loss of tax base, and decline in the quality of services.

Unemployment and underemployment rates are already critically high in inner-city black and Appalachian neighborhoods. The 1970 *Census Employment Survey* for Cincinnati documented a 10 percent unemployment rate and a 61.6 percent underemployment rate (based on $3.50 an hour for an eight-hour-day) for a target area that included most of the low-income black and Appalachian neighborhoods (U.S. Bureau of the Census, 1970b). Continued loss of manufacturing jobs may cause these indicators to look even worse in 1980. It is extremely important, then, that midwestern centers maintain and expand, where possible, their base of manufacturing jobs.

The educational crisis for urban Appalachian youth may get worse before its gets better. In Cincinnati, and very likely in many other Appalachian migrant receiving centers, the most dramatic difference between social indicators for Appalachian areas and those for other areas of the central city occurs in the area of education. In the percentage of high school dropouts (Maloney, 1974: 52–55) or the percentage of the population sixteen to twenty-five years old, not high school graduates and not attending high school (McKee, 1978), Appalachian neighborhoods in Cincinnati rank dramatically higher than either black areas or other white areas.

The rate of decline in the percentage of population over twenty-five with less than a high school education (education index) was lower for Appalachian areas than for other areas. I fear that during the next two decades the situation of central-city schools may deteriorate further as a result of the loss of industrial tax base described above coupled with the trend toward a reduction of the share of educational taxes paid by business and industry. Other aspects of the failure of urban public school systems to respond to the needs of central-city Appalachian youth have been described in the work of Thomas Wagner (1974) of the University of Cincinnati.

It should be pointed out that the failure of Appalachian neighborhoods to show greater improvement over the past decade may have been influenced by an influx of recent migrants with lower educational levels than longer term residents of the neighborhoods. Ornati (1968) has mentioned the need to know "which of the urban 'newcomers' are poor and which of the poor are 'newcomers.' " A recent Dayton survey states that 27 percent of Appalachians who have lived in Dayton all their lives have less than twelve years of school while 45 percent of recent migrants (one to five years in residence) have at least twelve years of schooling (Office of the City Manager, 1977: 13). These data indicate that in-migration should actually raise aggregate educational levels. If it is true, as Philliber's paper indicates, that educational and occupational levels are closely linked, then perhaps our primary concern should be to provide better education for youth, both in rural Appalachia and in the cities.

There are many concrete expressions of the Appalachian migratory-stream systems in the cities of Ohio, Indiana, Illinois, and Michigan and in the cities that ring the mountain region. There are factories, schools, and churches that are predominantly Appalachian. Union and civic halls resound with "down home" accents. Bluegrass, gospel, and country and western music dominate radio dials and the stage of many a night spot. Much of Ohio, especially, speaks with an Appalachian accent.[6]

One much neglected yet very important feature of the migratory-stream systems that link cities politically, economically, and culturally to Appalachia is the urban neighborhood.[7] Ethnic neighborhoods are often perceived as slums to be cleaned up through massive urban renewal or gentrification processes, as hotbeds of racism, and more generally as an environment counterproductive to upward mobility and social integration. Without denying the kernel of truth in each of the above concepts of urban neighborhoods, it is necessary to assert that these neighborhoods represent much more than this list of negative stereotypes. Fundamentally, the urban neighborhood is a primary sphere of social interaction within and without the ethnic kinship networks and a primary focus for the consumption of goods and services.

Planners of schools, community development projects, and social services need to be aware of the positive functions of urban neighborhoods. Planner-sociologist Herbert Gans (1960) is a pioneer in developing a critique of urban development projects which often destroy as much as they create. James Brown has stated that if the government had had to finance the social welfare functions provided by the stem-and-branch family system for millions of Appalachian migrants, the costs would have been staggering. The mutual aid functions of working-class family, peer group, and church systems which, for example, have helped urban newcomers to find housing, employment, and other needed services, have been largely ignored in studies that tend to focus only on pathology and dysfunctional elements of community life.

Perhaps the greatest fear of Appalachian migrant leaders in Columbus, Dayton, and Cincinnati is that urban social policy in the next decade will have the effect of massive destruction of inner-city neighborhoods and their system of social networks. The most threatening of these emerging policies is that of "planned shrinkage," which involves writing off "nonviable" neighborhoods, denying them services, and letting them die. Historic preservation and other gentrification projects pose an additional threat to urban minority neighborhoods. Several Appalachian areas of Dayton and Cincinnati have already been displaced by such projects. It is likely that the kinds of prejudice and stereotyping described by Clyde McCoy and Virginia McCoy Watkins in this volume are very much involved in deciding which neighborhoods are to be subjected to triage (another word for planned shrinkage) or gentrification projects.

The prescription, offered by such organizations as the National Center for Urban Ethnic Affairs, is to take the positive aspects of neighborhood life (culture, social structure, and so forth) as basic in the development of program policy.[8] If urban neighborhoods are not respected in the formulation of policies and plans, the dislocation of inner-city, working-class Appalachians could disrupt indigenous social networks and create a new round of social problems that would be too costly to these communities and to society in both human and economic terms.

In Cincinnati, Appalachians have begun to organize at both city and neighborhood levels to fight for better schools, jobs, housing conditions, and social services. Self-help programs and inner-city cultural and educational centers have been established. If this trend continues and spreads to other cities, it will be another vital step in their adaptation to urban society. In Ohio, especially, where there are such large numbers of transplanted Appalachians, mountain people have the capacity to become a significant political force. A "cultural revitalization movement" is a possible and perhaps necessary requirement for inner-city Appalachians in order to overcome the barriers to upward mobility which they, along with the rest of the urban poor, now face.

It is possible to derive two quite different pictures of the status of Appalachian migrants from the papers in this volume. One says that the majority live in suburbia, enjoy gradual upward mobility, are more and more employed in skilled occupations (Schwarzweller), are not alienated from urban society (Photiadis), and increase their income after migration (Schwarzweller et al. and Morgan). The other says that migrants concentrate disproportionately in low-status areas of the central city where they are discriminated against by established ethnic groups, have limited access to good schools, jobs, housing, and social services (Fowler), have high unemployment rates (Schwarzweller), and are worse off than nonmigrants (Photiadis). All of the authors seem to reject the stereotypes of Appalachian migrants as unambitious, welfare-malingering slum dwellers who are a tremendous economic burden to the receiving cities and a threat to the social order.

The conclusion is that we still do not know all that we need to know. Most of the data in these studies are based on surveys of recent migrants. The peak period of Appalachian migration was the 1940s and the early 1950s. We still lack a comprehensive survey that includes the people who migrated before 1955 and their descendants. I am convinced that when such data become available, they will show that a large percentage of first- and second-generation Appalachians still live in central-city low-status areas and that, in some cases, the status of the second generation will be lower than that of the first generation. Another important characteristic of the needed studies should be that they compare Appalachians to other groups. A base of information is being developed, for instance, showing that the status of Cincinnati's Appalachian population is comparable to that of the black population.

Until surveys are available for several entire metropolitan areas that include household data on at least two generations of urban Appalachians, there will be a serious gap in information concerning multigenerational ethnic neighborhoods as we learn more and more about recent migrants and return migrants. The Urban Appalachian Council in addressing this issue was instrumental in encouraging a United States senator from Ohio to submit an amendment to the Appalachian Regional Commission to conduct research to determine the health and welfare status of Appalachian migrants. The ARC's response to the mandate has been to prepare a bibliography of literature and to collect existing data on recent migrants. This type of research does not give a realistic account of urban Appalachians who are second- and third-generation, nor does it exemplify conditions of Appalachians who migrated out of the region in the 1940s and 1950s and stayed in the cities. The health and welfare status of these earlier migrants, as well as of second- and third-generation migrants, may differ vastly from that of recent migrants. Since ARC has shown little interest in responding realistically to the mandate, a more appropriate federal agency should be assigned to conduct the research and to play an advocacy role for urban Appalachians within the federal government.[9]

Although the most dramatic phases of the "great migration" from Appalachia (1940–70) are now a matter of history, an enormous reality remains. Rural Appalachia and many metropolitan centers outside the region are linked together economically, socially, culturally, and politically through various migratory-stream systems. Social planners and policy makers at both ends of these systems need to develop a more complete understanding of how this social reality operates; this understanding can guide the formulation of programs and policies. So far the data suggest that the emphasis of social policy should be on the provision of education and jobs for those who, without special assistance, may become casualties of the rural-to-urban shift. Although there are many facts that destroy most of the stereotypic myths concerning urban Appalachians, there is still an urgent need for more knowledge to address the remaining questions. At stake, ultimately, is the social welfare of many thousands of families who have not shared in the general success story of Appalachian migrants.

NOTES

1. The concept of assimilation used here is the one developed by sociologists Robert E. Park and Ernest W. Burgess in *Introduction to the Science of Sociology* (Chicago, University of Chicago Press, 1921), p. 735. "Assimilation is a process of interpenetration and fusion in which persons and groups acquire the memories, sentiments, and attitudes of other persons or groups, and, by sharing their experience and history, are incorporated with them in a common cultural life." It should be noted that this broad concept of assimilation implies what is sometimes meant by "acculturation" and also a degree of social structural relationship as well as cultural sharing with other individuals and groups.

2. The work on migration streams by James Brown and his colleagues describes the process by which urban ethnic enclaves are established and maintained. Fowler's chapter in this volume shows that many first- and second-generation Appalachians still live in low-status areas. Philliber's monograph on a Hamilton County (Cincinnati) survey may show that on some social indicators second-generation migrants are worse off than the first generation. Dan McKee's study (1978) shows that in Cincinnati's multigeneration neighborhoods severe problems persist.

3. The term "urban village" as used by Herbert Gans in *The Urban Villagers* (1962), p. 4, implies an area in which recent urban migrants adapt their nonurban institutions and cultures to an urban milieu.

4. Mass migration is a sociological phenomenon which, once begun, is not totally dependent upon economic or social opportunity. In Appalachia, youth are still being socialized to become migrants and they will continue to migrate within established migration-stream systems. Even if opportunities in Appalachia expand rapidly it may take the socialization process some time to adapt to the new reality.

5. The reference here is to statements by Cincinnati's former housing director and Cincinnati and Dayton newspapers, in particular.

6. The Urban Appalachian Council estimates that one million Ohioans are first- and second-generation Appalachians (from other states). An additional 1.2 million Appalachians live in Ohio's twenty-eight Appalachian counties.

7. The function of migratory-stream systems in linking urban areas to Appalachia is described in "Southern Appalachian Migration and Metropolises, a Study of Migratory-Stream Systems" an unpublished paper by James Brown. An unpublished paper by Michael Maloney entitled "The Mountaineer as Industrial Worker" describes two types of urban Appalachian neighborhoods.

8. The National Center and the Urban Appalachian Council recognize that broad questions of social change such as open housing and school desegregation are in some tension with the concept of strengthening ethnic neighborhoods. Their appeal is that working-class ethnic neighborhoods not be forced to endure the entire cost of social change. Rather, the cost should be borne fairly by the entire metropolitan community.

9. For a more complete statement on how the federal government could help Appalachian migrants see "Appalachia 1978: A Statement from the Colony," Appalachian Alliance Steering Committee, February 1978.

References

Adams, James L. 1971. "Nuns at Work in Changing World." *Cincinnati Post*, December 11, p. 1.

American Jewish Committee Institute of Human Relations. 1972. *Group Life in America: A Task Force Report*. New York: American Jewish Committee of Human Relations.

Appalachian Regional Commission. 1970. *Appalachian Data Book*, 2nd ed. Washington, D.C.: G.P.O.

———. 1975. *Annual Report*. Washington, D.C.: Appalachian Regional Commission.

Arnowitz, Stanley. 1973. *False Promises: The Shaping of American Working Class Consciousness*. New York: McGraw-Hill Book Company.

Backes, Clarus. 1968. "Uptown: The Promised Land." *Chicago Tribune Magazine*, September 22, pp. 26–33.

Ball, Richard A. 1971. "The Southern Appalachian Folk Subculture as a Tension Reducing Way of Life." In John Photiadis and Harry Schwarzweller, eds., *Change in Rural Appalachia*, pp. 69–84. Philadelphia: University of Pennsylvania Press.

Banas, Casey. 1969. "Uptown: Mecca for Migrants." *Southern Education Report* 4:10–13.

Berry, Brian J.L., and Horton, Frank. 1970. *Geographic Perspectives on Urban Systems*. New York: Prentice-Hall.

Blevins, Audie L. 1971. "Socioeconomic Differences between Migrants and Non-migrants." *Rural Sociology* 4:509–20.

Bogue, Donald J. 1951. *State Economic Areas: A Description of the Procedure Used in Making a Functional Grouping of Counties of the United States*. Washington, D.C.: G.P.O.

Bogue, Donald J, and Beale, Calvin L. 1961. *Economic Areas of the United States*. Glencoe, Ill.: Free Press.

Bordeaux, A. Frank, Jr., and Morgan, Larry C. 1973. "Sources of Job Information for Migrants." *Southern Journal of Agricultural Economics* 5: 211–16.

Branscome, James. 1972. "The Crises of Appalachian Youth." In David S. Walls and John B. Stephenson, eds., *Appalachia in the Sixties*, pp. 224–31. Lexington: University Press of Kentucky.

————. 1976. "Appalachian Migrants and the Need for a National Policy." In
Bruce Ergood and Bruce Kuhre, eds. *Appalachia: Social Context Past and
Present*. Dubuque, Iowa: Kendall/Hunt Publishing Company.

Brown, James S. 1967. "Population and Migration Changes in Appalachia."
Paper presented at the Conference on Rural Appalachia in Transition, West
Virginia University.

————. 1970. "Southern Appalachian Migration and Metropolises: A Study of
Migratory Stream-Systems, 1955–1960." Paper presented at the Annual
Meeting of the American Sociological Association.

————. 1968. "The Family Behind the Migrant." *Mountain Life and Work*
44:4–7.

————. 1971. "Population and Migration Changes in Appalachia." In John
Photiadis and Harry Schwarzweller, eds., *Change in Rural Appalachia*.
Philadelphia: University of Pennsylvania Press.

Brown, James S., and Hillery, George A., Jr. 1962. "The Great Migration,
1940–1960" In Thomas R. Ford, ed., *The Southern Appalachian Region: A
Survey*. Lexington: University of Kentucky Press.

Brown, James S.; Schwarzweller, Harry K.; and Mangalam, Joseph J. 1963.
"Kentucky Mountain Migration and the Stem Family: An American Variation on a Theme by LePlay." *Rural Sociology* 28:48–69.

Bruno, Hal. 1964. "Chicago's Hillbilly Ghetto." In H. H. Meisner, ed., *Poverty in the Affluent Society*, pp. 102–07. New York: Basic Books.

Campbell, John C. 1921. *The Southern Highlander and His Homeland*. New
York: Russell Sage Foundation.

Choldin, Harvey M. 1973. "Kinship Networks in the Migration Process." *Inter-
national Migration Review* 7:163–75.

Cincinnati Public Schools. 1973. "Estimated Memberships, Percent, and Number of Appalachian Pupils, by School, December, 1973." Cincinnati: Cincinnati Public Schools.

Cloward, Richard, and Ohlin, Lloyd. 1960. *Delinquency and Opportunity*.
New York: Free Press.

Coles, Robert. 1971. *The South Goes North*. Vol. 3 of *Children of Crisis*. Boston: Little, Brown and Company.

Crowe, Martin J. 1964. "The Occupational Adaptation of a Selected Group of
Eastern Kentuckians in Southern Ohio." Ph.D. dissertation, University of
Kentucky.

Cunningham, Earl Harold. 1962. "Religious Concerns of Southern Appalachian Migrants." Ph.D. dissertation, Boston University.

Davies, Christopher Shane, and Fowler, Gary L. 1972. "The Disadvantaged
Urban Migrant in Indianapolis." *Economic Geography* 48: 153–67.

Dayton Human Relations Commission. 1966. *Southern Appalachian Migration: A Descriptive Study*. Dayton, Ohio: Human Relations Commission.

Deaton, Brady J. 1972. "The Private Costs and Returns of Migration from Eastern Kentucky to Cincinnati, Ohio." Ph.D. dissertation, University of Wisconsin.

Deaton, Brady J., and Anschel, Kurt B. 1974. "Migration and Return Migration: A New Look at the Eastern Kentucky Migration Stream." Paper presented at the annual meeting of the Southern Agricultural Economics Association.

Dreyer, James Teufel. 1977. "Ethnic Relations in China." *Annals of the American Academy of Political and Social Science* 433 (September):100–111.

Duncan, Otis Dudley, et al. 1960. *Metropolis and Region*. Baltimore: Johns Hopkins Press.

Edwards, N.F., and Krislov, J. 1971. "Three Local Employment Service Offices in Appalachia." *Journal of Human Resources* 2: 237–43.

Elgie, Robert. 1970. "Rural In-migration, Urban Ghettoization, and Their Consequences." *Antipode* 2: 35–54.

Ergood, Bruce. 1976. "Toward a Definition of Appalachia." In Bruce Ergood and Bruce E. Kuhre, eds., *Appalachia: Social Context Past and Present*, pp. 31–41. Dubuque, Iowa: Kendall/Hunt Publishing Company.

Ford, Thomas, ed. 1962. *The Southern Appalachian Region: A Survey*. Lexington: University of Kentucky Press.

Fowler, Gary L. 1973. "Locating Southern Migrants in Northern Cities." Paper presented at the Symposium on Southern White Rural Poverty and Urban Migration, Central States Anthropological Society Meeting.

———. 1976a. "Residential Mobility among Appalachian People in Central Cincinnati." *Research Bulletin, Urban Appalachian Council* (May).

———. 1976b. "Up Here and Down Home: Appalachians in Cities." In Bruce Ergood and Bruce Kuhre, eds., *Appalachia: Social Context Past and Present*, pp. 77–82. Dubuque, Iowa: Kendall/Hunt Publishing Company.

Fowler, Gary L., and Davies, Christopher Shane. 1972. "The Urban Settlement Patterns of Disadvantaged Migrants." *Journal of Geography* 17: 275–84.

———. 1973. "Southern White Migrants in Northern Cities: Residential Search and Urban Settlement." Paper presented at the Symposium on Southern White Rural Poverty and Urban Migration, Central States Anthropological Society Meeting.

Freedman, Ronald. 1964. "Cityward Migration, Urban Ecology, and Social Theory." In Ernest W. Burgess and Donald J. Bogus, eds., *Contributions to Urban Sociology*. Chicago: University of Chicago Press.

Gans, Herbert. 1962. *The Urban Villagers*. New York: Free Press.

Gianutsos, Pete. 1978. "Bench's Ethnic Jokes Strike Out." *Cincinnati Post*, January 10.

Giffin, Roscoe. 1957. "Newcomers from the Southern Mountains." Paper presented at the Institute on Cultural Patterns of Newcomers, Migration Ser-

vices Committee of the Chicago Commission on Human Relations, Welfare
Council of Metropolitan Chicago.

————. 1962. "Appalachian Newcomers in Cincinnati." In Thomas R. Ford,
ed., *The Southern Appalachian Region: A Survey*, pp. 79–84. Lexington:
University of Kentucky Press.

Gitlin, Todd, and Hollander, Nanci. 1970. *Uptown: Poor Whites in Chicago*.
Evanston: Harper and Row.

Glazer, Nathan. 1976. "Liberty, Equality, Fraternity—and Ethnicity." *Daedalus* 105 (Fall): 115–27.

Granovetter, Mark. 1975. "On Ethnicity and Cultural Pluralism." *Change* 7
(Summer): 5–6.

Greeley, Andrew M. 1976. Letter to Urban Appalachian Council. January 28.

Hanrahan, Charles E. 1973. "Public Budget Effects of Eastern Kentucky Migration to Cincinnati, Ohio." Ph.D. dissertation, University of Kentucky.

Henderson, George. 1966. "Poor Southern Whites: A Neglected Urban Problem." *Journal of Secondary Education* 41 (March): 111–14.

Hillery, George A., Jr.; Brown, James S.; and DeJong, Gordon F. 1965. "Migration Systems of the Southern Appalachians: Some Demographic Observations." *Rural Sociology* 30:33–48.

Howell, Joseph T. 1973. *Hard Living on Clay Street: Portraits of Blue Collar
Families*. Garden City, New York: Anchor Press/Doubleday.

Huelsman, Ben R. 1969. "Urban Anthropology and the Southern Mountaineer." *Proceedings of the Indiana Academy of Science for 1968* 78: 97–103.

Hyland, Gerard A. 1970. "Social Interaction and Urban Opportunity: The Appalachian In-migrant in the Cincinnati Central City." *Antipode* 2:66–83.

Hyland, Gerard A., and Peet, Richard. 1973. "Appalachian Migrants in
Northern Cities." *Antipode* 5 (March): 34–41.

Isajiw, Wasvelod W. 1974. "Definitions of Ethnicity." *Ethnicity* 1 (July):
111–24.

Jackson, Agnes Moreland. 1973. "To See the 'Me' in 'Thee.'" *Soundings*
56:21–43.

Kain, John F., and Persky, Joseph J. 1968. "The North's Stake in Southern
Rural Poverty." In President's National Advisory Commission on Rural
Poverty, ed. *Rural Poverty in the United States*, pp. 288–308. Washington, D.C.: G.P.O.

Keyes, Charles F. 1976. "Towards a New Formulation of the Concept of Ethnic Group." *Ethnicity* 3 (September):202–13.

Killian, Lewis M. 1970. *White Southerners*. New York: Random House.

Kunkin, Dorothy, and Byrne, Michael. 1973. *Appalachians in Cleveland*.
Cleveland: Institute of Urban Studies, Cleveland State University.

Lee, K.W. 1972. "Fair Elections in West Virginia." In David S. Walls and
John B. Stephenson, eds., *Appalachia in the Sixties*, pp. 164–76. Lexington: University Press of Kentucky.

Lex, Barbara W., and Hartman, David W. 1974. "The World of the Appalachian Migrant: Review of the Literature." In David W. Hartman, ed. *Immigrants and Migrants: The Detroit Ethnic Experience*, pp. 142–64. Detroit: New University Thought Publishing.

Leybourne, Grace. 1937. "Urban Adjustments of Migrants from the Southern Appalachian Plateaus." *Social Forces* 16: 238–46.

Lieble, Charles. 1976. "Appalachian Region—Myth or Reality." In William Plumley, ed., *Things Appalachian: A Handbook*. Charleston, West Virginia: MHC Publications.

Long, Larry H. 1974. "Poverty Status and Receipt of Welfare among Migrants and Nonmigrants in Large Cities." *American Sociological Review* 39 (February):46-56.

McCoy, Clyde B.; Brown, James S.; and Watkins, Virginia McCoy. 1975. "The Migration System of Southwest Ohio and Its Relation to Southern Appalachian Migration." *Research Bulletin, Urban Appalachian Council*, October.

McKee, Dan. 1978. "A Time Series Comparison of Cincinnati Neighborhoods." Cincinnati: Urban Appalachian Council Working Paper.

Maddox, James G. 1960. "Private and Social Costs of the Movement of People out of Agriculture." *American Economic Review* 50: 392-402.

Maloney, Michael E. 1974. *The Social Areas of Cincinnati: Towards an Analysis of Social Needs*. Cincinnati: The Cincinnati Human Relations Commission.

———. 1976. Statement made during a lecture, University of Cincinnati, August 10.

Maloney, Michael E., and Huelsman, Ben. 1972. "Humanism, Scientism, and Southern Mountaineers." *Peoples Appalachia* 2:24-27.

Mangalam, J.J. 1969. *Human Migration*. Lexington: University of Kentucky Press.

Marra, John L. 1971. "Career Orientations of High School Seniors in an Appalachian Coal Mining County." M.A. thesis, West Virginia University.

Miernyk, William H. 1975. "Coal and the Future of the Appalachian Economy." *Appalachia* 8 (October-November):29-35.

Miles, Emma Bell. 1976. *The Spirit of the Mountains*. Knoxville: University of Tennessee Press.

Miller, Jim Wayne. 1976. "Appalachian Values/American Values: The Role of Regional Colleges and Universities." Unpublished paper.

Miller, Tommie R. 1976. "Urban Appalachians: Cultural Pluralism and Ethnic Identity in the City." M.A. thesis, University of Cincinnati.

Montgomery, Bill. 1968. "The Uptown Story." *Mountain Life and Work* 44:8-18.

Morgan, Larry C. 1973. "An Economic Analysis of Out-Migration from a Depressed Rural Area." Ph.D. dissertation, University of Kentucky.

Morgan, Larry C., and Bordeaux, Frank, Jr. 1974a. "Selectivity of Out-Migration from a Depressed Area." Paper presented at the Annual Meeting of the Southern Regional Science Association.

———. 1974b. "Urban Public Service Costs and Benefits of Rural-to-Urban Migration." Paper presented at the Annual Meeting of the Southern Agricultural Economics Association.

Morris, Molly. 1970. *The Appalachian Migrant in Columbus, Ohio*. Columbus: Junior League of Columbus.

Murdock, Steven H., and McCoy, Clyde B. 1974. "A Note on the Decline of Appalachian Fertility, 1930-70." *Growth and Change* 5 (October):39-42.

Myrdal, Gunnar. 1974. "The Case against Romantic Ethnicity." *Center Magazine* 7(July-August):28.

Novak, Michael. 1976. "The 1980 Census." *EMPAC* 10:4-5.

Office of the City Manager. 1977. *Demographic and Socioeconomic Characteristics of East Dayton Residents*. Dayton: Office of the City Manager.

Orlov, Ann. 1976. Letter to the Urban Appalachian Council. August 10.

Ornati, Oscar. 1968. "Poverty in the Cities." In Harvey S. Perloff and Lowdon Wingo, eds., *Issues in Urban Economics*, pp. 335–62. Baltimore: Johns Hopkins Press.

Osburn, Donald D. 1966. "Returns to Investment in Human Migration." Ph.D. dissertation, North Carolina State University.

People's Appalachia. 1972. Special Issue on Urban Migrants. Vol. 2 (July).

Peterson, Gene B., and Sharp, Laura M. 1969. *Southern Migrants to Cleveland*. Washington, D.C.: Bureau of Social Science Research.

Peterson, Gene B.; Sharp, Laura M.; and Drury, Thomas. 1977. *Newcomers to Northern Cities: Work and Social Adjustment in Cleveland*. New York: Praeger.

Photiadis, John D. 1965. "Corollaries of Migration." *Sociological Quarterly* 6: 339-48.

———. 1970. *Social and Sociopsychological Characteristics of West Virginians in Their Own State and in Cleveland, Ohio*. Morgantown: Appalachian Center, West Virginia University.

———. 1975. *West Virginians in Their Own State and in Cleveland, Ohio*. Rev. ed. Morgantown: Appalachian Center, West Virginia University.

Photiadis, John D., and Schwarzweller, Harry. 1971. *Change in Rural Appalachia*. Philadelphia: University of Pennsylvania Press.

Pille, Bob. 1978. "Woody Lectures on War," *Miami News*, October 25.

Plumley, William. 1977. *Things Appalachian: A Handbook*. Charleston, West Virginia: MHC Publications.

Powles, William E. 1964. "The Southern Appalachian Migrant: Country Boy Turned Blue Collarite." In Arthur B. Shostak and William Gomberg, eds., *Blue Collar World: Studies of the American Worker*, pp. 270–81. Englewood Cliffs, New Jersey: Prentice Hall.

President's National Advisory Commission on Rural Poverty. 1968. *Rural Poverty in the United States*. Washington, D.C.: G.P.O.

Price, Daniel O., and Sikes, Melanie M. 1974. *Rural-Urban Migration Research in the United States: Annotated Bibliography and Synthesis*. Washington, D.C.: G.P.O.

Rainwater, Lee. 1968. "Social and Cultural Problems of Migrants to Cities." In President's Advisory Commission on Rural Poverty, eds., *Rural Poverty in the United States*. Washington, D.C.: G.P.O.

Rieger, Jon; Beegle, J.A.; and Fulton, P. 1973. *Profiles of Rural Youth: A Decade of Migration and Social Mobility*. East Lansing: Michigan State Agricultural Experiment Station, Research Report 178.

Schrag, Peter. 1972. "The School and Politics." In David S. Walls and John B. Stephenson, eds., *Appalachia in the Sixties*, pp. 219–24. Lexington: University Press of Kentucky.

Schwarzweller, Harry K. 1963a. *Research Design, Field Work Procedures, and Data Collection Problems in a Follow-up Study of Young Men from Eastern Kentucky*. Lexington: Kentucky Agricultural Experiment Station, Bulletin RS 21.

————. 1963b. *Sociocultural Origins and Migration Patterns of Young Men from Eastern Kentucky*. Lexington: Kentucky Agricultural Experiment Station, Bulletin 685.

————. 1964. *Family Ties, Migration, and the Transitional Adjustment of Young Men from Eastern Kentucky*. Lexington: Kentucky Agricultural Experiment Station, Bulletin 691.

————. 1973. "Regional Variations in the Educational Plans of Rural Youth." *Rural Sociology* 2: 139–58.

Schwarzweller, Harry K., and Brown, J.S. 1962. "Education as a Cultural Bridge between Eastern Kentucky and the Great Society." *Rural Sociology* 4: 357–73.

Schwarzweller, Harry K.; Brown, J.S.; and Mangalam, J.J. 1971. *Mountain Families in Transition*. University Park: Pennsylvania State University Press.

Schwarzweller, Harry K., and Crowe, M.J. 1969. "Adaptation of Appalachian Migrants to the Industrial Work Situation." In Eugene B. Brody, ed., *Behavior in New Environments*. p. 99–116. Beverly Hills, California: Sage Publications.

Schweiker, William F. 1968. *Some Facts and a Theory of Migration*. Morgantown: Appalachian Center, West Virginia University.

Sessions, Robert Paul. 1977. "Appalachians and Non-Appalachians: The Common Bond." In J.W. Williamson, ed., *An Appalachian Symposium*, pp. 92–101. Boone, North Carolina: Appalachian State University Press.

Shannon, Lyle W., and Shannon, Magdaline. 1967. "The Assimilation of Migrants to Cities: Anthropological and Social Contributions." In Leo F.

Schnore and Harry Fagin, eds., *Urban Research and Policy Planning.* Beverly Hills, California: Sage Publications.

Sharp, Laura M., and Peterson, Gene B. 1967. "The Cleveland In-migrant Study: An Overview." Paper presented at the Seventeenth Meeting of the National Manpower Advisory Committee's Subcommittee on Research.

Smith, Eldon D. 1953. "Migration and Adjustment Experiences of Rural Migrant Workers in Indianapolis." Ph.D. dissertation, University of Wisconsin.

———. 1956. "Nonfarm Employment Information for Rural People." *Journal of Farm Economics* 38:813–37.

Snuffer, Fred. 1976. "Appalachia Is Bicultural." In William Plumley, ed., *Things Appalachian: A Handbook.* Charleston, West Virginia: MHC Publications.

Sowell, Thomas. 1978. "Ethnicity in a Changing America." *Daedalus* 107 (Winter):213–37.

Stekert, Ellen J. 1971. "Southern Mountain Medical Beliefs in Detroit: Focus for Conflict." In Otto Feinstein, ed., *Ethnic Groups in the City*, pp. 231–76. Lexington, Mass.: Heath Lexington Books.

Stephenson, John B. 1976a. "Appalachia and the Third Century in America: On the Eve of an Astonishing Development—Again." *Appalachian Journal* 4:34–38.

———. 1976b. Statement at the University of Cincinnati, December 11.

Sunquist, James L. 1970. "Where Shall They Live?" *The Public Interest* 18:88–100.

Thompson, Bryan. 1974. "Newcomers to the City: Factors Influencing Initial Settlement and Ethnic Community Growth Patterns: A Review." *East Lakes Geographer* 10:50–78.

U.S., Bureau of the Census. 1960. *1960 Census of the Population, Alphabetical Index of Occupations and Industries.* Washington, D.C.: G.P.O.

U.S., Bureau of the Census. 1967. *U.S. Census of Population, 1960, Subject Report, Final Report PC(2)-2E, Migration between State Economic Areas.* Washington: G. P. O.

———. 1970a. *Census Employment Survey.* Washington, D.C.: G.P.O.

———. 1970b. *Data Uses in School Administration.* Report No. 10, *Census Use Study.* Washington, D.C.: G.P.O.

———. 1972a. *Census of Population, 1970, Detailed Characteristics; Final Report PC(1)-D37, Ohio.* Washington, D.C.: G.P.O.

———. 1972b. *U.S. Census of Population, 1970, Subject Report, Final Report PC(2)-2E, Migration between State Economic Areas.* Washington, D.C.: G.P.O.

———. 1972c. *Census of Population and Housing, 1970, Census Tracts; Final Report PHC (1)-44, Cincinnati, Ohio-KY-IN.* Washington, D.C.: G.P.O.

U.S., Congress, House, Committee on Agriculture. 1972. *Hearings before the*

Committee on Agriculture, House of Representatives, on H.R. 12931. Rural Development Act of 1972. Washington, D.C.: G.P.O.

U.S., Department of Agriculture. 1935. *Economic and Social Problems and Conditions of the Southern Appalachians*. Washington, D.C.: G.P.O.

van den Berghe, Pierre L. 1976. "Ethnic Pluralism in Industrial Societies: A Special Case?" *Ethnicity* 3(September):242–55.

Varady, David P. 1975. "Determinants of Mobility in an Inner-City Community." *Regional Science Perspectives* 5: 154–78.

Votaw, Albert N. 1958. "The Hillbillies Invade Chicago." *Harpers* 216:64-67.

Wagner, Thomas. 1974. "Urban Appalachian School Children: The Least Understood of All." Cincinnati: Urban Appalachian Council Working Paper.

Waites, Nancy Hane. 1976. *Demographic Status of Appalachians in Clermont County, [Ohio,] 1965–1970*. Cincinnati: Urban Appalachian Council Research Department.

Walls, David. 1976. "Appalachian Problems are National Problems." *Appalachian Journal* 4(Autumn):39–42.

———. 1977. "On the Naming of Appalachia." In J.W. Williamson, ed., *An Appalachian Symposium*, pp. 56–57. Boone, North Carolina: Appalachian State University Press.

Watkins, Virginia McCoy. 1976. *Demographic Status of Appalachians in the Model Neighborhood*. Cincinnati: Urban Appalachian Council Research Department.

Wertheimer, Richard F. 1970. *The Monetary Rewards of Migration within the United States*. Washington, D.C.: Urban Institute.

Whisnant, David. 1973. "Ethnicity and the Recovery of Regional Identity in Appalachia: Thoughts upon Entering the Zone of Occult Instability." *Soundings* 56(Spring):124–38.

Williams, Cratis. 1976. "Who Are the Southern Mountaineers?" In Bruce Ergood and Bruce Kuhre, eds., *Appalachia: Social Context Past and Present*. Dubuque, Iowa: Kendall/Hunt Publishing Company.

Index

West Virginia, 5, 10, 20, 22-23, 35-36, 38, 39, 41-52 passim, 54, 55, 59, 75, 76, 134, 140-53 passim, 164. *See also* Charleston; Huntington
Winston-Salem, N.C., 62-71 passim
Wisconsin, 57
work visits, 131
World War II, 116, 154

youth: Appalachian, 87, 167, 168, 173; college students, 132; high school students, 131; in population, 96, 97; in urban schools, 163

Contributors

JAMES S. BROWN is professor of rural sociology at the Kentucky Agricultural Experiment Station of the University of Kentucky.

GARY L. FOWLER is associate professor of geography at the University of Illinois at Chicago Circle.

MICHAEL E. MALONEY is director of the Urban Appalachian Council.

CLYDE B. McCOY is associate professor of sociology in the Department of Psychiatry at the University of Miami.

LARRY C. MORGAN is associate professor of agricultural economics at Texas A. and M. University.

PHILLIP J. OBERMILLER is a member of the board of the Urban Appalachian Council.

WILLIAM W. PHILLIBER is associate professor of sociology at the State University of New York at New Paltz.

JOHN D. PHOTIADIS is professor of research and sociology at the Center for Extension and Continuing Education at West Virginia University.

JEROME P. PICKARD is director of research at the Appalachian Regional Commission.

HARRY K. SCHWARZWELLER is professor of sociology at Michigan State University.

VIRGINIA McCOY WATKINS is director of research at the Urban Appalachian Council.